e Klossowski

CULTURAL INTERACTIONS
Studies in the Relationship between the Arts

Edited by J.B. Bullen

Volume 22

PETER LANG
Oxford · Bern · Berlin · Bruxelles · Frankfurt am Main · New York · Wien

Hervé Castanet

Pierre Klossowski

The Pantomime of Spirits

With a Foreword by Sarah Wilson

Followed by an interview with Pierre Klossowski
by Judith Miller

PETER LANG
Oxford · Bern · Berlin · Bruxelles · Frankfurt am Main · New York · Wien

Bibliographic information published by Die Deutsche Nationalbibliothek. Die Deutsche Nationalbibliothek lists this publication in the Deutsche Nationalbibliografie; detailed bibliographic data is available on the Internet at http://dnb.d-nb.de.

A catalogue record for this book is available from the British Library.

Library of Congress Control Number: 2014936228

ISSN 1662-0364
ISBN 978-3-0343-0209-8

Cover Image: *La Monnaie Vivante*, Pierre Klossowski, Pierre Zucca, Ed. Eric Losfeld, 1970. Courtesy of Sylvie Quesemand-Zucca.

Hochfeldstrasse 32, CH-3012 Bern, Switzerland
info@peterlang.com, www.peterlang.com, www.peterlang.net

This publication has been peer reviewed.

Printed in Germany

Jacques-Alain Miller, hunc librum, quem mihi ante mandavit,
gratiae debitum solvendo dedico

Contents

SARAH WILSON

Foreword: Klossowski our Contemporary

> The simulacre in its meaning as *imitation* is the actualisation of something in itself incommunicable or unrepresentable: properly speaking the phantasm in its obsessional *constraint.*
>
> KLOSSOWSKI, GALERIE LE BATEAU-LAVOIR, Paris, 1975[1]

Pierre Klossowski is a writer, artist, filmmaker and translator of huge renown; a *philosophe scélérat* – a perfidious and rascally philosopher – and a *théologien pornologue* who broaches God through the word made flesh … Klossowski's thought and art live among us. 'Sade my contemporary', *Sade mon prochain* often translated as 'Sade my neighbour', is a concept at the heart of some of his most important work.[2] Hervé Castanet's *Pierre Klossowski: The Pantomime of Spirits* reinforces the artist's presence today for a new generation of English-speaking readers. It follows several Klossowski publications by the author.[3]

1 *Le simulacre au sens imitatif est l'actualisation de quelque chose d'incommunicable en soi ou d'irreprésentable: proprement le phantasme dans sa contrainte obsessionnelle …* 'La description, l'argumentation, le récit' Galerie Le Bateau-Lavoir, Paris, 1975 in *Pierre Klossowski, Tableaux vivants, Essais critiques, 1936–83,* Le Promeneur, Paris, 2001, p. 131.

2 The notion of 'Klossowski our contemporary' contains a certain *renvoi* to Jan Kott's celebrated *Shakespeare our contemporary* (New York, Doubleday, 1964), where the *oeuvre,* read 'in the present' was rich with political metaphor.

3 See Castanet, Hervé, *Regard et perversions. À partir des* Lois de l'hospitalité *de Pierre Klossowski,* Z'Éditions, Nice, 1992; *Pierre Klossowski. Le Regard à la lettre,* Anthropos-Economica, Paris, 1996; *La Manipulation des images. Pierre Klossowski et la peinture,* La Lettre volée, Brussels, 2001, prior to *Pierre Klossowski, La Pantomime des esprits,*

Klossowski was always contemporary. After a precarious childhood expelled from Paris in 1914, surviving in wartime Berlin and then Geneva, he returned in 1923 as André Gide's schoolboy 'secretary', to become part of the glittering literary milieu that would frequent his artist-mother Baladine's salons. In 1930s Paris his first translations of German literature coincided with work for the psychoanalyst René Laforgue and his initiation into psychoanalytic literature; he would subsequently become involved with German *emigré* intellectuals in Parisian exile (including Walter Benjamin), their precarious lives and often tragic fates.[4] In 1940s Paris, Klossowski's pre-war writings reappeared as the volume *Sade mon prochain*; in 1950s Paris, his first silvery pencil drawings were exhibited in his brother Balthus' former studio in the Cour de Rohan. This was the era of great creativity: *La Vocation suspendue* (1950) was followed by *Roberte ce soir* (1954), *Le Bain de Diane* (1956) and *La Révocation de l'Édit de Nantes* (1959). Klossowski, by now in his own mid-century, was perhaps not entirely a 1960s man: the optimism of Pop, Op and kinetic art were surely alien to him – yet 1960s Paris marked an explosion of discourse on the Marquis de Sade and Klossowski's prefaces to new and definitive versions of his works.[5] In 1967 a new essay on Sade appeared as 'Le philosophe scélérat' in the structuralist-orientated review *Tel Quel* and for *Sade mon prochain*'s second edition.[6]

---

suivi d'un entretien de Pierre Klossowski avec Judith Miller, Cécile Défaut, Nantes, 2007; *Le Savoir de l'artiste et la psychananlyse*, Cécile Défaut, Nantes, 2009. See also *Pourquoi écrire? Artaud, Jouhandeau, Genet, Klossowski* (with Alain Merlet), Éditions la Différence, Paris, 2010.

4 Scheler, Max, *Le Sens de la Souffrance*, Paris, Aubier, 1936, trans. Pierre Klossowski.

5 Marquis de Sade, *Œuvres, Justine ou les Malheurs de la vertu* and other texts, with Klossowski's 'Essai sur Sade', Club français du livre, Paris, 1960; *Œuvres complètes* 3, *Justine ou les Malheurs de la vertu* and other texts, with Klossowski's preface to 'La philosophie dans le boudoir'; *Œuvres complètes* 6–7, *La Nouvelle Justine ... Histoire de Juliette ...* prefaces by Blanchot, Bataille, Klossowski and the late Maurice Heine, both Cercle du livre précieux, Paris, 1963; *Œuvres complètes* 10 *Les Crimes d'amour* ... and 13 *Les 120 journées de Sodome ou l'École du libertinage*, with prefaces including Klossowski, Cercle du livre précieux, Paris, 1964.

6 Klossowski, 'Le Philosophe scélérat' (*Tel Quel*, 28, 1967) in *Sade mon prochain*, précédé de *Le Philosophe scélérat*, Seuil, Paris, 1967, pp. 48–9.

Klossowski joined Philippe Sollers' theoretical study group and in 1968 exhibited in Geneva.

Klossowski's wife Denise was tall and enigmatic. In contrast with the 1960s new woman, she was older, more severe; she was a survivor of the Ravensbruck concentration camp. Denise was the focus of Klossowski's writings and drawings, which were representations – simulacra – of her living, breathing body traversed with myriad palimpsests of great art from the past.

In the 1970s, Klossowski became even more topical, the contemporary of Michel Foucault and Roland Barthes, who so appreciated *La Monnaie Vivante*, the purple picture book whose black and white *tableaux vivants* denoted the female body as 'living currency'. Woman in her plural manifestations became sign of the motor of desire traversing all hierarchies, all institutional infrastructures. Jean-François Lyotard's *Libidinal Economy* appropriated and reformulated Klossowski's ideas.[7] This generation turned from the collision of Marx and Freud ('the personal is the political') to Friedrich Nietzsche, to a darker philosophy and darker sexualities.

Klossowski abandoned literature from 1972 onwards, in favour of an art practice that was secret, obsessive and amateur in the truest sense, conducted without conventional materials or (for many years) an artist's studio. This was also the era of his collaboration as producer and actor on three films, Raoul Ruiz's *La Vocation suspendue*, 1977, *L'hypothèse du tableau volé*, 1979 and Pierre Zucca's *Roberte*, filmed in 1977 (released 1979) where Denise rather than a professional actress played Roberte. Klossowski's influence on filmmakers such as Pier Paolo Pasolini (*Salo*) or Michelangelo Antonioni was important; he frequented the Villa Medici in Rome, directed by his brother Balthus at this time. At the 'moment of postmodernism' (Lyotard's *Postmodern Condition* was published in French in 1979), France selected the powerful yet bizarre combination of Daniel Buren and Pierre Klossowski's large-scale drawings for the international Kassel Documenta

7 For Klossowski and Lyotard, see Wilson, *The Visual World of French Theory Figurations*, Yale University Press, London, 2010, Ch 5, 'Lyotard, Monory Postmodern Romantics', pp. 164–6 ff.

exhibition of 1982: late conceptual art met the simulacra. Klossowski of course anticipated Jean Baudrillard's *Simulacres et simulation* (1981) and its repercussions in France and America in the era of posthumous tributes to Andy Warhol ...[8]

Five years younger than the century, Klossowski was by now in his eighties: these were the years of consolidation and the beginnings of his world-wide fame amongst a select, but different generation of intellectuals writing and thinking in English, who were rediscovering Klossowski's peers such as Maurice Blanchot (not to mention the *doyens* of 'French theory' ...). I was both mystified and elated by Klossowski's 1990 Paris retrospective, where I first met the artist.[9] Later in the decade, Klossowski crowned the short-lived bilingual series of texts I edited with his own 'Decadence of the Nude' (first published as 'The Falling Nymphs') and other art writings in conjunction with Maurice Blanchot's analysis: 'Laughter of the Gods'.[10] Alas, Klossowski would not live to see our retrospective of his paintings and curious sculptures, nor meet his first cousin the artist Peter Spiro, still living in London, whose testimony at the time was – and is – invaluable.[11] The exhibition travelled from London to Cologne and to Paris: Klossowski became once more a contemporary of the twenty-first-century art world.

* * *

8 Baudrillard, Jean, *Simulacres et simulation*, Galilée, Paris, 1981; *Simulations*, Semiotext(e), New York, 1983. *Andy Warhol, rétrospective*, Centre Pompidou, Paris, 1990, generated Baudrillard's essay 'Le Snobisme machinal', *Les Cahiers du Musée National d'Art Moderne*, 34, Winter 1990, pp. 35–43.

9 Grenier, Catherine, et al., *Pierre Klossowski*, Éditions la Différence, Paris, Centre National des Arts Plastiques, 1990.

10 Wilson ed., Maurice Blanchot, *Laughter of the Gods* ('Le rire des Dieux', *Nouvelle Revue Française*, 151, July, 1965, pp. 91–105); Klossowski, Pierre, *Decadence of the Nude*, Sarah Wilson ed., Alyce Mahon intro., Black Dog, London, 2002 (bilingual). 'La Décadence du nu' appeared as 'The Falling Nymphs. A Survey of the Nude as a Subject in Modern Painting from Ingres to Our Contemporaries', *Portfolio or Art News Annual*, 3, 1960; hence between 'Balthus' (1957) and 'La Judith de Frédéric Tonnerre' (1865), (1961). (See 'La Décadence du nu', *Les Cahiers du chemin*, 27, April, 1976; in *La Ressemblance*, Ryôan-Ji, Marseille, 1984).

11 Another conversation with Peter Spiro, 9 April, 2013.

Klossowski's *oeuvre* traverses disciplines: literature, philosophy, film, art and art history; he is surely a gift to psychoanalysis, with his early initiation into its texts and practitioners, his fascination with childhood, sexual fantasy, pederasty, wife swopping and above all the tropes of rape and voyeurism, which problematise the notion of the gaze. Politically incorrect *par excellence*, he offers via his writings and drawings an extraordinary psychoanalytic 'place' for reflection.[12]

Hervé Castanet is a practising psychoanalyst in Marseille – not the easiest of France's port cities with its histories of plagues and prostitutes, exiles and immigrations, poverty and folklore: its glorious moments, and unexpected rebirths. I witnessed the great period of Marseille's restored hospice-museum complex, La Vieille Charité in the late 1980s and early 1990s: it hosts Marseille's vibrant literature and poetry scene, where Castanet plays an important role. In 2013 Marseille became European City of Culture, showcasing many new projects.

Castanet's attitude towards 'applied psychoanalysis' – the transfer of the 'cure' from speaking patient to the narratives of text or image – is ambiguous: 'Rightly, *applied psychoanalysis* has a bad press and its results are vain' he argues ... 'The psychoanalyst becomes a detective and slides imperceptibly from the product, the work, to its producer, the creator's unconscious'.[13] He takes issue with the notion of 'application' and the production of a parallel narrative that might 'explain' what the work or the artist 'really' means; yet he throws the option back as a possibility – provided we deal with '*un réel nouveau*' ... (To what extent might this 'new real' be defined as a work of collaboration between author, critic/

12 For Klossowski within a psychoanalytical frame, see also Marroni, Aldo, 'Laws of Perversion and Hospitality in Pierre Klossowski', *Journal of European Psychoanalysis*, 25, 2007.

13 '*La* psychanalyse appliquée, *à juste titre, n'a pas bonne presse et ses résultats sont vains.*' [...] '*Le psychanalyste se fait détective et insensiblement glisse du produit/l'œuvre, à son producteur/l'inconscient du créateur*'. Castanet, Preface to 'Un réel nouveau produit par le théâtre? Une thèse, un exemple', in Christiane Page ed., *Écritures théâtrales du traumatisme, Écritures de la résistance,* Presses Universitaires de Rennes, Rennes, 2012, p. 7.

psychoanalyst, audience or reader?)[14] Klossowski engaged from the start of his career with applied psychoanalysis and with its origins: Freud himself. As we know, besides Freud's use of classical myth as trope with which to condense contemporary behaviour (such as the Oedipus complex), he analysed Wilhelm Jensen's Pompeian novel *Gradiva*, with its archaeological metaphor for the unconscious and its dream frame.[15] He then turned to painting: Leonardo da Vinci's *Virgin and Child with Saint Anne* (making a 'Freudian' error based on mistranslation around the famous inverted vulture he perceived in the work ...).[16] Freud saw the painting as the *locus classicus* for Leonardo's conundrum of 'two mothers', not to mention his speculations on the artist's homosexuality. Stepping outside the frame, as it were, Klossowski depicted Freud himself gazing at Leonardo's painting more than once – drawings all the more disconcerting when rendered with his habitual children's coloured crayons.[17] Following the striking precedents of applied psychoanalysis in Freud's review *Imago* (founded 1912), René Laforgue, Klossowski's mentor, analysed the poet Baudelaire's neuroses in 1930; and Freud's *Essais de psychanalyse appliquée* (including studies on Moses and Goethe) were published by Gallimard in 1933, yet Klossowski's 'applied' psychoanalysis of the Marquis de Sade met with opprobrium.[18]

14 *Ibid.*, p. 9.

15 Jensen, Wilhelm, *Gradiva: a Pompeian Fancy* (Vienna, 1902), Moffat and Co., London, 1918; Sigmund Freud, *Delusion and Dream in Jensen's 'Gradiva'* (1907) appeared as *Délire et rêves dans la 'Gradiva' de Jensen*, trans. Marie Bonaparte with E. Zak and G. Sadoul, Gallimard, Paris, 1931.

16 Freud, *Leonardo da Vinci and a Memory of His Childhood* (German 1910), *Un souvenir d'enfance de Léonard de Vinci*, trans. Marie Bonaparte, Gallimard, Paris, 1927.

17 See Klossowski, *Le Grand enfermement* (Foucault's phrase from *Histoire de la folie ... Madness and civilisation*) or *The Great Lock-up*, two versions, 1973 and 1988.

18 See Rank, Otto and Hanns Sachs eds., *Imago Zeitschrift für Anwendung der Psychoanalyse auf die Geisteswissenschaften*, introduction by Sigmund Freud, 1912–37; Laforgue, René, 'Devant la barrière de la névrose. Étude psychanalytique sur la névrose de Charles Baudelaire', *Revue Française de Psychanalyse*, 2, 1930–1, pp. 245–58 and 276 ff; *Essais de psychanalyse appliquée*, trans. M. Bonaparte and E. Matty, Paris, 1933; followed by Klossowski's 'Éléments d'une étude psychanalytique sur le Marquis de Sade', *Revue française de psychanalyse*, IV, 3–4, 1933.

As far as art history is concerned, Hervé Castanet is perfectly 'at home' with the discipline, most notably in his essays on Asger Jorn and the Bauhaus *imaginiste* or the artist-architect Constant's 'New Babylon'. He is happy with photography – Joel-Peter Witkin – and has written about photographic self-portraiture (Michèle Sylvander) for an exhibition in Marseille. These texts conform to the genre of the French *essai*: they are written in the historic present, highly conscious of their construction, style and elegance, with minimal footnoting and no ostensible engagement with specific theorists or art historical traditions; Castanet's first book on Klossowski's art, *La Manipulation des images, Pierre Klossowski et la peinture* (2001) is also in *essai* mode. In *The Pantomime of Spirits*, Castanet often performs as the learned exegete of 'difficult texts', offering penetrating summaries and analyses for the non French-speaking reader. The title of his collected essays on art, *S.K.beau*, – a Lacanian pun on the question 'is it beautiful?' (*est-ce que c'est beau?*) – refers us to Lacan's stepping-up of the meaning of *escabeau* (stepladder) with more complex associations of the work as sublimation and self-investment for the artist (initially Joyce); the work as elevation then, but also distortion, and a 'real' (Lacanian of course) whose 'S.K.' interrupts and precedes any simple perception of the *beau*. Here, the gaze itself is a construct – a dark hole that occludes at least part of the field of visibility, inciting painter, photographer or filmmaker to make a 'show'.[19]

References to Lacan or his epigones such as Jacques-Alain Miller pepper Castanet's writing; he offers us, then, his post-Lacanian Klossowski. Yet Klossowski evades us all: his mindset and profound involvement with multiple languages, with pre- and post-linguistic thought and imaging, call to us from another era. In fact the situations that a psychoanalyst might indeed work through with a 'Klossowski-as-analysand' are not treated explicitly: multiple or absent parenting and intense sibling rivalry (the painter Balthus, who usurped the position of 'elder' brother taking

19 '*... l'image se construit à partir d'un trou qui a nom regard. C'est ce pas-tout visible qui pousse le peintre, le photographe ou le cinéaste à montrer*', Castanet, 'L'*Escabeau* et la sublimation', *S.K.beau*, Éditions la Différence, Paris, 2011, p. 9.

the title of 'Count') are the most egregious of these; and though the voyeuristic obsession, woman as mother, wife, mistress and castrator are obvious issues, dominating all is surely the problem of 'art as a substitute for life' … If Klossowski's multiple voices emanating from one source are not the talking that solicits a 'talking cure', then what is, in fact, the status of his work – or the status of art itself, from a classic psychoanalytic perspective?

Klossowski never ceases to surprise and to reverse critical expectations. With our Whitechapel catalogue at proof stage, Thadée Klossowski, the artist's nephew, allowed me access to Klossowski's love letters to Betty, the English *Alice* painted by his brother Balthus in 1933 (beloved by visitors to the Centre Pompidou) – a canvas Castanet has also analysed, embracing the Pygmalion-like dream narratives of the poet Pierre-Jean Jouve who once owned the work.[20] Betty Holland married Pierre Leyris, Klossowski's school friend, and later France's greatest translator of English poetry and prose.[21] Klossowski's letters to Betty, extending from 1930 to 1945, fundamentally change our perception of the 'cult of Denise' accepted by generations of Klossowski scholars.[22] For it was Betty who occasioned Klossowski's blinding encounter with female sexuality: his escape from the heady homosexual world of André Gide (to whom his mother Balandine and her lover Rainer Maria Rilke had astonishingly confided her young son …) and the interwar Parisian world of erudite misogyny and *mascarade*, typified by André Breton and the surrealists. This erudition was predicated, of course, upon female disempowerment and male fear (see the surrealist panoply of male writers with closed eyes surrounding Magritte's naked woman in *Je ne vois pas la femme cachée dans la forêt …*).[23] This disempowerment subtends the

20 Castanet, 'Alice – image manipulée', *Il particolare. Art – littérature – théorie critique,* 24, 2010/11, pp. 7–11 (see Pierre-Jean Jouve, 'Le tableau', *Balthus,* Centre Georges Pompidou, Paris, 1983, pp. 64–5); it is in this review, run by Castanet in Marseille, that he published 'Pierre Klossowski, le passage au spéculaire' (*Il particolare,* 1–6).

21 See Leyris, Pierre, *La Chambre du traducteur,* José Corti, 2007.

22 See *Pierre Klossowski intégral,* Serge Fauchereau ed., including vol II: *Pierre Klossowski: cartas a Betty,* Circulo des Bellas Artes, Madrid, 2007.

23 See Wilson, 'Feminities/Mascarades, '*Rrose is a Rrose is a Rrose: Gender Performance in Photography*', Solomon R, Guggenheim Museum, New York, 1997, pp. 135–55.

canon of great male writers and artists into which Klossowski inscribed himself, firstly as a translator, then via his own creative writings.

In the letters to Betty, Klossowski registers his moments of despair and unrequitable distance from his love (his 'love object'), a woman so different, so kindred he could write to her in German. He himself asks what a psychoanalyst would make of his predicament: 'My dear Betty, you have departed, leaving me face to face with my appalling feebleness – here a psychoanalyst would say 'Aha! Aha! (the imbecile) the appalling feebleness I was forced to experience in front of you this dreadful morning'.[24] His intimate knowledge of Sade as both writing, *écriture*, and as active, visualised fantasy – and a frightening sociological 'Sade-in-context' he translated from the German – preceded his physical intimacy with this notionally correct English woman.[25] He sent Betty Sade's *Les Infortunes de la vertu* as early as 1930: 'You'll find there an innocent young girl, continually condemned, pursued, persecuted, whipped, bitten, violated and dishonoured, who, in love with her virtues, is unaware of the greatest, her only vice: curiosity'.[26]

Included with the letters are inkblot ghosts and occasional watercolours, amateurish and delightfully apt: a priapically erect and delicately feathery Papageno, Mozart's bird-catcher, for example. These anticipate his later practice, while referring us back again to the children's books and

24 '*Ma chère Betty, vous êtes partie en me laissant face à face avec mon affreuse faiblesse – ici un psychanalyste dira Ah! Ah! (l'imbécile) – l'affreuse faiblesse dont il m'a fallu faire l'expérience devant vous, au cours de cette matinée râtée*', Klossowski, Letter 8, 7 rue de l'Estrapade, Whit Saturday, Sunday and Monday, 1934, *Lettres à Betty/Cartas a Betty*, 2007, p. 62.

25 Otto Flake's *Le Marquis de Sade*, translated by Klossowski (Grasset, Paris, printed 16 February 1933) contains harrowing descriptions of both *ancien régime* debaucheries and revolutionary atrocities including *La Terreur de la prostitution* (p. 156) and a disquisition on the iniquitous Palais Royal – site of Klossowski's future erotic fictions.

26 '*Vous y trouverez une jeune fille innocente continuellement condamnée, poursuivie, persécutée, fouettée, mordue, violée et déshonorée, qui tout éprise de ses vertus ignore la plus grande ou son seul vice: la curiosité*', Klossowski, Letter 7, 13 October, 1930, *Lettres à Betty*, p. 56.

other images that constantly peopled his imagination.[27] It is the Whitsun letter of 1934 (first quoted) which opts for explicit excess: a long drawn out fantasy in which Betty, overpowered by a group of half-naked boys, has her blouse ripped to shreds and is rammed by a huge organ while Pierre, the onanistic onlooker, narrator and author is likewise violated, then engages in various practices with her, both Sadean and tender … (Here we – a notionally male we – become spies reading private correspondence, joining Klossowski as *voyeurs* of the imagination …) Betty, pleasured, furious and shamed is calmed ultimately by the sight of the pure waters of the Palais Royal … 'Betty, I have pursued you for years, pursued you through city quarters, great capitals, hotel rooms, stations, novelty shops, forests. Everywhere one of your objects, forgotten somewhere, bears witness to your recent passage; I have descended into subterranean galleries, I have long wandered in obscure labyrinths giving soon onto a phosphorescent lake where you were boating with Sade'.[28] So many of Klossowski's future themes, themes woven around the trope of Denise/Roberte, are played out here.

The passion for Betty – and its fulfilment – extends to the point of primordial encounter: not a postulated Lacanian 'lack' but *le sexe de la femme*, the place of genesis itself: 'that which the eye should not see'. Freud used the classical metaphor of the Medusa's head for this encounter.[29] Klossowski would work through the experience, repeatedly using the tropes of rape

27 For inkblots, see Letter 4, 1938–9 and cover *Lettres à Betty*; watercolour *Beth je vous attends,* Letter 7, 13 October, 1930, p. 60; Letter 8 (19, 20, 21 May 34) manuscript, p 61; *Papageno* Letter 11, 27 July 38, pp. 86–7. My 'Pierre Klossowski, epiphanies and secrets', *Pierre Klossowski*, ed. Wilson, Whitechapel Art Gallery and Hatje Cantz, London, 2006, pp. 13 ff., discusses the child Klossowski and German children's book sources.

28 '*Betty, je vous aie poursuivie durant des années, poursuivie à travers des quartiers, de grandes capitales, des chambres d'hôtel, des gares, des magasins de nouveautés, des forêts : partout un objet vous appartenant et oublié en tel lieu témoignait de votre récent passage; je suis descendu dans des galeries souterraines, je me suis longtemps égaré dans des labyrinthes obscurs, débouchant bientôt sur un lac phosphorescent, où vous canotiez avec Sade.*' Klossowski, *Lettres à Betty,* Letter 8, p. 70.

29 Sigmund Freud, '*Medusa's Head*' (1922) was not translated into French until 1981.

and castration such as Tarquin and Lucretia, first gloriously embodied for the princes of Renaissance Italy. It was after our London show that the drawings in pale pencil – magnificence fallen from grace – *Roberte and the Colossus* and *Judith and Holophernes* (1956) were rediscovered and shown in Paris.[30] Klossowski in ekphrastic mode would address these tropes in writing: their afterlives in memory becoming present; a present where the hyperintellectual and hypersexual intertwine like bodies with the past. Notably his 'Judith by Frédéric Tonnerre' (concurrent with 'Decadence of the Nude') 'opens' out the *tableau* of a voluptuous Judith, her long fingers piercing the decapitated Holophernes' half-opened eyelids, which still yearn to gaze, even in death, upon her sex. This 'unbearable vision enclosed within the *chiaroscuro* of the tabernacle' unfolds onto a scene where a bourgeois family (contemporary with Tonnerre, the fictive nineteenth-century painter) buys lemonade on the Champs Elysées ... the bathos, too, is almost unbearable: is this the eruption of the 'real' world for Tonnerre, for Klossowski or ourselves?[31]

For me the key to Klossowski's later work of the 1970s is a constellation of thought of the 1930s where Sade, Max Scheler (the sense of suffering), Benjamin (aura and reproduction) and the encounter with a living female body (Betty) come together.[32] The frame is another translation project Klossowski evidently discussed with Benjamin, who had published a long article on the matriarchal theories of Johann Jakob Bachofen's *Mutterrecht* (he was fascinated by the role of the feminine within modern capitalism at this time ...).[33] Only in 1965 did Klossowski publish an article on the

30 *Judith et Holopherne, Roberte et le colosse,* catalogue numbers 7 and 8, in *Pierre Klossowski*, ed. Agnès de la Beaumelle, Centre Georges Pompidou, Paris, 2007, pp. 92–5.

31 See 'La Judith de Frédéric Tonnerre', 'Frédéric Tonnerre's Judith' (1865) trans. Annette Michelson, *Figures* no 1, 1961, in Pierre Klossowski, *Tableaux vivants, ibid.*, pp. 120–5.

32 Besides Benjamin on reproduction (1936, see discussion in Wilson, 2006), Klossowski translated the phenomenologist Max Scheler, *Le sens de la souffrance*, Paris, Montaigne, 1936, with additional essays 'Repentir et renaissance', 'Amour et connaissance'.

33 Benjamin, 'Johann Jacob Bachofen' in *Ecrits Français, op. cit.*, 1991, pp. 91–113 (he notes Erich Fromm's *Signification psychologico-sociale des théories matriarchales* on Bachofen and fascism, and the patriarchal *détournement* of the swastika). He was reading

mythical and cult origins of a 'certain behaviour of Roman ladies', which appeared as a book in 1968, its frontispiece his *Diana and Acteon* (becoming a stag) of 1954.[34] Here, he summarises Bachofen and issues of the sexual differentiation in effigy and legend of once androgynous gods: the long debate involved the congruence of nineteenth-century classics, anthropology, the history of religions and language with a focus, too, on etymology. The argument, the practice and the fantasy of female-dominant societies are still topical.[35] Evidently the modern Rome, whose vices were castigated by Saint Augustine in his *City of God*, was horribly 'contemporary'; yet it was there, in theatres or circuses, that the evolution of the Asiatic Mother Goddess was played out in debased versions of divine adultery, where the celebrations of hierogamy became a performance of painted courtesans, a mythological grotesque. The once-Augustinian analysis applies to our celebrity culture today ...[36]

Klossowski's 'mislaid' translation of Saint Augustine's *City of God* surpasses the story of T.E. Lawrence and *The Seven Pillars of Wisdom* manuscript lost at Reading station as an *acte manqué* ... His Latin translations included Tertullien in 1948 and Suetonius in 1959 and his controversial rendering of Virgil's *Aeneid* in 1964, respecting the Latin word order.[37] The bizarre masquerade of a Roman orgy with black and white photographs by Pierre Zucca accompanies the propositions – in a sexual sense – of *La Monnaie Vivante*, 1970. It was in fact a highly political text. While France produced Pierre Klossowski and Michel Foucault, Britain at the same time enjoyed televised bathos: Frankie Howerd and *Up Pompei!*,

---

Ludwig Klage, *Vom kosmogonischen Eros*, Munich, 1922 at this time. Klossowski's archives (Bibliothèque Jacques Doucet) contain the cover of Bachofen's *Mutterrecht und UrReligion*, Alfred Kroner Verlag and a proposal (unsigned and undated) for a translation to be called *Les amazones.*

34 Klossowski, *Origines culturelles et mythiques d'un certain comportement des dames romaines* (*Nouvelle Revue Française,* 1965), Fata Morgana, 1968, 1986.

35 See the exhaustive historiography in Chris Knight, 'Early Human Kinship Was Matrilineal', N.J. Allen et al. eds., *Early Human Kinship*, Blackwell, Oxford, 2008, pp. 61–82.

36 Klossowski, *Origines culturelles, op. cit.*, p. 71 ff.

37 *Virgile, L'Enéide*, trans. Pierre *Klossowski*, Gallimard, Paris, 1964.

with Senator Ludicrus Sextus, his daughter Erotica, the slave Lurcio … The BBC series, *I, Claudius* prolonged our Roman fever (we too were once subjects of Hadrian …). Yet fictional time warps, the tantalising meanings of historical kitsch and recognition of the actor or actress in and out of role, were problematics that the most banal British TV viewers shared with Klossowski at this time.[38]

Finally, why is 'Sade my neighbour' Klossowski's most important concept? We must return to the first appearance of his essay 'Who is my neighbour?' *Qui est mon prochain?*, written in October 1938. Klossowski's matrilineal Jewish descent was a perpetual secret. Referring to the French terror, he declares: 'the revolutionary government found its most original and most concrete expression in the extermination of the aristocrats, while the national-socialist government found this expression in the extermination of the Jews, these two categories of the "exterminated" in fact giving a living signification to the principles evoked: the people as sovereign, and race.' Klossowski made the impermissible parallel between Sade's description of France as a regicide nation, and contemporary nazism: a 'nation whose republican model could be maintained only through many crimes because it is already in the realm of crime.' Klossowski's thought was honed at this moment by the lectures of Alexandre Kojève, and besides the works he translated, he was surely aware of the disturbing political theology of Carl Schmitt and his distinction between the *inimicus* (individual enemy) and the *hostis* (collective enemy).[39] Herein lies the uncanny twinning of the words for enemy, 'host' and 'hospitality', a proximity haunted by the fantasy of the 'enemy' within our midst. The trope of *Flûchtlingspolitik* (the politics of the exile) is permanently entwined here with that of *Feindkonstruction*:

38 See Howerd, Frankie, *Up Pompei!* series, 1969–70; Jack Pulman's *I Claudius*, BBC TV mini-series, 1976 was based on the 1934 novel by Robert Graves. On the doubling of Denise as actress/Roberte, see Klossowski's 'L'indiscernable', *Nouvelle Revue Française*, June 1978; 'The indiscernable', *Decadence of the Nude*, 2002, pp. 142–59.

39 Klossowski quotes Carl Schmitt's *Der Begriff des Politischen*, Duncker und Humblot, Munich and Leipzig, 1932; see 'Qui est mon prochain', *Esprit*, December, 1938, in Klossowski, *Écrits d'un monomane, Essais, 1933–9*, Jean Decottignies ed., Gallimard, Paris, 2001, pp. 161–82.

the construction of the enemy: friend or fiend? The paradigms of etymological reversal – the *pharmakon* of words with opposite meanings – were at their origins linked to ritual and sacrifice: hence the French Revolution's killing of a king and the Nazi's desire for the 'sacrifice' of an entire race become coeval ... In both Popular Front celebrations such as Jean Renoir's film *La Marseillaise*, 1938 (with citizen extras) and the 150th anniversary celebrations of 1939, the French Revolution was currently being re-enacted on the streets. Klossowski's Sade addressed his contemporaries in this context.[40]

Klossowski, writing from the perspective of his entangled personal and intellectual identities, Polish, German, French, Catholic and Calvinist – and his Jewish secret – saw his text become prophecy. From Christ to *Kristallnacht* ... While he begins and ends 'Who is my neighbour?' with the parable of the Good Samaritan and Christian love, it was published under a rubric 'The Forces of Hatred' in December 1938 in the aftermath of the Nazi's 'Night of Broken Glass': anti-Semitism become terrifyingly 'real' in the destruction of synagogues and shops and deportations, one night that was the harbinger of the internecine destruction of nations. 'Who is my neighbour?' is the germ of 'Sade my neighbour', their genesis a few months apart.[41] Within the College of Sociology, 'the Sadian secret society par excellence', the Society of the Friends of Crime, Klossowski lectured on Sade amidst the Revolutionary celebrations of 1939, citing the eighteen hundred acts of guillotining that the Marquis witnessed from his window in the Picpus prison ... 'All in all, the vision of society in a permanent state of immorality is presented as a *utopia of evil*;

40 Klossowski, 'Sade et la Révolution', *Sade mon prochain, ibid.*, pp. 183–204. Lecture for the College of Sociology, 7 February, 1939: this became the introduction to *Sade mon prochain*, 1947 and the preface to 'La philosophie dans le boudoir' (*Œuvres complètes* 3, see note 5). René Girard's, *La Violence et le sacré*, Grasset, Paris, 1972 – without reference to Schmitt – pursues the notion of *pharmakos*, and the *homo sacer* – anticipating the writings of Giorgio Agamben.

41 Klossowski, 'Qui est mon prochain?' (*Esprit*, 75, December 1938, pp. 402–33), in *Ecrits d'un monomane, Essais 1933–9*, Jean Decottignies ed., pp. 173–5.

this paradoxical utopia corresponds to the virtual state of our modern society. [...] Method is put to the service of regression'.[42]

This is why Sade is our contemporary; why the Iranian artist, Barbad Golshiri, uses the tropes of Sade and Revolutionary bloodbath in the political works he smuggles into the 'rest of the world' for us to see.[43] Precisely as a novelist and artist of cruelty and the immoral, of collaboration, of *jouissance* in shame and impotence rather than resistance, Klossowski is our contemporary today.

* * *

During the Second World War Balthus, Klossowski's brother, would seek refuge in neutral Switzerland; Klossowski's spiritual refuge was the Catholic church, which harboured for a while his religious and sexual conundrums. 'Defrocking' became the trope of his autobiographical novel, *La Vocation suspendue*, 1950.[44] Even when, with the title *La Révocation de l'Édit de Nantes*, the displaced reference to religious persecution is explicit, exegetes remain fascinated by Roberte's seduction and the 'parallel bars scene' – at the expense of her memories, her 'Roman impressions'.[45] Klossowski's

42 '*Somme tout, la vision d'une société à l'état d'immoralité permanent se présente comme une utopie du mal; cette utopie paradoxale répond à l'état virtuel de notre société moderne ... La méthode est mise au service de la régression*', Klossowski, 'Sade et la révolution', *Sade mon prochain*, *ibid.*, p. 200.

43 Barbad Golshiri (whose father, the writer Houshang Golshiri, survived the 'Chian murders of Iran') presented the one-man show *L'Inconnu de la Scéne* (sic) in a David-like bloodbath, 'Iranian Arts Now', Paris, Cité des Arts, 28 June, 2012, and has a project, 'Sade et Eyck', involving the broadcast of Sade's works for the Jan Van Eyckplein, Bruges.

44 Curiously Foucault 'forgets' the tabernacle's content for the 'void left behind by the division of Christian theology [...] the void of the sign and the artwork', Michel Foucault, 'The Prose of Acteon', (*Nouvelle Revue Française,* March 1964) in Klossowski, *The Baphomet*, trans. Sophie Hawkes and Stephen Sartarelli, Eridanos Press, Colorado, 1988, p. xxxiv.

45 Following the massacre of Protestants by Catholics in 1572 (c. 25,000 in Paris ...) the Revocation of the Edict of Nantes by Louis XIV in 1685 withdrew the rights granted to Protestants by King Henri IV in 1598 (which had ended decades of religious wars).

later drawings of this scene are not merely simulacra in their own terms but 'screen memories': his title is the key which remains the explicit blind spot of his exegetes. In psychoanalytic terms it is astonishing that the clue at the dark vortex of this fiction of collaboration remains 'not perceived' by Michel Foucault in his celebrated essay 'The Prose of Acteon'. Foucault displaces the list of saved Jewish children hidden in a tabernacle in a church in Anzio with 'the void left behind by the division of Christian theology [...] the void of the sign and the artwork'.[46] The 'oversight' is blotted out by the intoxication of intellectual thought, the displacement of theology by structuralism, content by exegesis, life and lives by the *postfactum*, by intellectual afterlife. Klossowski would rejoice in the repetition of his compulsions, where the simulacrum multiplies to hide the meaning at the heart of the abyss: he is master of displacement, condensation and, above all, the *mise en abyme*.

The marital and adulterous relations which fascinate Klossowski posit alternative trinities: 'obscene' repetitions of the notion 'Three in One and One in Three'. The deceived host, the enemy within, the laws and transgressions of 'hospitality' confound the regimes of art, society, Christendom. With wicked, lubricious or mischievous pleasure, interjecting at will, Klossowski conflates the sacred with the staple of fairy tale, of legend and of vaudeville. We relish the svelte beauty or sudden shocks of his prose, the apparently uncensored fantasies of the drawings, so light, yet worked so laboriously. His bestowal of attention on these works involves time of an order which is no longer ours. Klossowski splices the banality of our everyday lives or loves with their sacred and cultic origins, with perceptions of hidden coercion, political horror. This is why he has been so inspiring to cutting-edge contemporary artists linked to performance and public spectacle such as Pierre Bal Blanc or indeed Santiago Serra.[47]

46 Foucault, Michel, 'The Prose of Acteon', in Klossowski, *The Baphomet, ibid.*

47 Choreographer Pierre Bal Blanc staged 'La Monnaie Vivante/The Living Currency' in Paris, 2006; Leuven, 2007; Tate Modern, London, 2008 (where I lectured on Klossowki's *La Monnaie Vivante* in the presence of Santiago Serra); and at the 6th Berlin Biennale, 2010, with his CAC Bretigny troupe.

It is psychoanalysis itself, vaunting its own myths, its short history, which is 'put to work' by Klossowski's seventy-year œuvre. It is interesting to see his narratives themselves as a work of unravelling: the refiguration of psychoanalytic knots. 'It is the work which makes the enigma erupt, on the side of a psychoanalysis henceforth in labour' says Hervé Castanet: *S'il y a énigme, c'est au côté de la psychanalyse. C'est l'*œuvre *qui fait surgir cette énigme au côté de l'analyse désormais mis au travail.*

... If there is enigma, it is with psychoanalysis ...[48]

48 Castanet, preface to *Écritures théâtrales du traumatisme*, *op. cit.*, p. 9.

Introduction to the English-language Edition: Why a book about Pierre Klossowski in 2013? A Brief Biography

Pierre Klossowski was born in Paris in 1905 and died in 2001. He was a writer, translator, essayist, actor and painter. He had never been at the forefront of the social scene nor celebrated by the larger, popular media. He had no experience with television studios. He lived quietly in Paris, yet he was not unknown and reclusive. On the contrary, he was a major twentieth-century writer, translator, essayist and painter and was recognised as such by his peers; he was the favourite interlocutor with many of them. He is what one would call a great figure in French culture. Numerous texts and theses have been published about his work, and his books have been translated into many languages. All the same, Pierre Klossowski continues to be considered a difficult and unclassifiable author.

Of Polish origin, he was the eldest son of the painter and art historian Erich Klossowski, author of a monograph on Honoré Daumier. His mother, Baladine, was a student of Bonnard. When she died in 1969 the writer and critic Jean Cassou said of her, 'Baladine was the most adorable, playful and spontaneous woman in the world – ingenuous in her own way'. Pierre Klossowski's parents were married in 1903 and separated in 1917. His younger brother was Balthus, an artist loved by the media and, at the end of his life, considered by celebrity magazines to be one of the greatest, most highly valued painters of the twentieth century. Pierre grew up surrounded with his parents' friends – the writers and thinkers that made Paris the intellectual capital of the world between 1910 and 1930. In the twenties, Baladine and her sons left Paris for a few years to live in Geneva, then Berlin, where Pierre learned both German and Latin.

During his youth, Pierre Klossowski became close to Rainer Maria Rilke, his mother's lover from 1920 to 1926. Baladine described her sons as 'my teachers and my joys, and I was their playmate. When Rilke would join us we were like four happy children'. Back in Paris, Klossowski worked as secretary for André Gide, the future Nobel laureate in Literature, who helped the young man in his studies; both Gide and Rilke were father figures to him. He received his diploma from the *École des Hautes Études* in 1928 after writing a thesis on the Scout movement in Germany. He started translating from German during this period, an activity he would keep up for decades. His friends were intellectuals, including Georges Bataille and others associated with Surrealist groups. In 1929 he fell in love with Elizabeth (Betty) Holland, Pierre Leyris' future wife, to whom he wrote numerous letters that have been preserved. He was obsessed with Betty for many years. Later, in 1939 Klossowski affirmed his pronounced attraction to religion, an interest that proved to be difficult and hesitating at times. He took classes in theology intending to become a priest; a spiritual crisis caused him to abandon this project. In 1947 he met and married Denise Morin, a widow with two children deported to Ravensbrück during the war. The following year they had a son, Matthieu.

This was the beginning of a productive period. That same year he published the notable essay *Sade My Neighbor* with Éditions du Seuil. In 1950 he wrote his first narrative, *La Vocation suspendue*, in which he played out the story, through the character of Brother Jerome, of the throes of his own spiritual crisis, his complicated love affair with a nun, and his decision not to be ordained. He continued his translations, especially of Nietzsche who had a strong influence on the intellectual scene in which Klossowski was important. In 1952 he published *Roberte Ce Soir*, the first narrative of what would be called the *Roberte* trilogy or *Les lois de l'hospitalité*. He illustrated this piece with a few pencil drawings. Three years later he wrote *Diane at Her Bath*, a re-examination of the ancient myth of Diane and Actaeon. This was followed by the two other pieces in the trilogy, *The Revocation of the Edict of Nantes* and *Le Souffleur*, released in 1959 and 1960 respectively. In these works Klossowski indulgently describes his heroine Roberte, whose physiognomy had become the *unique sign* around which his life and thought incessantly turned. Roberte is captured in erotic and pornographic scenes that her husband Octave contrived in an effort to grasp her soul. Klossowski wrote these pieces in a sober, Jansenist style; the characters discuss theology without the slightest vulgarity. The philosopher

Gilles Deleuze was inspired by these works to write an important article on Roberte and the parallels between body and language. Other philosophers such as Michel Foucault and Jean-François Lyotard also admired and were influenced by Klossowski. Other friends of his in the 1960s were Roland Barthes and Philippe Sollers. Sollers asked Klossowski to contribute to the avant-garde review *Tel Quel* and invited the author to organise a conference on Sade in 1966.

His 1964 translation of Virgil's Aeneid created a polemical reaction: he had striven to imitate the Latin phrasing so closely that it became almost unreadable in French, offending some Latin scholars. The following year he wrote his last work of fiction, *The Baphomet*, an outlandish tale of the erotic and spiritual adventures of a young page during the Middle Ages. He also played a role that year in Robert Bresson's film *Au hasard Balthazar*. In 1969 a collection of his articles on Nietzsche were published under the title *Nietzsche and the Vicious Circle*. In them, Klossowski recounts his own experience of the 'vicious circle', extensively described by the philosopher. He comments on the deterioration of the logical forms of Nietzsche's rational thinking, which he relates to his own subjugation to the image of Roberte as the *unique sign*. What remains are intensities associated with the flow of images that dissolve the unity of language and one's individual, psychic identity.

After *The Baphomet*, Klossowski chose silence, or what he would later call 'muteness'. He stopped writing fiction and lived the next thirty-five years creating full-scale coloured crayon drawings, his *grandes machines*. These drawings, purposely awkward, represent characters usually – but not always – played by Roberte in the scenes of his stories, and in them Pierre gives Roberte the explicit physiognomy of his wife, Denise. The film director Raoul Ruiz made two films from his narratives: *La Vocation suspendue* in 1977 and *L'Hypothèse du tableau volé* in 1978. That same year, Pierre Zucca, who had already put together a series of photographs to illustrate *La Monnaie Vivante* in 1970, filmed Pierre as his character Octave, and Denise as Roberte; this film was released in the cinemas as *Roberte*.

Numerous exhibitions made Klossowski a well-known artist, and his work is still shown in major museums and galleries of contemporary, avant-garde art. In 1984 he had a show at the Holly Solomon Gallery in

New York – others followed, including at the Maeght Lelong Gallery in Paris. A reviewer wrote: 'Pierre Klossowski, better known in Paris for his prestigious erotic fictions, is seen here to be an exciting draughtsman … The almost life-size characters are drawn with a softness that is the exact opposite of what the situations could have called for.' Even after his death, his success did not wane, but rather increased in intensity. More recently, in 2006–7 his work was exhibited in London's Whitechapel Gallery in a show entitled *Pierre Klossowski and the Vicious Circle*, also presented in Cologne's Ludwig Museum and modified for the Centre Georges Pompidou in Paris.

At his death, the testimonies were unanimous about the grandeur of his oeuvre, a work not bound to a single medium. Klossowski had been a *monomaniac* throughout his long life. His words were an attempt to describe the visions that obsessed him. His concepts were tools to tackle the workings of the image. His coloured drawings closely and directly depicted the visions of his childhood and their magical power. Pierre Klossowski, firmly enshrined within the literary and art historical canon in France, continues to gaze at our century's creations. This is why a book that takes into account the entirety of his work, and not just the literary, conceptual or artistic dimension, is pertinent today.

Introduction

This book examines the work of Pierre Klossowski (1905–2001) in its *entirety*. His work revolves around the *gaze*, a gaze heated to glowing point, transforming all who meet it. The focal point is the destiny of Actaeon, a figure with whom the author and his male heroes identify. Rarely has an artist's oeuvre interpreted the gaze in such a radical way – as an active, mobile and evanescent object that picks apart the coordinates of representation and the visible. How is one to *see* the invisible divinity (the eye being the noble organ according to Doctors of the Church)? This question plagued Klossowski, and he displaced it onto the pornographic rituals of a woman being violated (a new Diana). Faced with these tirelessly repeated scenes, a subject becomes a pure gaze object. Once a hunter, he is now the prey.

This book is not a monograph on Pierre Klossowski. A monograph has the task of relating an oeuvre back to itself. This does not rule out situating the oeuvre in political, literary, art and other contexts, though nothing will be said here of the literary style of the author. The writing will not be related back to what was at stake in mid- to late-twentieth century literature (Klossowski's first narrative piece, *La Vocation suspendue*, dates from 1950). His artwork will not be examined from the point of view of the European avant-garde. Finally, nothing will be mentioned of the impact, which was major, of his works dedicated to Sade, Nietzsche or utopia. Nonetheless, in each case (narratives, painting, theory), Klossowski was known and admired by his peers (Bataille, Blanchot, Parain, Gide, Foucault, Deleuze and Lacan): he is a *major* writer, a *major* theoretician, and a *major* painter. He is also a *major* translator of Latin and German.

The approach we have chosen is different: Pierre Klossowski accomplished a real feat in the field of culture and creation; to the best of our knowledge, he is unique. From 1972 onwards (he was already sixty-seven years old), he stopped writing fictional narratives and theoretical texts. He gave up writing, in which he had acquired an uncontested reputation, to devote himself to what he called his *muteness*: his 'painting', which consisted of large, coloured drawings. He had started making drawings, initially without colour, in the early 1950s. The feat does not lie in the switch whereby a former writer subsequently only paints. It lies in the following: Klossowski became just as famous as a painter as he was as a writer and theoretician. His painting found a new public of collectors, galleries, curators and critics, some of whom were unaware – or virtually unaware – of his literary oeuvre. This switch towards painting exclusively was an *absolute break* with writing. What logic governs this switch? What necessity can be read in it? What is at stake here in terms of creation? In what way does this switch to the *pictorial* – which constitutes the conclusion of Klossowski's oeuvre – imply an advancement of his earlier work (from the 1930s to the 1960s) on the Marquis de Sade, the philosopher Nietzsche, and utopian fiction (through a parody of Charles Fourier)?

Today, Klossowski is still just as famous as a writer, and his valuation as a painter is high enough to make his works inaccessible to the enthusiast of his narratives. The likes of Artaud and Michaux also have an art oeuvre, but one that remains overshadowed by the renown of their texts. Klossowski has managed not to be a *writer-who-draws-and-paints*; he now holds his rightful place in the art sphere. Klossowski has two types of commentator and critic: those who speak about his writings and those who comment on his painting. Between the two, there is little exchange.

In the work that follows, this separation is explicitly done away with. The *entire* (fictional, theoretical and artistic) oeuvre will be tackled. Of course, Klossowski very often moved from the *speculative* to the *specular*, to use his terms. Rather than saying something of the *powers* that made him speak, he wanted to show what was imposed upon him as *visions*. These visions provide the conjunction between the *forces* that make up the being of any subject (forces that he called, following his extended readings of Sade and Nietzsche, imponderable, obscure, irrepressible, impulsive forces, in a word, forces of *non-speech*) and the staging whereby, in transforming and falsifying them, they find a place. Klossowski gave them a name: it is the obsessive constraint of the *phantasm* that subjugates him without respite. To exorcise the visions and the constraint of the phantasm, he would turn himself into the creator of *simulacra*: fictions, paintings, even concepts.

Taking on the entire oeuvre means examining what the words of fiction fail to depict, forcing him to call upon concepts and images. The inverse is also true: the image shows, but it does not display everything, hence the return to words and concepts. Yet concepts are abstract and cannot completely convey visions and unexchangeable intensities, hence the return to fiction and painting. This interplay of word/concept/image is decisive for his oeuvre. Each text (whether fictional or theoretical) has its own blind spot, its fault line. The same goes for the image: something escapes and comes crashing down in a paralysing silence.

A paramount expression emerges in Klossowski's writing: *the pantomime of spirits*. It denotes the moment when, in an encounter between a man and a woman (*the husband/the wife*), words cease to be uttered. Klossowski's fictional scene, which opens onto the sexual meeting of bodies, freezes into silence. The wife's body, taken over by desire – Klossowski says *demons* – becomes the site of a singular experience, an encounter where desiring body ties in to dogmatic theology: her bodily enjoyment marks the abjection of her soul. *God is evil*, and the wife's soul is given a taste of it. The true conversation is a silent one, a pantomime. Klossowski's spectacle – his phantasm – unfolds under the gaze of the husband (or Actaeon): *The truth of theology is pornography*. The *pantomime of spirits* is this truth become both pornographic spectacle and logical proof – between image and word – of the exigency of this new *Supremely Evil Being* (to use Sade's expression), the Klossowskian God.

In his theoretical works, Klossowski often commented on what was at stake in his monstration/demonstration. He constructed concepts with their own meanings: simulacrum, perversion, tableau vivant, obsessional phantasm, (libidinal) economy of impulses, stereotype, Gulliverian vision, monomania, solecism, value, evil, and so forth. These concepts are tools for thinking through the pornographic *specular* as theological truth.

Is Klossowski to be considered an *eccentric* of thought, a *fringe element* of culture, a *hapax* in the world of arts? Not in the slightest. How about a *singular* theoretician with whom concepts, words and images assume a new and unheard of value? A practitioner of the letter, written and shown, in which the object gaze is isolated? Quite so!

Klossowski as Reader

In the 1930s, when he was twenty-five years old, Pierre Klossowski began translating German (Hölderlin, Kafka, Benjamin, Scheler, etc.).[1] It was during those years that he first came across Sade. In 1934 he began reading Nietzsche, whom he would also go on to translate. Klossowski became a prestigious commentator on these two authors, each of whom overshadowed their respective centuries, and his works on them are by no means marginal in his oeuvre. They are recognised and cited by specialists. Above all, they are not to be separated from his fictional works. For Klossowski, activities are never separate, nor held at a distance from one another. He insisted on this:

> The presence of these works of imagination (*Diana at her Bath*, The *Roberte* trilogy, *The Baphomet*) necessarily reacts on the notional plane, allowing for the conception of *The Philosopher Villain* and *The Vicious Circle*. This completely changes the perspective of what is thought, felt and said, taking away, even annulling, the false perspective of a complete bibliography.[2]

Even the most cursory reading of Klossowski's work on Sade, Nietzsche or utopia (Charles Fourier), from 1933 to today, reveals an instantly recognisable style that will take on its full extent in the fictional narratives. Style, however, is not to be understood solely in its literary aspect, but also in its theoretical questioning. What unfolds here is initially worded in theological terms: the content of being is not exchangeable. The subject is an enigma to himself; he is not for all that condemned to powerlessness. What can be deduced from that unavoidable torment – 'the presence in his soul of those forces and energies that constitute an

1 See the list of Klossowski's translations in Arnaud, A., *Pierre Klossowski*, Les contemporains, Seuil, 1990, pp. 202–3.

2 Klossowski quoted by Arnaud, [translated from] *ibid.*, p. 199.

irreducible totality, impossible to communicate […]?'[3] Klossowski's oeuvre gives a reply to this question: exchange the unexchangeable. Admittedly, this reply fails: the unexchangeable remains, but so does the desire to know, which traces out its path, creating 'equivalents', or 'stand-ins' for that which is incommunicable.

We shall take our bearings from a question: how does Klossowski read Sade and Nietzsche? What does our author uncover in commenting on these two philosopher-writers? First of all, he discovers that his question was already a question for them. Next, he experiences the fact that an oeuvre is inseparable from a subjective experience. Both of them, in their own way, try to say and write that for which there are no words: the vanishing point of being.

One notion overshadows his reading: that of forces. He will call them by turns psychical, sensible, polymorphous, diffuse, impulsive, obscure, from within, impenetrable, irrational, solvent, hostile, subversive, sterile, individual, transgressive, monstrous, foreign, animal, affirmative, chaotic, occult, demonic, perverse, etc. His decisive formulation is 'forces of non-speech'.[4] Here, then, are the forces – real forces – that stir the soul. The Church fathers spoke of them at great length. They will be examined in terms of evil, perversion (Sade), and madness (Nietzsche), where God (uncreated yet creator) or any divine or moral (ego) unity is abolished.

The forces of non-speech are, by definition, unexchangeable, indiscernible, and ungraspable, hence the equivalents, the stand-ins, or better still, the simulacra that are used to communicate and produce a social bond nevertheless. The concept of *simulacrum* is surely Klossowski's most profound. He uses it to account for his literary and art oeuvre. The simulacrum is an authentic method of exposition:

> The simulacrum has the advantage of not claiming to fix down what it presents of an experience and what it says about it; far from excluding the contradictory, it naturally implies it. For if it cheats on the notional level, it is because it is faithfully miming the

3 *Ibid.*, p. 8.
4 *Ibid.*

> part that is incommunicable. The simulacrum is all that we know of an experience; a notion is only its waste matter calling upon other waste matter.[5]

The simulacrum has an opening function that calls upon accomplices (the readers and viewers). Why 'opening'?

> Language is left wanting because it is made up of propositions that lead identities to intervene. And from the moment that, due to the bulging sums to be spent, one is forced to spend not for gain but for the sake of spending, one can no longer stay on the plane of identity. One is forced to open up the notions beyond themselves. What does that mean, 'to open up the notions beyond themselves'? Or rather: to what does language correspond when its propositions no longer have identities that intervene? A language freed of all notions no longer corresponds to being, having abolished itself along with the identities: and indeed, by eluding any supreme identification (under the name of God [...]), being can only be grasped as perpetually fleeing everything that exists, just at the point where notion pretends to explain being [...], and so existence falls back into discontinuity, where it had never ceased 'being'.[6]

For Klossowski, both Sade and Nietzsche are 'openers' of 'notions beyond themselves', masters in the use of simulacra as operators that make the reader an accomplice. It is as one such accomplice that Klossowski reads them and gives his commentary. We are not to expect fixed notions from our author that annul the very experience they speak of, but rather simulacra that mimic the incommunicable! Examining the concept of simulacrum, in Sade and in Nietzsche, is indispensable when it comes to grasping how it is used in Klossowski's painting. The pictorial simulacrum is mute; it carries out a truly silent conversation on a screen displaying frozen, immobile representation. Such are Klossowski's pictures.

This book concerns Klossowski – his reading – and not the authors he reads. There will be no reference to the numerous critical books and essays on Sade and Nietzsche. Nevertheless, all the quotations from Sade and Nietzsche given by Klossowski are to be found here so as to determine a context.

5 [Translated from] Klossowski, P., *La Ressemblance*, Éditions Ryôan-ji, Marseille, 1984, p. 24.

6 *Ibid.*, pp. 26–7.

Three chapters order our reading:

In the first, dedicated to Sade, the presence of evil (perversion) is looked at in particular through the way it is brought to light in an apathetic accomplishment of integral monstrosity. It will be demonstrated how Sadean perversion, willed into existence on a wide scale, thenceforth implies atheism, which is likewise integral. A new face of the Marquis emerges, that of a genuine theologian.

In the second chapter, which focuses on Nietzsche, we single out the abolition of the very agencies that allow for unity of centring and order: God, the ego, reason, language, and so on. The subject is reduced to a sheer fortuitous moment at which the forces of Chaos return incessantly in the shape of the Same – the Same as an impulse that is henceforth goalless and shapeless. Nietzsche was to realise (because he was mad?) what Sade had always come up against (because he was submitted to the Law of the Name-of-the-Father?[7]): the impossibility of escaping the logic of outrage in so far as it must necessarily maintain what it is fighting against; the impossibility of freeing oneself from a 'counter' thought and a 'counter' practice.

The third chapter introduces a utopia – whose content is negative – that Klossowski invented in 1970, *Living Currency* (*La Monnaie Vivante*). It is an ideal society where the world of needs and commercial exchange are replaced by impulses. It is constructed in reference to Charles Fourier and his world of the passions of love. It stands out, in its impossibility of ever coming about, as a sharp criticism of the world, revealing its bitter truth: perversion has become the reason behind our industrial society – its radical un-thought.

Klossowski's thought is difficult – it is not dialectical. It sometimes displays condensed wording that verges on the unreadable. Above all, it is not just one thought. Klossowski often returns to his texts and modifies his sentences, but in each case showing great rigour. Is his thought to be summed up and simplified in order to make it smooth and monolithic?

7 The failing of the signifier of the Name-of-the-Father is the sign of psychosis. See Lacan, J., *The Seminar Book III, The Psychoses, (1955–6)*, trans. R. Grigg, Norton, New York, 1993.

No. On the other hand, one of the challenges is to avoid making it more complex. We shall take our bearings from one specific part of his thought: the author's *difficulties* in his readings of Sade and Nietzsche, spanning more than sixty years. Now, these difficulties are the very same that both of the two philosopher-writers braved. We will be taking up the terms that spell out these difficulties, as well as the contradictions within the texts. Klossowski's various viewpoints and angles of attack will be brought to light. The objects are seemingly the same, and yet, by changing the point of view and tilting the light, new truths arise. They will set the conceptual markers that signal the switch from the *speculative* to the *specular*.

Sade: Evil, Perversion

Pierre Klossowski is a renowned specialist on Sade's oeuvre. His works are classics that are routinely cited. It is the perversion in Sade that fascinates him. This fascination is not focused on the description of perverse acts singled out for their crudity. Its object is rather the way Sade's (philosophical and political) thought ties in with the integral monstrosity that he claims to bring about by introducing it into this thought. This is an examination of the presence of *evil* – its possibility, its quest, its concrete manifestations – in so far as perversion carries it to its full pitch.

How is a singular experience to be translated into writing? asks Klossowski, in regard to Sade the writer. The perversion presented in the fiction cannot be isolated from the text that records it, nor from the theoretical function that it occupies. Klossowski does not comment on the sadistic scenes as such. His line of attack is different. What does thought become once perversion is no longer simply the privilege of an aristocrat on the eve of the Revolution, but is established as a concept? There is a cutting edge to Sade that the Enlightenment sought to render obsolete, in vain.

In 1962, Jacques Lacan wrote of *Sade My Neighbor* that it has no need to resort to the 'same things as the highbrow literati'.[1] This is a sizeable compliment. Lacan is designating the fact that Klossowski is not obsessed with the Marquis's odd sexual manias, but is perplexed by a thought that, through the rational knowledge and reasoning maintained in classical language,[2] tries to communicate the incommunicable part of an anomaly:

1 Lacan, J., 'Kant with Sade' in *Écrits, The First Complete Edition in English,* trans. B. Fink, Norton, New York/London, 2006, p. 666. Lacan also speaks of Klossowski's 'extreme perspicacity'.

2 Sade lends to his protagonists 'a rigour of expression and argumentation which is perfectly rational, and does not himself invent some code language,' Klossowski, P., 'The

perversion. This perversion is not moralised, is not viewed through the lens of the Oedipus complex, nor is it reduced to any abnormal particularity in the slightest. It takes on meaning only when referred to the norms of reason – the very same reason that the Enlightenment thinkers and French Revolutionaries daubed on their banners. How is one to write, in the terms of reason, about that which exceeds and transgresses this same reason? This was Sade's absolute choice. Sade's object, perversion, pushes the thinking of reason to its point of impossibility, causing it to implode. What is a thinking that implodes? What remains of reason when it has fallen apart? These are the questions that fascinate our commentator who took the trouble to read Sade, and all of it.

The 1947 publication of *Sade My Neighbor* influenced the arrival of Sade's oeuvre on the centre stage of contemporary reflection. The title hints that the question posed by Sade's writing is not distant, outdated, or anachronistic – it lies close at hand. It is in this respect that Sade is his neighbour. In May 1966, at the behest of the editors of the journal *Tel Quel*, Klossowski gave a lecture, 'Signe et perversion chez Sade', later developed and published under the title, *The Philosopher Villain*. In his foreword to this book, Klossowski has very harsh words for his previous works, and one could say that *The Philosopher Villain* stands as the critique of *Sade My Neighbor*. We shall be going over these crucial criticisms.

Sade My Neighbor examines 'Sade's thought'; on the other hand, *The Philosopher Villain* describes the logic and the deadlocks of 'Sade's sadism'.[3]

Phantasms of Perversion: Sade and Fournier' in *Art & Text*, 18, July 1985, pp. 23–34. 'It is unheard of – into what an abyss of folly one is hurled when, in reasoning, one abandons the aid of reason's torch!' Marquis de Sade, 'Philosophy in the Bedroom', in *Justine, Philosophy in the Bedroom and Other Writings*, Grove Weidenfield, New York, 1965, p. 326.

3 Klossowski, P., *Sade My Neighbor*, including 'The Philosopher Villain', trans. A. Lingis, Northwestern University Press, Evanston, 1991, p. 6.

Impossible Revolution

Sade was part of the historic Revolution, yet as a witness rather than a main player. The Revolution results from a '[...] vast combination of contradictory demands [...]'.[4] This remark will not surprise the historian. However, what does come as a surprise, right in the opening lines, is the reference to 'psychic forces'.[5] The expression is barely explained, and yet it is of great importance. Here lies our author's originality. Certain 'psychic forces' come to inscribe themselves in a determined historical moment where they have a causal place. Perversion is a choice operator for producing and intensifying these silent, subterranean psychic forces, with unheard of consequences.

Klossowski depicts Sade as a privileged aristocrat who is thus in a subjective position that stands in opposition to that of the 'amorphous mass of average men'.[6] For their part, the people demand that 'Natural man'[7] should prove himself – Natural man being ordinary man in an idealised form. Contrary to this, Sade – who developed, because of the inequity of his level of life, 'a supreme degree of lucidity' – wants '[his] own problematic structure [...] [to be] admitted as a universal necessity, and [awaits] the Revolution as something that would bring about a complete remoulding of the structure of man'.[8] On one side, there is Natural man, on the other, 'the image of integral man, a man of polymorphic sensibility'.[9] Sade believed that the adventure would now be possible. Klossowski takes pleasure in imagining this hopeful euphoria. That was Sade's error, and the error of his peers too. The Revolution renders these great lords obsolete, outdated and finished in as much as their days are drawing to an end. '[...] [T]hey will fall because they are an end, not a beginning, the end of a long evolution'.[10]

4 *Ibid.*, p. 47.
5 *Ibid.*
6 *Ibid.*
7 *Ibid.*
8 *Ibid.*, p. 48.
9 *Ibid.*
10 *Ibid.*

The evolving world quickly reduces them to rotten fruit. 'Their dream of giving birth to a humanity like themselves is in contradiction with the very basis of their ripeness, or their lucidity'.[11] These remarks run counter to Sade's positive vision. The aristocrats' immorality had been sustained by values (the king, nobility, etc.) that the Revolution cast aside. Being symptoms of the break-up of historical society, they have no place in the new social scheme where the Sovereign People, the general will, holds pride of place. Sade's transgression was in solidarity with and inseparable from the *ancien régime*, and it was perhaps he who drew back the curtain on it more than anyone else.

The contradiction between Sade and the Revolution is not relative or contingent, but structural. The problem is 'insoluble'.[12] The very person who single-handedly managed to discover what was really at stake in the Revolution finds himself cut off from the very social forces that brought it on. The masses do not know; they are fairly narrow-minded and blind to what they are building and developing. The 'man of privilege',[13] and he alone, is lucid; only he has an acute awareness of what is being hatched. In this capacity, Sade was a real danger for the Revolution.

Klossowski has scant sympathy for the amorphous mass, for the natural man desired by the new wildly excited social forces. For him the Revolution is on Sade's side – on the side of his oeuvre: 'he made of the virtual criminality of his contemporaries his own personal destiny [...]'.[14] Sade would bring about the Revolution – its un-thought, its virtuality.

In the midst of the revolutionary fury, Sade kept rather to himself. He wrote: 'Amid everything I am not well; my state detention, with the guillotine right under my eyes, made me suffer a hundred times more than all the imaginable Bastilles ever had'.[15] What does him harm is not the Reign of Terror with its multiple, bloodstained acts of violence, but the prevailing *not wanting to know anything about it* – its blindness. Faced with this

11 *Ibid.*
12 *Ibid.*, p. 49.
13 *Ibid.*
14 *Ibid.*, pp. 49–50.
15 *Ibid.*, p. 50.

Terror, Sade wrote *Justine*, where he pushed the horrors contained in his doctrinal analyses to their limit. He felt compelled to lay bare 'the secret impulse of the revolutionary mass'.[16] Now, what was the Reign of Terror doing, what was it saying? It was proclaiming that the horror it was bringing stemmed from the will of the sovereign people! The sovereign people, revolutionary lawfulness and natural man are merely concepts built for the occasion, so as not to say what is really at issue: *evil*. The Revolution and the Reign of Terror, concretising this evil day in day out, do not want to know anything about it. They repress it.

We can see a radical opposition here: the Republican State wants the public good, and yet Sade is asserting that the State 'in its depths [...] nurtures the germs of evil'.[17] Thus its action is reduced to preventing evil from hatching out. This is a permanent threat in the Republican State. Evil can erupt at any time, although it never does, for evil is not in a position of exteriority with regard to the Republican State. It lies at its centre. This is what is eating away at Sade: may this evil finally come to be!

> [...] evil has to break out once and for all, the tares have to flourish so that the spirit can tear them up and destroy them. It is necessary to make evil reign once and for all in the world in order that it destroy itself, and Sade's mind find peace at last.[18]

Fundamentally, Sade is anti-Republican. He knows that freedom, proclaimed by the Republican State, 'refuses to recognize that it lives only through evil and claims to exist for the sake of good'.[19] The Marquis's strategy would be to show the Republican State its unknown cause, tracking down the cause of the revolutionary Reign of Terror, and becoming the one to reveal evil's work. His job was twofold: first to track down this evil, then to present it to the Revolution as its own face.

Sade yearns for the reign of the integral man. But where does this man come from, a man who could never be a Natural man from a happy

16 *Ibid.*
17 *Ibid.*, p. 51.
18 *Ibid.*, p. 51.
19 *Ibid.*

age when natural innocence existed? The response is precise: he was produced by an act. 'Integral man thus bears the seal of crime, of the most redoubtable of all crimes: regicide'.[20] To kill the king is to kill God's temporal representative. To kill the king, or to kill God in people's consciousness, is an incommensurable act that brings with it an incommensurable consequence. For Sade, 'The putting to death of the king by the nation is then only the final phase of the process whose first phase is the putting to death of God by the revolt of the libertine great lord'.[21] Without this murder in consciousness, no regicide is possible. 'The execution of the king thus becomes the simulacrum of the putting to death of God'.[22] The place that Sade attributes to the great lord – in other words, to himself – is that of a logical precedence that makes the Revolution possible. The error of the revolutionaries is to fail to spot that while Louis XVI dies by means of the guillotine, it is not the traitor who is passing away, the tyrant who is being punished, but rather God's representative that is dying. The Republic on the other hand judges him an enemy who sold his people to foreign despots. Louis must die because he has destroyed the social pact. He must therefore first be judged, then sentenced, for his high treason. Because he broke the social pact, his person is no longer sacrosanct, and can be judged and sentenced like anyone else. Robespierre delivers this logic when he issues his sentence – 'Louis must die in order that the country live'.[23] The cement of the Republic finds its foundation. Only the likes of Danton will indicate a different logic with the proclamation: 'We do not wish to condemn the King, we wish to kill him'.[24]

The consequence of this regicide/patricide is the integral man, the criminal man par excellence. Instigating Revolution is not about putting the people in the place of the aristocracy; it is about pushing 'monarchical corruption [...] to its limit'.[25] Perpetrating regicide allows for the construction

20 *Ibid.*

21 *Ibid.*, p. 55.

22 *Ibid.*

23 *Ibid.*, p. 56.

24 *Ibid.*

25 *Ibid.*, p. 52.

of a Republican State synonymous with 'heightened criminality'. In this respect (and here we meet Sade's new but terrible thesis), the

> [...] revolutionary community will then be at bottom secretly, but inwardly bound up with the moral dissolution of monarchical society, since it is through this dissolution that the members have acquired the force and energy necessary for bloody decisions.[26]

The act of regicide vouches for the moral disintegration of monarchic society. By effectively bringing this about, it opens a door not to the future – not in the slightest – but to the prior logic that made it possible. It reveals how society was still limited in its criminality by the idea of God in every consciousness. Committing crime would amount to leaving behind monarchic inertia, to becoming truly republican. Regicide is the first of these crimes – the most radical one, the most decisive one – the one that will make all the others possible.

God is the keystone to the whole system. Regicide brings down this hierarchical system of reciprocal interlocking levels. The result for the Revolution is a vicious circle. Already steeped in crime, an aged and corrupt nation that has rattled its monarchical yoke can be sustained only by more crimes. For Sade, the French Revolution – the one before his eyes – actually never got going. 'The Republic, in short, can never begin'.[27] To come about, it would have had to commit the crime *absolutely*. Integral man might then have come into being. However, in principle, the Republic annuls the very thing it discovers by promoting the good of the people. Oriented in this way, such a State will be neither republican nor revolutionary. '[...] the Revolution is truly the Revolution only in as much as it is the monarchy in perpetual insurrection. A sacred value can be trampled underfoot only when one has it under one's feet'.[28] Klossowski excels in isolating this point of contradiction in Sade's thought: in wiping out what has been transgressed, in laying to waste what has been trampled underfoot, transgression, blasphemy, and provocation immediately disappear. In other words, as Sade puts it himself,

26 *Ibid.*
27 *Ibid.*, p. 55.
28 *Ibid.*

society 'would fall into an inertia whose result would soon be its certain ruin.'[29] It would be a matter of maintaining Monarchy in order to ceaselessly fight against it. Regicide must be continuously repeated so that each time its power of revival may be renewed. The Republic does not come in the wake of the Monarchy; it is Monarchy flouted in permanent insurrection. Inertia is in store should one go about things any other way.

In his tract 'Yet Another Effort, Frenchmen, if You Would Become Republicans', Sade broaches first religion, then morals. In the first chapter it is stated that, 'theism in no way suits a republican government.'[30] To affirm this, Sade employs 'positive rational arguments'.[31] For him, 'Christianity must be rejected because its social consequences are immoral'.[32] He affirms, *a contrario*, atheism, or a form of atheist morality. What is surprising is the second chapter, which draws fresh consequences from this morality: 'The point is not at all to love one's brethren as oneself [...] since that is in defiance of all the laws of nature [...]'.[33] The death of God (and its actualised simulacrum: the death of the King) entails 'freedom of conscience':[34] a tyranny has fallen. But this freedom of conscience does not suffice for a truly Republican State. For Sade, to act is to commit crime. Consider the terms of the moral change he wanted: yes to the community of women for men and to the community of men for women 'but in order to fill the public palaces of national prostitution';[35] yes to the community of children, but so as to deliver them up to 'sodomy';[36] yes to the removal of the family, but yes, too, to incest; yes to the community of wealth, but with theft, and so on. In a Republican State, '[...] calumny, theft, rape, incest, adultery, and sodomy are not to be sanctioned [...]'.[37]

29 *Ibid.*, p. 52.
30 *Ibid.*, p. 59.
31 *Ibid.*
32 *Ibid.*
33 *Ibid.*, p. 60.
34 *Ibid.*
35 *Ibid.*
36 *Ibid.*
37 *Ibid.*

Likewise for the crime *par excellence*, murder:

> A government that was born from the murder of God and that continues to exist through murder has lost in advance the right to inflict capital punishment; it consequently could not pronounce sanction against any other crime [...].[38]

Sade draws out all the consequences of the regicide/parricide that presided over the constitution of the Republican State, thus reasserting his notion of permanent insurrection:

> Insurrection [...] is not at all a *moral* condition; however, it has got to be a republic's permanent condition [...] the state of a moral man is one of tranquillity and peace; the state of an *immoral* man is one of perpetual unrest that pushes him to the necessary insurrection in which the republican must always keep the government of which he is a member.[39]

When applied, the consequences of atheism drive society towards perpetual movement. Each citizen must be immoral in order to implement the movement, the insurrection. Choosing permanent immorality sets out the logic of a social system heading to its destruction. Sade does not want to build a new society on the old one. He wants to destroy everything to create a truly new society. Otherwise the Republican State would only be a monarchical system plastered over with modernist ideas, a mere facelift.

Permanent immorality as the basic principle of a Republican society is a '*utopia of evil*'.[40] However, a new contradiction is pointed out. Such a utopia is limited by what cannot fail to arise once it has been accomplished: 'ennui'.[41] Endlessly committing crimes would only lead to boredom. How is one to get out of this? 'Against disgust and ennui there can be no remedy save to go yet further into new crimes ad infinitum'.[42] Proceeding thus, the way out is forever deferred, forever pushed back. More crimes lead to

38 *Ibid.*, p. 61.
39 *Ibid.*, p. 62.
40 *Ibid.*
41 *Ibid.*, p. 63.
42 *Ibid.*

more boredom that itself leads to the realisation of more and more crimes in order to combat it. Sade's utopia runs aground on this contradiction that paralyses all practice.

In a note from 1967, Klossowski comes back to the 1947 analysis to show its limits. He speaks of the 'tendentious deviation'[43] of his reasoning, which maintains Sade's system in a perpetuation of the same where change is impossible. Here lies the error: the utopia of evil does not leave out ennui, but the 'functional, or utilitarian, character that the institutions of a given social milieu give to the exercise of impulsive forces'.[44] Disgust and ennui follow crime 'only in the existing institutional world [...] [where] there arises the idea of such a crime'.[45] It has to be supposed that the state of perpetual motion would change the world in which it would begin its destructive course. The dark forces would be liberated. Permanent criminality would no longer have anything to do with the society of today. To generalise crime would no longer be simply to multiply it (a quantitative vision) but, through this crime, to change the society that promulgates it (a qualitative vision therefore). But Klossowski's 1947 analysis misses this option on the qualitative change obtained by permanent insurrection. A question arises as to what shape the criminal acts would take in an insurrectional state where dark forces hold the ground. *The Philosopher Villain* is devoted to this analysis.

The relations between Sade and the Revolution are ambiguous and complex. The Marquis' objective is to take off the mask of an idea or a doctrine in order to show its limits and contradictions, thereby making a radical internal critique of it. By adopting the very reasoning he is combating, he makes it implode. Our author is a true double agent, a spy on the enemy lines of reason. Hence the following question: doesn't Sade 'espouse the philosophy of the Enlightenment solely in order to reveal the darkness of its foundations'?[46] Klossowski's analysis answers in the affirmative.

43 *Ibid.*, p. 140.
44 *Ibid.*
45 *Ibid.*
46 *Ibid.*, p. 63.

There are two ways to grasp what is at stake in Sade's thought:

i. Sade is 'one of the most searching and most revealing epiphenomena',[47] of social decomposition. He is an 'executor'[48] that actualises the hesitations of the Revolution. He is the hidden face of the Revolution, its dark angel.
ii. Sade is a genuine player not in the Revolution but in the 'dark forces',[49] whose camouflaging as 'social values'[50] he dedicates his life and work to denouncing. This camouflaging is brought about by a community looking out for its own survival. The Marquis clamours as much, loud and clear:

> I wish formally to certify here and now that I have none of these perverse intentions; I set forth the ideas which, since the age when I first began to reason, have identified themselves in me, and to whose expression and realisation the infamous despotism of tyrants has been opposed for uncounted centuries.[51]

The Marquis' System

Klossowski notices psychical forces in the Marquis' work that are both obscure and impulsive. They are manifested as diffuse, unconstrained energies that, being incompatible with any social-political organisation, remain concealed. These forces, appearing as impulses, are what make one's experience singular and unique. Sade found himself confronted by them, and he decided not to keep quiet about it. Was it necessary for Sade to be of a polymorphous sensitivity – a problematic structure – in order

47 *Ibid.*
48 *Ibid.*, p. 65.
49 *Ibid.*
50 *Ibid.*
51 *Ibid.*, p. 64.

to be familiar with these dark forces? It is here that the history of the Revolution and of Sade's social position ties in with the personal destiny of Sade the subject. Assuredly, perversion frees these psychical forces; they can manifest in a manner of acting and thinking that specifies the perverse subject. Dark psychical forces and perversion are inextricably bound. However, this relationship between Sade and the Revolution should not lead us to forget that Sade's doctrine is no such thing; a dialectical process structures it.

To take Sade at his word is to notice the terms he uses to carry out his demonstrations. Klossowski describes Sade's line of attack as a commentator:

> Magnetised by the events that are getting underway outside (the assault on the principles of religious and social authority), dark forces arise within a man, who then feels himself forced to declare them to his contemporaries, even though he must live among them as a moral smuggler.[52]

But how is one to go about making such a testimony? Sade preferred to express himself in accepted terminology. The Marquis' originality lay in postulating that:

> it is temperament that inspires the choice of a philosophy, and that reason itself, which the philosophers of his time invoked, is but a form of passion.[53]

A philosopher's text cannot be reduced to a series of statements disconnected from he who states them. On the contrary, the choice of an idea is made and mobilised by passion, even if the subject concerned is unaware of it. Psychical forces drive the subject and determine his choices. This is the drama of the Marquis: Sade was a prisoner,

> in the name of reason and the philosophy of the Enlightenment, because he wished to translate into the terms of common sense what must pass over in silence and abolish in order to stay common, lest it be itself abolished.[54]

52 *Ibid.*, p. 67.

53 *Ibid.*, pp. 67–8.

54 *Ibid.*, p. 68.

By showing and demonstrating through his life and oeuvre that temperament and dark forces govern the subject, and not our all-powerful reason, Sade attacks reason head on, along with those who promote it. He is the enemy of rational revolutionaries because he claims to reveal what reason conceals and annuls – the psychical forces that are, unto themselves, their own goal.

Sade is not showing any theoretical originality when he notes that

> religion is an enterprise of mystification and […] human actions have no other motive than self-interest.[55]

Such were the conclusions of rational materialism which already had its rightful place in philosophy with the rationalism of Voltaire and the encyclopaedists, along with the materialism of d'Holbach and La Mettrie, and which gives a mechanistic explanation of man and nature. Sade adds nothing to demonstrations of this kind, but rather distorts their normal use. For example, regarding *suspicion*,[56] he stated:

> I am being deceived? Then I must deceive. Others are dissimilating? Then I must dissimulate. Others are pretending and masking themselves? Give us simulacra and masks.[57]

By employing his interlocutor's classic reasoning and language only to use it against him, Sade provocatively ups the stakes. This is why he follows set terminology and its logical forms. His goal is straightforward enough: to make reasoning in language 'convey all it is capable of conveying'.[58] In this way, 'he will push the mechanistic explanation of man to the point of delirium,'[59] demonstrating the absurdity of reasoning. Condemning the lie and the other's cheating is his goal. Sade reveals the dark forces present in the materialist and mechanistic philosophy of his time.

55 *Ibid.*
56 *Ibid.*
57 *Ibid.*
58 *Ibid.*
59 *Ibid.*

Continuing along this path of destruction, materialist atheism is also examined anew. 'Does not the denial of God involve the denial of the neighbour?'[60] The supposition is a terrible one, for if the neighbour is denied, what becomes of the citizens' liberty, equality and fraternity? 'When the existence of God, that is, the judge, is denied, what becomes of the culprit?'[61]

Klossowski insists on the presence of a dialectic process in Sade's doctrine. In the *Dialogue between a Priest and a Dying Man*, written in 1782, Sade 'still believes in the possibility of maintaining moral categories without drawing out the consequences that can result from the non-existence of God'.[62] Five years later (1787), in *The Misfortunes of Virtue*, the problem of evil takes on a different hue.

> A work of a quite new taste; from one end to the other vice triumphs and virtue is humiliated. The denouement alone renders to virtue all the lustre due it. No one who finishes reading this book fails to abhor the false triumph of crime and cherish the humiliations of virtue.[63]

Sade's advance sets off from the question of evil, a questioning that constituted his own subjective drama. One would nevertheless have to wait for his first major work, in 1785, *The 120 Days of Sodom*, which develops a genuine 'theory of perversions',[64] before one meets a precise definition of evil as subjectified by Sadean consciousness: 'the misfortune of *being virtuous in crime and finding oneself criminal in the practice of virtue*'.[65]

At the start of his oeuvre, Sade was as yet dissatisfied with the negation of evil. What complicated his reasoning was the presence of the neighbour: 'As long as the neighbour exists for the ego, he reveals the presence of God'.[66] How is this new aporia to be resolved? Our commentator

60 *Ibid.*, p. 70.
61 *Ibid.*
62 *Ibid.*, p. 71.
63 *Ibid.*
64 *Ibid.*, p. 73.
65 *Ibid.*
66 *Ibid.*

sets down three phases in the resolution of the notion of evil: destructive theology, the materialist theory of pure crime, and asceticism and apathy. We shall examine them each in turn.

Destructive Theology

According to Klossowski, Sade's destructive theology is spawned by the 'bad conscience of the debauched libertine'.[67] This is a 'transitional state of mind',[68] between two key elements in the Marquis' thought: on one hand, social man, on the other, the atheist conscience of the philosophy of Nature that leads to the morality of perpetual motion.

Being a theology, the question of God lies at its very heart. But it is a destructive theology; its relationship with God is a negative one. This atheism is not cold-blooded, but is driven by resentment. 'Its atheism is but a form of sacrilege. Only the profanation of the symbols of religion can make its apparent atheism convincing to itself'.[69] A theology that admits the presence of God in order to annul Him is one whose combat implies God's existence. Here, atheism takes the form of 'provocations addressed to the absent God, as though scandal were a means to force God to manifest his existence'.[70] Paradoxically, this atheism gives consistency to what it claims is absent. Sade's God, at this point in his dialectic advance, consists through His absence. This God takes on an imaginary form as an adversary that must be forced out of the woods where he is hiding. 'Were there a God', claims the Marquis, '[...] would he permit [...] this feeble creature to insult him, to flout him, to defy him, to challenge him, to offend him as I do, wantonly, at my own sweet will, at every instant of the day?'[71] The strict recognition of formulations such as this leads Klossowski to ascertain

67 *Ibid.*, p. 74.
68 *Ibid.*
69 *Ibid.*
70 *Ibid.*, p. 75.
71 *Ibid.*

a theology in Sade, effectively a destructive one, being negative, but a theology nevertheless.

At this point, libertine debauchery is not yet the atheist philosophy it will become in Sade's mature work. The lord and lover of vice is fascinated by evil in so far as it is the means by which God can be given consistency in a negative way. However, there is no response from God; libertine crime goes unpunished. The effect of this impunity is immediate: the crimes run amok. Sade admits: 'What animates us is not the object of libertinage, but rather the idea of evil'.[72] Evil is done under God's watchful eye; evil doing is addressed to him as a provocation. All the libertine's action is conducted under this watchful eye of the divine Other who is ceaselessly summoned and compelled to be witness to his own supposed radical underbelly: evil! This theology maintains the classical categories of Christian morality. Within this reasoning, the possibility of doing good is not ruled out. On the contrary, it is in relation to good that practicing evil takes on its full negative value. This theology maintains free will: the subject can choose *either* good *or* evil. Such a position stands in opposition to atheism. Here, the existence of God is maintained in order to go against him.

This point is particularly important. It is in reference to this destructive theology that the following contradiction, often noticed in Sade's works, can be understood: the affirmation of atheism on one hand, the development of the *Supremely Evil Being* on the other.

> This religion of evil does not yet consist in denying crime, as the philosophy of perpetual motion will, but consists in admitting crime as proceeding from the existence of an infernal God.[73]

What is Sade discovering? Not the absence of God that he had been searching for, but the presence of an infernal God, of an absolute realisation of evil. There is a mirrored relationship between the libertine and God, which lies on the dual axis of imaginary rivalry. God is the 'original culprit who

72 *Ibid.*
73 *Ibid.*, p. 76.

attacked man before man attacked him'.[74] Here then is the apotheosis of this struggle to the death between God and the depraved lord. How is he to fight effectively? From this conception of a guilty God, Sade deduces a consequence:

> [...] man would have acquired the right and the strength to attack his fellow. And this divine aggression would be so incommensurable that it would legitimate the impunity of the guilty one and the sacrifice of the innocent.[75]

We have come full circle. God and one's fellow man – the neighbour – are tied together inseparably. To attack one is to fight the other. Sade insists on this point:

> [...] and if I receive *evil* from others, I enjoy the right to pay them back in kind, to be the first to cast the stone: so, henceforth, *evil* is a good, just as it is for the author of my existence, [...]: the *evil* I do others makes me happy, as God is rendered happy by the *evil* he does me.[76]

The dual, symmetrical and reciprocal logic could not be clearer, could not be any more explicit than in such formulations as this. Evil comes first, it is the cause of everything. God incarnates it, carries it through: evil 'is [...] an eternal and not a perishable entity: it existed before the world; it constituted the monstrous, the execrable being who was able to fashion such a hideous world'.[77] Man, unless he repudiates what constitutes him, lives in and of this evil. Sade hammers this home: '[...] God who is only *evil*, who wants nothing but what is *evil*, who requires *evil* alone'.[78]

What may be deduced from these affirmations is that the libertine acknowledges and accepts God, with all His vices and horrors, as absolute evil. Strictly speaking, Sade is neither an atheist nor a deist in the generally

74 *Ibid.*
75 *Ibid.*
76 *Ibid.*, pp. 76–7.
77 *Ibid.*, p. 77.
78 *Ibid.*

accepted sense. But in a singular way he is a deist nevertheless, a very peculiar one, who abhors the original culprit, who loathes the eternal criminal.

Let us clarify the consequences of this for the relationship with the neighbour. Sade is obviously taking up the Christian formula: 'Thou shalt love thy neighbour as thyself' in order to reduce it to nothing by seizing its nether side. The relationship with the neighbour is modelled on the relationship with God – it is its negative. The category of the fellow man, of the alter ego, is perfectly maintained. In saying, 'the *evil* I do others makes me happy, as God is rendered happy by the *evil* he does me',[79] the libertine debauchee maintains the moral categories by inverting them, as far as their value is concerned. Klossowski points out this purely imaginary logic:

> [...] by comparing his situation to that of the wretched, the fortunate man ineluctably identifies himself with the wretched one. In torturing the object of his lusts in order to derive pleasure from his suffering, the debauchee will represent to himself his own suffering, his own being tortured, and in so doing will also represent his own punishment.[80]

This sliding of one ego into the other, and the reversibility that results from it, is decisive when it comes to broaching the subjective logic at work. It is an intensified imaginary inter-subjectivity – the very same, Lacan reminds us, back in his first Seminar in the lessons from June 1954,[81] that specifies the perverse structure and accounts for its concrete phenomenological manifestations. Klossowski comes back to the example of Saint-Fond who, after attacking a poor family, got himself attacked, on his own order, by two louts. Whatever for? He replies: 'I love to make them experience the sort of thing that troubles and overwhelms my existence so cruelly'.[82] A system of reciprocity is confirmed, and eternity enlisted. Taking into account an

79 *Ibid.*, p. 78.

80 *Ibid.*, p. 79.

81 Lacan, J., *The Seminar Book I, Freud's Papers on Technique, 1953–4*, trans. J. Forrester, Cambridge University Press, 1988, chapters XIII to XVIII.

82 Klossowski, P., *Sade My Neighbor, op. cit.*, p. 79.

imaginary identification with the partner is crucial when it comes to grasping this inter-subjectivity.

The reference to hell or to the possibility of a torture inflicted eternally upon the victim, a surprising feature in Sade's writing, is a result of the place that is given to the neighbour in this inter-subjective logic. The libertine's mind

> [...] cannot renounce the singular hope of a future, infernal, life, that is, it cannot consent to the annihilation of his 'body of sin' because of its mad desire eternally to hurl its furies upon the same victim.[83]

The libertine's practice of evil corresponds to the Evil that characterises God, just as the perpetuation of evildoing corresponds to eternity, and so on.

Klossowski's merit is to have singled out this genuine theological position of Sade's, a position that ties in with Saint Augustine's analysis of Evil for Evil's sake. He has not allowed himself to be fascinated by the Marquis' atheist proclamations. He has found a way to spot the undeniable theological moments in this thinking, in particular the moment at which it overturns all the moral values established by religion under royalty. At this moment, our Marquis has a subjective experience of the fact that there exists an exercise of the '*right to forbidden experiments*'.[84] Sade experiences this possibility of thought in his own conscience. This is the libertine Sade, not yet the sadist Sade. But without the libertine Sade, without Sade the debauchee, the sadist Sade could never come to be.

The Materialist Theory of Pure Crime

Ten years after drafting his *Dialogue between a Priest and a Dying Man*, Sade makes a reversal. Around 1792, he takes on board the ideas of the materialists of his time (notably La Mettrie, Helvétius and d'Holbach):

83 *Ibid.*
84 *Ibid.*, p. 80.

the universal agent that makes the material and social world go round is the state of perpetual motion. This thesis, which thus constructs a universal cause, excludes the logical necessity of the existence of God. For the materialists and the Encyclopaedists, the thesis of perpetual motion signifies the establishment of a happier humanity. Sade adopts this theme, although its consequences, for him, bring about something very different: '[…] the beginning of tragedy and its conscious and deliberate acceptance'.[85] The Marquis' atheism is profoundly different from that of his contemporaries: 'To admit matter in the state of perpetual motion as the one and only universal agent is equivalent to consenting to live as an individual in a state of perpetual motion'.[86] Now, this incessant movement, applied to a life, is the opposite of any pastoral of happiness regained in the wake of the tyrannical interlude of masters and priests. Sade is foreshadowing formulations worthy of Nietzsche – the Nietzsche of the Vicious Circle and the glorification of the changes of eternal return:

> […] dissolution is a very great state of motion. There is, therefore, no moment when the body of the animal is at rest; it never dies; but because it no longer exists for us, we believe that it no longer exists at all: that is the mistake. Bodies are transmuted … metamorphosed, but they are never inert. Inertia is absolutely impossible for matter whether matter is organized or not. Weigh these truths carefully, and you will see where they lead and what a twist they give to human morality.[87]

On reading these sentences, a dramatic issue comes to the fore: affirmation through a thought (which is indeed a thought because it thinks itself as such) of that which repudiates it: dissolution and destruction. Hence the following question from Sade: is this movement really free of any will, or is it ordered? To the extent that movement specifies nature, Sade finds himself insulting nature and scoffing at it, as beforehand he had insulted and scoffed at God.

85 *Ibid.*, p. 81.
86 *Ibid.*
87 *Ibid.*

> Her barbarous hand can only nourish evil; evil is her entertainment. Should I love such a mother? No, but I will imitate her, all the while detesting her. I shall copy her, as she wishes, but I shall curse her unceasingly.[88]

It is a return to evil, the same that gives order to movement, and orients and curbs matter. Sade's materialism is inseparable from this vector of evil. Nature is evil, just as God was Evil.

This reference to nature will be constant. Its laws must constitute the only principles to which each person must submit himself and to which a State must refer. Nature wants, exacts, and commands: 'One motor alone acts in the universe, and this motor is nature'.[89] Perversion itself is no longer an anomaly. It comes from nature, it is nature manifested. It becomes a virtue because henceforth there are only natural virtues.

Klossowski draws two consequences from this new conception of nature:

Firstly, insulting nature limits the libertine's action to a 'revolt'.[90] Clearly, nature is pure silence; it does not respond to any provocation or blasphemy. Unlike God, it cannot take revenge. To annihilate it by fighting it is senseless because '[the] notion of perpetual motion absorbs every idea of annihilation, which now becomes nothing but a modification of the forms of matter [...]'.[91] Destroying nature would only confirm its existence since nature itself is incessant destruction, transmutation and metamorphosis.

Secondly, there is a dynamic dimension to Sade's description: 'Aware of her frightful secrets, I have fallen back on myself and I have felt [...], I have experienced a kind of pleasure in copying her foul deeds'.[92] Nature is set out as knowledge that is already constituted ('foul deeds') from which, through imitation, knowing is possible. The mind, in as much as it is an

88 *Ibid.*, p. 82.

89 Sade, 'Philosophy in the Bedroom', *Justine, Philosophy in the Bedroom and Other Writings, op. cit.*, p. 360.

90 Klossowski, P., *Sade My Neighbor, op. cit.*, p. 83.

91 *Ibid.*

92 *Ibid.*, p. 82.

integral part of nature, may find in nature's blind and necessary laws the logic of its own suggestions. Crime and knowledge become inseparable. Now, this new knowledge will have a far greater power than that which we possess today.

Klossowski will pursue this thought to the point of isolating positions that tie in with those of Nietzsche and which he will examine in the staged scenarios of his fiction. Through Sade, Klossowski is posing his own question. He reads Sade's oeuvre from the point of view of his own private and phantasmatic obsession: *What is an individuality? What of the being and its thinking?* How far does he push his reading? One observes a 'transcendental fatalism'[93] in the Marquis' work. Sade allows for the existence of an 'original and eternal nature',[94] independent of its concrete effects – the three kingdoms of species and creatures. Human beings are merely the result of 'blind laws'. Mankind has no purpose; it is profoundly useless in the scheme of the universe. Sade then comes to affirm that

> [the] most wicked individual on earth, the most abominable, the most ferocious, the most barbarous, and the most indefatigable murderer is therefore but the spokesman of his desires, the vehicle of his will, and the surest agent of his caprices.[95]

Klossowski insistently shows us the dialectical evolution of the Sadean oeuvre. First of all, there is the affirmation of the theology of the *Supremely Evil Being*. God is evil and eternally guilty. Next, this God is reduced to nature which is just as maleficent. This is the 'satanization of nature'.[96] Finally, nature is pure motion; it is dehumanised and constructed as a metaphysics. This third phase is essential. Mankind is submitted to 'the categorical imperative of a cosmic tribunal that demands the annihilation of all that is human'.[97] Sade will go on to speak of disease, cataclysms, war, discord, and of course the crimes of villains:

93 *Ibid.*, p. 84.
94 *Ibid.*
95 *Ibid.*, p. 86.
96 *Ibid.*
97 *Ibid.*, p. 87. This instance of the categorical imperative is to be found perfectly, for example, in the following quotation: 'Then act [...] act and fear nothing; [...] it is

> Therefore is crime necessary in the world. But the most useful crimes are without doubt those which most disrupt, such as *refusal to propagate and destruction* [...] and thus you see these crimes [...] essential to the laws of nature.[98]

Here we meet Sade's transcendental position. Through integral cruelty, rather than achieving a singular destiny, the individual satisfies an aspiration that outstrips his individual self. He achieves the law of nature. For Sade, there is but one principle:

> In all living beings the principle of life is no other than that of death; at the same time we receive the one we receive the other, we nourish both within us, side by side. At the instant we call *death*, everything seems to dissolve; we are led to think so [...]. But this death is only imaginary; it exists figuratively but in no other way. Matter [...] merely abandons its form, it decays – and in decaying proves that it is not inert; it enriches the soil, fertilizes it [...].[99]

What can be deduced from such a remark? Sadean nature is an interplay of dark, impulsive forces; human creatures are merely particular moments at which these different forces are embodied by means of an agent.[100] Creatures are merely 'changing phases'.[101] This is a point in the Marquis' work that fascinates our commentator. Only motion, in as much as it is tantamount to these forces, is real.[102] It is movement that is determinant at the end of the day – that is the absolute cause. Creatures are merely accidents, consequences of this flux made manifest.

---

impossible for man to commit a crime [...]. The blind instruments of [nature's] aspirations, were she to order us to set fire to the universe, the only crime possible would be in resisting her: all criminals on earth are nothing but the agents of her caprices [...]', Sade, 'Philosophy in the Bedroom', *Justine, Philosophy in the Bedroom and Other Writings*, *op. cit.*, pp. 360–1.

98 Klossowski, P., *Sade My Neighbor*, *op. cit.*, p. 88.

99 *Ibid.*, p. 89.

100 [TN, Klossowski frequently employs the term *suppôt*, which has previously been translated as both 'agent' and 'henchman'. Here and hereafter, we have opted for the former.]

101 Klossowski, P., *Sade My Neighbor*, *op. cit.*, p. 90.

102 [TN, *Le réel*, as opposed to *la réalité*, as in the teaching of Jacques Lacan.]

Asceticism and Apathy

Sade introduces the question of apathy based on the relationship with the neighbour – a relationship that has been modified by his new conceptualisation of the eternal, aimless movement of nature.

To naturalise cruelty, or to re-articulate it within the system of a universe emptied of any divine presence, 'will be to deny the reality of the neighbour, to empty the notion of the neighbour of its content'.[103] Sade's theological error was to convert neighbourly love into its opposite. He affirmed the hatred of this same neighbour, a hate that stemmed from the hate addressed to God. But the hate of the neighbour – an inverted and thus ambivalent love – maintained the reality of both the other party and oneself, both caught up in an imaginary dialectic. Hence the following question: how, in order to adhere to a strict materialism, is one to do away with the (moral) category of the neighbour, and, therefore, with one's ego? Sade begins – this is one step in his thought – by establishing 'between the self and the other a negative reciprocity'.[104] The effects of this mirroring need to be done away with:

> What, after all, are all the earth's creatures when measured against a single one of our desires? And by what right should I deprive myself of the least of my desires in order to please a creature who is nothing to me and who holds no interest whatsoever for me?[105]

The other party must no longer be a constraint, an entity that holds back and curbs. Compared to desire, he is nothing. 'But if the other is *nothing* for me, henceforth I am not only *nothing* for him but also *nothing* before my own consciousness – and in fact that consciousness is no longer still *mine*'.[106] The ego's ownership of consciousness must be destroyed – '[for]

103 Klossowski, P., *Sade My Neighbor*, *op. cit.*, p. 91.
104 *Ibid.*, p. 92.
105 *Ibid.*
106 *Ibid.*

if I break with the other on the level of morality, I will have broken with my own self-possession on the level of existence itself'.[107]

It is not enough to negate God, the guarantor of the responsible ego and the respected, even loved, neighbour. It is the ego – and the neighbour – that has to be radically destroyed. Sade will go so far as to question the normative principle of individuation in order to give free rein to the 'forces of dissolution'.[108] Forces are not only dark and impulsive; they also have a function of dissolution. And what do they dissolve? They dissolve the very locus in which they exert themselves, because they are psychical forces; they dissolve the ego in as much as it is the explicit seat of reflexive consciousness and thought. To opt for these forces – the eternal movement in the subject's psychical life – amounts to choosing 'the perversions, the anomalies – the emergence in the individual of sensuous polymorphy, at whose expense conscious individuation is accomplished in beings'.[109]

This is why perversion – anomaly in relation to the norm of reason – interests Klossowski in his reading of Sade. He considers that perversion has its rightful place in the Marquis' work, which affirms, on a case by case basis, 'sensuous polymorphy',[110] or the embodied presence of impulsive forces when they are no longer centred, developed, and strung together by the ego of consciousness. Perversion is the name of the individuated forces that cast doubt on the unity of the rational ego of which God was the guarantor, just as the neighbour was the guarantor of the imaginary double. In this capacity, perversion annihilates God, the neighbour, and the ego; not by virtue of the idea, but through private practices. Perversion is the appearance of the eternal movement of destruction 'in the individual', in his heart of hearts.

Perversion in Sade is above all a writing that spells out this perversion by describing it in the postures commented on by its own agents of realisation. The presence of both described postures and argued out reasoning

107 *Ibid.*
108 *Ibid.*, p. 93.
109 *Ibid.*
110 *Ibid.*

make them part of a legitimate doctrine, while at the same time piercing through their closed and reflexive images. Hence the following contradiction in the Marquis' text when taken literally: perversion is only an anomaly for the discourse of reason. This is why Sade develops his texts with the rational logic of exposition and the classical language of the eighteenth century. Perversion as an anomaly of reason will always be postulated as negative. Reason would never be able to account for the positive content of perversions. The paradox lies here: perversion is pure positivity because it carries through the emergence of impulsive forces, but, on being spoken, it takes on a negative status in the words of reason. This is the drama of the subject Sade – his relation to traditional thought: the 'forces hostile to individuation', on being uttered, find themselves 'in an inverted form, in a discourse that requires a bearer'.[111] Sade's drama consists in this contradiction between reason, which is universalising by definition, and the particular case of the anomaly. How is one to translate into terms of universal and duly shareable communication that which destroys, de facto, all unity – including the ego of the thought that achieves, for an individual, shared common reason?

In so far as they exemplify the contradictions of the Marquis, the fictional characters ceaselessly proclaim this misunderstanding in their dialogues and exchanges. The libertine who exclaims, 'What, after all, are all the earth's creatures when measured against a single one of our desires?' is questioning desire as the desire of an individuated entity. However, on manifesting itself, this desire would destroy the unity of the ego. The ego is the 'plaything of an impulse'[112] from the start. As Klossowski notes, 'the impulse of desire can give its own absolute character to the individual, who in return speaks for the desire that has no language'.[113] Let us take up these terms and especially the chiasmus that articulates them: desire is wordless, it is the name for what shows itself to the subject as *forces*; in return, language excludes these same forces. Desire silences. It emerges as

111 *Ibid.*
112 *Ibid.*, p. 94.
113 *Ibid.*

the impossible of articulated speech – the nameless, formless nether side of speech – the real.

And what of *apathy*? The 'therapeutics' of the morality of apathy must 'bring about this renunciation of the reality of self'.[114] Apathy is a means of doing away with the ego as an agency that curbs the dark forces and shuts them away. The ego filters impulsions, but how is the emergence of these forces in the ego manifested?

> Through images, which form prior to acts and incite us to act or to suffer acts, and through the images of acts committed which return to us and torment conscience with remorse as much as the idle impulses restore it.[115]

Hence the necessity of substituting acts for images. Sade says it is the cold-blooded act: '[...] to do, immediately, in cold-blood, that very thing which, done in the throes of passion, has been able to cause you remorse [...]'.[116] A difficulty arises. If the cold-blooded crime is accomplished, it necessitates the presence of the other party upon whom it is perpetrated; and yet, both the other and the ego must be destroyed.

> If the other is now nothing for me, and I nothing for the other, how could these acts, issuing from a nothing and directed upon another nothing, be brought about? If this nothing is never again to be filled by the reality of the other and the reality of myself, filled neither by enjoyment nor by remorse, it is necessary that I disappear in an endless reiteration of acts [...].[117]

If the act is suspended, the reality of the other returns as the pre-existing image reaffirming itself. In Sade there is an opposition between act and thought, between active crime and passive image. Pure crime, pure act, bring about the interplay of impulsive forces, while image and thought do the opposite. The act is a way of short-circuiting any possible return of the image as either enciphering, as remorse, or as an experience of voluptuous

114 *Ibid.*
115 *Ibid.*, p. 95.
116 *Ibid.*
117 *Ibid.*, p. 96.

jouissance.[118] Sade does not resolve this contradiction, but his ability to have isolated and staged it is to his merit. This contradiction is the ultimate point in the advance of his thought, his impassable point of real.

Klossowski resumes his train of thought:

> To get beyond the notion of evil, which is conditioned by the degree of reality accorded the other, we have seen this mind exalt the ego to the limit [its model being Saint-Fond's negative sympathy]. But the culmination of this exaltation was to be in the apathy in which, when the other is abolished, the ego is abolished at the same time, in which enjoyment is dissociated from destruction, and in which destruction is identified with desire in its pure form.[119]

The loop has practically come full circle. The libertine's acts would thus reproduce the laws of nature. He would accomplish himself by destroying his own works. Through apathy, the libertine annuls himself as a unity. Sade's dream – or better still, his myth – finds here its sharpest attack against the forms of reason and the consciousness that realises it: the production of a subject free of affect, free of remorse or pleasure – a subject who would no longer feel anything and who would reduce himself to the real of an endlessly reiterated act. Pure crime, pure act, designate a crime or an act beyond the signifier. The apathetic hero is no longer a *parlêtre*,[120] but a subject who has managed to abolish himself, to disconnect from the signifier that logically determines him as an effect. The apathetic libertine would be pure real, a pure absolute being henceforth emptied of all thought and reason. Materialism would meet its point of realisation. No subject can subjectively testify to this point. The very most he can do is create a myth about it.

118 [TN, Throughout this book, the French term 'jouissance' is reproduced as such, un-italicised, as is customary in English language psychoanalytic texts. The English term 'enjoyment' has long been recognised as a poor and misleading translation.]

119 Klossowski, P., *Sade My Neighbor, op. cit.*, pp. 97–8.

120 [TN, Jacques Lacan's neologism *parlêtre* includes a concentration of, on one hand, *parler* or *parlé* with *être*, thus giving 'speaking' or 'spoken' being, and on the other, *par lettre*, 'by letter'.]

The Place of the Subject Sade

What place does the subject Sade occupy in his system of thought? His fictional oeuvre has the following function: 'to make intelligible the unrelenting course of the life he lived'.[121] The oeuvre's function is to set down words where there has been a silent experience, a pathos. What Sade lived through inexorably was the 'mystery of being, which is the possibility of evil and of nothingness'.[122] His singular experience is the 'pathos of imprisonment and impotence [...]. For it is indeed being that is experienced here as the ultimate prison, the outermost wall'.[123] There is the problem of the fall of the spirit, a position that stands in opposition to the idea of progress in the way the Enlightenment understood it. The operations of creation, of writing, and of philosophical elaboration are inseparable from this context: 'The act of creation is itself a consequence of the fall; creating is the act of revolt of a demiurge against the pure God of the spirits. The whole of creation then bears the seal of the curse [...]'.[124] Creation has a positive function of exorcism, but in no way does it solve or lift the curse associated with that which is created – the creature. It exteriorises it. Creating becomes the mark of this original powerlessness that makes for the creature's pathos.

This purity, which has become inaccessible, haunts the subject Sade. Indeed, he has the particular experience of language perverting what he is speaking about. The referent is lost and being is thus contaminated, rendering it impossible to superpose onto itself. Being can only be conjugated as want-of-being.[125] This 'beforehand' of language – before the fall, the curse, the decline – is marked by the 'obsession with virginity'.[126] This obsession

121 Klossowski, P., *Sade My Neighbor*, *op. cit.*, p. 99.
122 *Ibid.*
123 *Ibid.*
124 *Ibid.*, p. 100.
125 [TN, Again, the term is borrowed from Jacques Lacan. Lacan himself approved this English rendering of *manque-à-être*.]
126 Klossowski, P., *Sade My Neighbor*, *op. cit.*, p. 101.

exists only because it is Sade's 'basic experience of [...] temperament'.[127] The purity of crime brings the subject who accomplishes it closer to the purity that existed prior to the fall, closer to this being that existed prior to the signifier that renders him incomplete.

A figure embodies this conjunction between destruction and purity: the virgin. But there is a contradiction: 'Purity is an absolute quality which the Sadean mind has dissociated from the creative God'.[128] With this reference to purity, materialist thought is brought back to the theological categories previously done away with.

> As an image of the purity of God, the virgin is excluded from possession by man; but man cannot forget that she is possessable. She becomes in Sade a motif of exasperation, and prohibition, of virility.[129]

Wanting to possess the virgin instantly taints her. The virgin, by definition, cannot be possessed. The loss is twofold. In the sacrilegious act of possession, the virgin is tainted, and the libertine who takes her loses this purity, becoming impure and cruel. Virility is accursed and frustrated in the face of its impossible realisation:

> Indeed, all of Sade's work has appeared to us as one desperate cry, hurled at the image of inaccessible virginity, a cry enveloped and as it were enshrined in a canticle of blasphemies: I am excluded from purity because I wish to possess the one who is pure. I cannot not desire purity, but by the same time I am impure because I wish to enjoy purity, which excludes enjoyment.[130]

Unattainable purity constitutes the absolute secret in Sade's female characters. Thus Justine's purity, which the libertines want to take from her, will remain inviolable. On the other hand, her sister Juliette, Justine's other, negative side, will persevere in vice to become the counterpoint to Justine's purity. Her secret too remains: 'One crime, or two, or a hundred

127 *Ibid.*
128 *Ibid.*, p. 103.
129 *Ibid.*
130 *Ibid.*, p. 105.

are not enough to reveal this secret; she must be pushed into ever greater crimes [...]'.[131] What Sade is depicting is not the secret of such a heroine, but the secret of purity in such a woman. Think of another character from Sade's fiction, the beautiful Florville. Klossowski notices that, 'Florville is an enigma to herself, as is the human soul at the beginning of its journey, before being able to know itself as God alone knows it'.[132] To possess Florville would be to find out the secret of evil – its emergence in an island of original purity.

> Why did it have to be that the unhappy Florville, the most virtuous, most loveable, and most sensitive of beings, finds herself, because of an unseemly evolution of fate, the most abominable monster nature could create?[133]

The emergence of evil in a virtuous agent is assuredly Klossowski's key question. It is the question he examines in his commentaries and which he will stage, tirelessly, with Roberte. What does Florville's undoing demonstrate? The young woman kills herself faced with the monstrosity of her evil deeds. Our commentator says that, 'it is the solution of an enigma. The turn of fortune has revealed a soul that was guilty before it had acted'.[134] Let us mark this term: *before* (her acts). In the beginning is evil. The path of the soul is to come face to face with itself – to the point at which evil is realised. Think of *Eugénie de Franval* where the father commits incest with his daughter. A series of horrors follow one after the other. Likewise, in *The Story of Justine and Juliette* each victim is violently assaulted, the libertine aggressors moving on to their next victim only with reluctance.

How is the escalation of crime to be explained in light of this question as to the virgin's purity? Sade's criminals do not reach their goal. Why not? Because what they are hunting for is immortal: it is the soul itself. Here we have a paradox: in his practice, the materialist atheist fails because of the immortality of the soul of his victims. '[...] the soul destroys the body

131 *Ibid.*
132 *Ibid.*, p. 107.
133 *Ibid.*.
134 *Ibid.*

because it does not succeed in destroying itself'.[135] Sade's characters spend their time wanting to kill the soul, but they fail. The characters' suicides at the end of the stories now take on their full value: since the soul cannot die, all that remains is the 'simulacrum of the death of the soul which is suicide'.[136]

The inviolable soul of the unpossessable virgins is the absolute and ultimate expression of the secret of being. The soul is what is dissociated from God the creator. It is eternal because it is a divine essence. Caught up in a problematic of decline, misfortune and malediction, the soul of creatures is used by God 'for his own redemption, his own deliverance. The economy of salvation is inverted; human sufferings redeem a fallen spirit by enabling it to purify itself'.[137] It is God who is evil. Here, then, lies the secret of the virgin. Here is what rouses the libertine in his crimes. But the demonstration is impossible. The soul, like God, cannot be destroyed. What remains is the simulacrum of death, the parody of the resolution of this contradiction in the Marquis' materialist position: suicide. It is no longer the body, the flesh, that corrupts; it is God himself!

Apathy is, therefore, affect par excellence – the affect that, not without paradox, signals the neutralisation of the passionate affects: rage, turmoil, embarrassment, anxiety, and so on. Klossowski isolates its equivalent in the perverse consciousness: *delectatio morosa*. The term was introduced by the mediaeval Church fathers. It designates not a delectation that would be sad, gloomy or morose, but a delectation of some duration (this is the first meaning of the Latin *mora*: 'delay', 'lateness'). *Delectatio morosa* names a particular relation to the passing of time. In the apathetic reiteration of crime, the hero experiences 'a deficiency in being and of time without eternity'.[138] *Delectatio morosa* is a response to the ennui of the soul cut off from God who nevertheless maintains its immortality. It is a practice that calls to mind that of the contemplative monk.

135 *Ibid.*, p. 109.
136 *Ibid.*, p. 110.
137 *Ibid.*, p. 102.
138 *Ibid.*, p. 112.

> Morose delectation consists in that movement of the soul by which it bears itself voluntarily toward images of forbidden carnal or spiritual acts in order to linger in contemplation of them. […] [T]he soul sets out to fix these images whenever they present themselves to chance reverie […].[139]

Therein lies the sin. In and of itself, the appearance of forbidden pornographic reveries is not sinful, but it become so when the dreamer, with eyes wide open, sets about maintaining it, when he makes it last (*mora*). For Sade, as read by Klossowski, making the reverie last amounts to accepting that dark psychical forces come about and begin their slow work of dissolving the unity of consciousness. The atheist libertine makes himself overtly complicit with this active deconstruction:

> […] the dreamer casts himself into time like the desperate man who, not having been able to decide on suicide, resolves at least to cast himself into the swirling ocean, leaving to the element its freedom to swallow him up […] Sade's consciousness watches its progressive invasion by the powers of the soul with all the objects that have affected them.[140]

The result is a desperate soul that 'feels itself alive only in exasperation'[141] of its break from contemplating and fusing with God. The soul of morose delectation is the soul of the fall, of decline. Morose delectation is a veritable worship of absence; its anchoring point is found, for the libertine, where his powerless virility is exasperated. In this respect, we cannot forget the long years the Marquis spent in prison. Morose delectation is above all his private, intimate experience, of which his writing is an account: 'I exist so as not to exist'.[142] *Delectatio morosa*, a jouissance of absence, invades the libertine's effective mental field. This passion will go so far as to make all concrete realisations thoroughly unsatisfying. Absence must be perpetuated, it is an 'expectation destructive of the present'.[143]

139 *Ibid.*, pp. 113–14.
140 *Ibid.*, p. 115.
141 *Ibid.*
142 *Ibid.*, p. 117.
143 *Ibid.*, p. 119.

Delectation nevertheless has an active function. It does not counteract the emergence of solvent forces in consciousness. In this capacity, it confronts the soul's lost possibilities, where God is to found again:

> By outraging God, it would cease to be a soul God has drawn from nothingness and would return at once to all the eventualities that nothingness contains prior to the soul's vocation, return to a pseudoeternity, to the atemporal existence of perverse polymorphousness.[144]

This leaves the door wide open to the possibility of integral monstrosity.

Through his imagination, Sade attempts to 'return to that atemporal state in which the possession of everything possible excluded the possibility of the painful experience of loss'.[145] The loss has occurred, irremediably. It is from this loss that, regressively, one can come back to the atemporal point from which everything would have been possible because nothing had yet taken place. The congruence between materialist atheism, ascetic apathy, and morose delectation finds here its strongest, as well as its most contradictory, justification. This congruence is the visage of the Marquis' subjective drama, of which his work is a testament.

These are Klossowski's main advances in his reading of Sade between 1933 and 1947. For Klossowski, Sade's oeuvre is not simply one amongst others; it is an essential one when it comes to speaking about his own drama from which his own work as a writer will be possible. He outlines a little known image of Sade the theologian whose exceptional merit is to demonstrate that perverse pornography and Sade's integral monstrosity are simply the underbelly of religious and theological discourse, or better still, the *truth* of dogmatic theology. People have admired Sade the theoretician and writer. Now meet Sade the theologian, a breed apart.

144 *Ibid.*, p. 120.
145 *Ibid.*

The Perverse Gesture

In 1967, Klossowski modifies his line of attack. Sade is no longer being examined in the name of theological discourse, but from the angle of the singular perverse act. In 1947 it was Sade and theology; in 1967 it is Sade and the perverse act.

Our commentator sets off from a question that touches on writing: 'What do thinking and writing – as opposed to feeling or acting – mean for Sade?'[146] In the fictional works, the invented characters philosophise before, during, and after their evil deeds. In the books that Sade agrees to sign in his name, the philosophers are 'decent people'.[147] But in the unsigned texts, they are 'villains'.[148] Why this difference? Whilst the 'decent gent' philosopher posits thought as his domain, the villain aims at obtaining 'the activity of the strongest passion'[149] – if need be, through the contribution of thought. The villain wants more, demonstrating, through the play of his sophisms, that the thought of the decent gent is merely the 'disguise of an impotent passion'.[150] Passion is posited as original and causal. Thought is only a travesty, a rational ordering of solvent and impulsive forces. This is Sade's question: what about the 'decision to think and write – particularly to think of and describe an act instead of committing it?'[151] The 'irreducible depth of sensitivity'[152] of a subject – in this case the libertine lord – can only come to light through acts. What place is there for philosophy, which always sees these acts from a position of exteriority in relation to this irreducible sensitivity, as thought and writing? As Klossowski quite rightly says, this is a 'dilemma'.[153]

146 *Ibid.*, p. 13.
147 *Ibid.*
148 *Ibid.*
149 *Ibid.*
150 *Ibid.*
151 *Ibid.*
152 *Ibid.*, p. 14.
153 *Ibid.*

The fact of writing presupposes partaking of a generality. In speaking as in writing, an individual enters the generality that makes for a social bond because it is common and therefore shareable. In this regard, Sade chooses the 'logically structured language of the classical tradition'.[154] The function of language 'reproduces and reconstitutes in the field of communicative gestures the normative structure of the human race in individuals'.[155] On one side there is the (physiological) function of reproduction that allows the species not to disappear, on the other side there is language. The former seemingly stems from the latter: one is perpetuated physiologically because language, by definition, creates the social bond – it 'makes possible the exchange of individual singularities in the circuit of generality'.[156] Therefore, any possibility of exchange stems from language, which brings about the affirmation of the 'principle of identity' and the 'principle of contradiction'.[157]

Sade would like to integrate into rational generality the very thing that eludes it: the singularity of perversion. To do so, he establishes perversion as a counter-generality. But how is one to turn anomaly – which is without norm, without order and without logic – into a countergenerality? To avoid this contradiction, the Marquis constructs 'integral monstrosity'.[158] To will the singular act of monstrosity as integral is to give it the status of an affirmation that is generalisable and exchangeable. Speaking and writing perversion are ways of bringing about the integration of perversion in normative reason. The result is that this reason is disassembled from within. The affirmation of atheism functions as an Archimedean vantage point. To the generality of deism there is the counterpart of its negative reverse side: atheism as counter-generality.

'How does reason arrive at atheism?'[159] The answer to this question is surprising. The notion of God is illogical, in contradiction with the

154 *Ibid.*
155 *Ibid.*
156 *Ibid.*
157 *Ibid.* [Where the translation gives 'principle of understanding'.]
158 *Ibid.*
159 *Ibid.*, p. 15.

principles of reason. To say that it is illogical is to point out that it is monstrous; the notion that God is illogical holds the same place as a perverse anomaly. We can immediately grasp the consequences: '[…] from the notion of God, which is arbitrary in itself, all arbitrary, perverse and monstrous conduct derives'.[160] Declaring atheism to be a 'decision of autonomous reason'[161] results in the suppression of all that is illogical in thought. In principle, rational atheism affirms normative reason, it upholds a principle of order. This is its impasse.

> […] this atheism is still nothing other than an inverted monotheism […] scarcely distinguishable from deism. Just as the deist certified the notion of God, this atheism stands as a guarantee of the responsible ego, its possession and individual identity.[162]

Sade's goal will be to deplete atheism of the deism of reason. Atheism will be integral, or it will not be at all. By choosing to bring about monstrosity, the Marquis encounters divine arbitrary power again, thereby demonstrating that the true goal is not to remove God from reason, but to free the act of thought from all established normative reason: 'integral atheism will be the end of anthropomorphic reason'.[163] The autonomy of reason must be destroyed by introducing the practice of perverse anomaly as a thought. This presents a new dilemma, one that Sade lives out in his flesh:

> […] either reason itself is excluded from its autonomous decision – atheism – which is to forestall monstrosity in man, or else monstrosity is once again removed from all possible argumentation.[164]

Choosing perverse monstrosity amounts to losing one's reason – and yet Sade wants to maintain this reason so as to be able to write and be read (the intrinsic dimension of the social bond). Choosing this reason so as to communicate with others is again to maintain perversion as a singular anomaly

160 *Ibid.*
161 *Ibid.*
162 *Ibid.*, pp. 15–16.
163 *Ibid.*, p. 16.
164 *Ibid.*

outside reason. Yet Sade wants to establish perversion as an exchangeable generality. This dilemma cannot be resolved. The internal exclusion between reason and perversion is structural. Sade's merit is to cover the two poles of the contradiction through his theoretical and perverse demonstrations (as seen in the logic of writing).

Sade's writing is 'interpretative'.[165] It does not make do with objectively describing monstrous acts by presenting them to the reader, rather it argues out what happens to the characters. It tries to tie in that which is 'sensuous in an aberrant act'[166] (i.e. a perverse act) with reason. In this regard, Klossowski speaks of 'perverse reason'[167] – a surprising expression but one that conforms perfectly to the Marquis' aim. Sensuous nature, which designates the 'propensity to act',[168] is never justified by Sade, for it is obvious that it is what drives one to act. Perversion will always be 'the fact of sensing'[169] – it is a sensuous impulse. Sade – and Klossowski after him – investigates the (moral, logical, and philosophical) nature of the aberrant act that is deduced from this. This act must be moralised. There is a perverse way of feeling and a perverse way of acting. Both act and reason are always in a position of exteriority in relation to the perverse interiority of the sensuous. Hence the following consequence: '[...] the sensuous (that is, the experience peculiar to Sade) is obscured to the extent that discourse has to justify the act'.[170] One must call on reason to justify the act, but this act ensues only from the perverse inner sensation that, because it is composed of untethered impulses, is without reason.

This system of tying-in and multi-causality allows us to grasp why the Marquis calls himself an atheist. His thought, which fights against deism and rational atheism, stems from his perverse way of feeling. It is because he is perverse that Sade is an atheist. He discovers within himself these sensuous forces that deny any centring by God. Klossowski does not say

165 *Ibid.*, p. 17.
166 *Ibid.*
167 *Ibid.*
168 *Ibid.*
169 *Ibid.*
170 *Ibid.*, pp. 17–18.

Sade is perverse *because* he is an atheist but, on the contrary, that he is an atheist *because* he is perverse. This remark carries great importance. The dilemma between perversion and reason explains why '[…] Sade did not seek a positive conceptual formulation of perversion [i.e. sensuous polymorphy] […]'.[171] Klossowski hammers this home: 'If Sade had sought […] a positive conceptual formulation of perversion, he would have passed by the enigma he sets up […]'.[172] His oeuvre would have been one utopia amongst others, fitting in with a positive logic – progress, happiness, and so on – the utopias of the Enlightenment. His own dilemma manifests itself in the form of a question, an enigma, a gap where being does not find its determinant. His life is caught up in the blankness of a chiasmus between reason and anomaly. Is there a way out? Outrage is part and parcel of this problem. Outrage maintains the necessity of what is outraged. '[…] if, in Sade, outrage is necessary, then transgression must prevail over the postulates that derive logically from his atheistic declarations'.[173] The Marquis' oeuvre – like his life – only ever inscribes itself negatively. There is no positive content to anomaly. Sade is counter-utopian.

What position does the pervert hold in Sade's work? Our commentator reminds us that 'the pathological sense of the term *perversion* is not to be found in Sade'.[174] The Marquis thinks in terms of a so-called 'moral' psychology whose model is the 'examination of conscience'[175] dear to Christian practice. In *The 120 Days of Sodom*, perversions are designated as passions and categorised. One term crops up regularly in the fictional texts: *maniac*, a word Klossowski will use in his own writings to designate subjects who carry out perverse acts. The pervert is he who has a mania; he 'subordinates his jouissance to the performing of one sole gesture'.[176] Klossowski is no

171 *Ibid.*, p. 18.

172 *Ibid.*

173 *Ibid.*, p. 19.

174 *Ibid.*, p. 22.

175 *Ibid.*

176 *Ibid.* [Where the translation gives: '… subordinates his pleasure …']. Like the sodomy practiced by Dolmancé. A reference to this gesture sparked off *Philosophy in the Bedroom*.

longer simply examining the place of perversion in rational thought; he is taking an interest in perverse practices themselves in so far as they are carried out by the character types.

The one sole gesture is a 'specific *fixed idea*'.[177] It is imposing and constraining – no gesture is less free. There is

> the scrupulous taste for, and search for, a detail, sated only in a gesture that advances scrupulously to this detail. This kind of concern escapes those who deliver themselves over to the outbursts of raw appetites.[178]

This is the mainspring of perverse practice. 'The pervert pursues the performance of one sole gesture; it is done in a moment. The pervert's existence becomes the constant waiting for the moment in which this gesture can be performed'.[179] No derogation is possible. The maniac waits to carry his gesture through – a *fixed idea* curbs him, indicating to him the only way he can achieve his sexual pleasure. Years later, Klossowski will call this idea the 'phantasm in its obsessive constraint'.

The pervert thus embodies perversion in the execution of his gesture. 'The pervert as such can signify himself only by this gesture; the executing of this gesture counts for the whole of his existing'.[180] He does not speak out, carrying his gesture through in silence. To exist – to be an individual singularity – is a mystery, an enigma for the subject. Since this question does not meet with any response in thought, the pervert finds consistency of being through the accomplished gesture. A gesture, in its particularity, can conjure an equivalence of being. Once enacted, it becomes an equivalent, a *stand-in* for the 'totality of the fact of existing'. The perverse gesture brings together what language delivers only in a partial way, whether in thought or in communicative reciprocity. Through its modality of exercise it devotes the centre stage, the only stage, to 'an arbitrary subordination of

177 *Ibid.*
178 *Ibid.*
179 *Ibid.*, pp. 22–3.
180 *Ibid.*, p. 23.

the habitual life functions to one sole insubordinate function'[181] and cuts itself off from all possibility of social bond. The gesture affirms sensuous polymorphy, the same whose emergence breaks down normative reason.

> Perversion would thus correspond to a property of being, a property founded on the expropriation of life functions. An expropriation of one's own body and of others would be the meaning of this property of being.[182]

This perverse gesture reveals a deed of existence that '[...] consecrates the death of the species in him as an individual'.[183]

However, this gesture in not comprehensible in and of itself. Its existence is enciphered by a *fixed idea*. This existence is unexchangeable and incommunicable. Although the being that creates existence is unknowable, the perverse gesture is visible and discernable. It 'does not yet belong to any code'[184] – and with good reason since it translates the emergence of an impulse that eludes any rational hold in language (i.e. code). 'It is not so much the pervert that recalls his gesture so as to unleash it again as it is the gesture itself that recalls the pervert'.[185]

There is no way out of such a position. If the perverse gesture is incomprehensible because the being that it achieves cannot be transmitted, then any possibility of saying something about it is futile. Sade does not accept this state of affairs. He will interpret what this gesture shows of the original impulse. He will render explicit what is sheer silence, what lies wide of the norm (i.e. anomaly). '[...] Sade will interpret the supposed interpretation of the pervert. He will do so on the basis of what he deciphers in the pervert's gesture'.[186] This gesture is a game of unknown, but also unknowable, hieroglyphs. Sade will be the one to decipher the hidden and, as yet, non-transmittable message. He makes himself the one who passes on what is unshareable in the dark and solvent impulse. This is what the perverse

181 *Ibid.*
182 *Ibid.*
183 *Ibid.*
184 *Ibid.*, p. 24.
185 *Ibid.*
186 *Ibid.*

gesture permits, the key place it occupies. Once interpreted, it allows for an understanding of the logic of a *stand-in*, an equivalent to the impulse itself. It is a revealing *simulacrum*.

The archetypal perverse gesture – on whose basis the code of perversion can be decrypted – is sodomy. The sodomite gesture would so fascinate Klossowski that it is the sole sexual act carried out in his narratives. It is likewise the only sexual act presented in his paintings. Sodomy is the paradigm of the genuine perverse practice. Why? It is the 'specific gesture of countergenerality' because it stands in opposition to the act of the law of the propagation of the species. It '[...] *bears witness to the death of the species in an individual*'.[187] Klossowski qualifies sodomy as simulacrum – it may well be his simulacrum princeps. Sodomy is a simulacrum, as well as a scorning, of the copulatory act. And when perpetrated on a subject of the other sex, it becomes the simulacrum of the metamorphosis of one being into another. This magical act, which annuls the differentiation between the sexes, allowing for their fusion and transformation, gives rise to the notion of abolishing the property of bodies as a closed and inviolable individuality. Sodomy is the perfect realisation of integral monstrosity and its institutional corollary, universal prostitution. The sodomite gesture is the 'key sign' of the code of perversion.

One can see the change Klossowski makes in 1967. The perverse gesture actualises the impulse in a concrete manifestation. It is a way of acting that translates a singular way of feeling. Given this gesture, what can reason do? What consequences will it draw from this, since reason, as a communicative generality, must dispute perversion? There exists a *perverse reason*. Sade's response is atheism: the counterpart, in rational thought, to the perverse and particularly to the sodomite gesture is the affirmation of God's death. '[...] reason, will adapt to the coded gesture of the pervert [...]'.[188] In return, what does the perverse gesture introduce into established reason? Answer: the 'non-language of monstrosity'.[189] It is not atheism that allows

187 *Ibid.*
188 *Ibid.*, p. 25.
189 *Ibid.*

for monstrosity, but the inverse. In 1967, it is Sade the pervert who is being examined, and no longer Sade the theologian.

How does Sade go about this in his fictional works? He brings the libertine out of a closed environment and puts him in the decent setting of the everyday world. This switch is a masterstroke. If the libertine finds himself at the heart of social life, then social life is the fertile ground on which perversion finds its origin and its substance. Sade does not criticise the institutions. By placing the libertine there he shows that our institutions 'ensure the triumph of perversions'.[190] Perversion is not kept at a distance. It is given the status of a universalising vocation in the form of a counter-generality.

Let us come back to the perverse gesture. Grasping its logic is crucial for the analysis of perversion. Though the perverse gesture is singular and undecipherable, it is only so with respect to the generality of everyday gestures that are named and explained by a word. The perverse gesture is not one gesture among others. On the contrary, it constitutes a break.

> [...] the singular gesture of the pervert is precisely not the gesture formed in the medium of generality that may accompany speech, is sometimes substituted for the word, and sometimes even contradicts it. The singular gesture of the pervert *empties all content out of speech at once, since it is by itself the whole of existence for him.*[191]

Whilst 'the generality of gestures is one with speech,'[192] the particularity of the perverse gesture is that it stands in opposition to speech. It strikes mute because it silences. It does not stop speech; it empties it out, reducing it to the real of an absolute silence. When taken up in Sade's fiction, the gesture cannot remain mute. It must speak out and can only do so in the name of the generality of gestures. The pervert knows 'that he is alone in acting in this way,' but in saying so, he affirms the contrary.

190 *Ibid.*, p. 26.
191 *Ibid.*
192 *Ibid.*

> How can he overcome this obstacle? If he speaks, can he show, in the name of generality, that there is no generality and that the norms of the species have no real existence?[193]

In maintaining this obstacle in thought, the gesture becomes impossible, left hanging from a contradiction perpetuated by the reasoning that posits it. It thereby remains opaque, absolutely singular, and indecipherable. The gesture, like perversion of which it is the key visible sign, cannot find a positive form. It is and always will be a negativity that pierces a hole in any linguistic argumentation and renders it indeterminate.

The gesture is performed unto an other, a fellowman. It is not cut off from the Other. What does it bring about when it is accomplished? In a word: persuasion.

> Persuasion can be brought about only if the interlocutor is in turn led to reject norms in himself. It is not by arguments that Sade's character can obtain the assent of his interlocutor but by complicity.[194]

This demonstrative value has its importance in the oeuvre, too. To make the other an accomplice is not to convince or persuade him with rational demonstrations. Sade's commentators recognise, as did the Marquis himself, that the reasonings of the libertine heroes are merely sophisms teeming with aporiae and contradictions. The accomplices must proclaim the absence of God, and profess their faith in atheism. This is not enough. Atheism must be a new form of generality to be fought against. The perverse gesture must necessarily be carried out – it is this, and this alone, that shows that atheism is integral, that it is not simply a new deism.

> [...] the coded gesture is disengaged from the logically structured language that, as an oratorical precaution, is put over it, and the key sign that this gesture represents appears in its true locus: the secret society.[195]

193 *Ibid.*, p. 27.
194 *Ibid.*
195 *Ibid.*

Case by case, the gesture demonstrates the abolition of generality. It demonstrates it in the act.

> [...] the gesture becomes a simulacrum, a rite, which the members of the secret society do not explain to one another otherwise than by the inexistence of the absolute guarantor of norms, an inexistence they commemorate as an event that one can represent only by this gesture.[196]

Bringing about integral atheism does not happen through rational decision making, through logical demonstration in language. Only the mute gesture, emptying speech of all content, can bring it into act. Only the silent and incomprehensible gesture proves that God does not exist and that reason is no more.

With the possibility of this secret society, the performed gesture has a necessary effect on the partner, the partner who is soon to be accomplice. This inter-subjectivity is indispensable if a dialectic is to be engaged, if a locus is to be established in which perversion will be realised.

> In order for complicity with the pervert to emerge in the normal interlocutor, the qua 'rational' individual must first be disintegrated. This is possible only by a leap of impulsion or of repulsion provoked in him by the word of the pervert.[197]

The gesture translates the fact that the one who accomplishes it annuls himself as a reasonable individuality. There is a singular actualisation of impulse which is real and which lies outside language. It provokes an effect in the partner: it tends to break him apart as a unity. The sodomite gesture thus represents the realisation of the transformation of beings, their metamorphosis, into one another.

Klossowski sums up this inter-subjective logic:

> How could the pervert recognise complicity in this 'normal' interlocutor? By a gesture a subject makes [...] in contradiction to what he says. The interlocutor who rejects the sophism of the pervert makes a gesture that is in this sense contradictory,

196 *Ibid.*, p. 28.
197 *Ibid.*

> for, notwithstanding the disavowal it expresses, it physically, hence corporeally, bears witness to his own singularity – latent in him as in everyone.[198]

The words 'as in everyone' need to be highlighted. There is a latent singularity in everyone. But language, society, God, and so on, proceed to reduce singularity to a normal or normalised element of generality. The pervert's gesture triggers in his partner this buried, hidden, and denied singularity; it gives rise to his unordered impulse that makes up his singularity. The partner is thus touched, though unaware of it, and he performs this contradictory gesture that demonstrates the chiasm between what he says (even what he proclaims in the assertive mode of reason and moral principles), and what he feels due to the emergence of the singular impulse that makes up his being. The function of the pervert unveils in the other party what reason eliminates, or would like to eliminate, but ever in vain.

> The pervert lays in wait for this contradictory gesture, this reflex gesture, this corporeal, thus mute, gesture, which he deciphers in these terms: 'Consider all the fatalities that unite us and see if Nature does not offer you a victim in my individual nature'.[199]

In this way, monstrosity could be integral. It is no longer a general principle to be deduced from integral atheism. On the contrary, an inverse causality is operative: the pervert brings about this singular impulse in the other party. The other party is unaware of this, but his contradictory gesture shows the goal has been reached. The secret society, made up of accomplices, is set up and becomes generalised. It is a society whose ethos is *We Are All Perverse!* With this realisation, the absence of God is proven as a concrete fact, making room for all that he censured – the dark, solvent, impulsive and duly silent forces.

Sade's goal is not to blow the isolated practice of such and such a case of perversion out of proportion, but rather to produce a doctrine of perverse monstration with an explicitly didactic aim. From the very first lines of 'Kant with Sade', Jacques Lacan insists on this point:

198 *Ibid.*
199 *Ibid.*

> I [...] maintain that the Sadean bedroom is of the same stature as those places from which the schools of ancient philosophy borrowed their names: Academy, Lyceum, and Stoa. Here as there, one paves the way for science by rectifying one's ethical position.[200]

What interests the Marquis are the 'doctors of monstrosity'[201] who constitute 'a space for minds that communicate with one another by the mutual understanding [...]'[202] of this key sign that the act of sodomy is. There is a progressive initiation into the role of doctor of monstrosity, culminating with the ascesis of *apathy*. With regard to apathy, what is interesting about the 1967 article (and this is a point that had already been commented on at length in 1947) is its explanation of the causal place of impulsive forces. These forces can be intimidated by the institutional system or, on the contrary, intensified by their internal pressure. What needs to be grasped is that 'it is always the same impulses that intimidate us at the same time that they raise us up in revolt'.[203] They intimidate us with images – images of executed or executable acts – in the form of fear, horror, compassion, remorse, and so on. No longer holding back the act is accomplished by short-circuiting the interplay of preliminary images. The image does not only halt the act, it also has the value of a project. In other words, the act is conditioned by an image. In this case, *to act* is taken up in an 'uncertain'[204] imaginary passion. The image preceding the act enciphers a promise of jouissance. The act is dependant on the 'primary benefit of transgression'.[205]

How is one to accomplish the act by disconnecting it from the images that condition it? It is at this point that we come across apathy again as the condition for the reiteration of the perverse act. Sade's demonstration is highly rigorous. Self-consciousness, where the images are formed and

200 Lacan, J., 'Kant with Sade' in *Écrits, The First Complete Edition in English*, *op. cit.*, p. 645.

201 Klossowski, P., *Sade My Neighbor*, *op. cit.*, p. 29.

202 *Ibid.*

203 *Ibid.*

204 *Ibid.*, p. 30.

205 *Ibid.*

actualised, is an individuated structure that, under the pressure of the institutional milieu and language, channels the forces. It puts them in order, brings them to heel, and localises them. But the forces continue their subterranean work. Self-consciousness cannot ensure its perfectly balanced stability. 'Sometimes these forces put the subject *outside of himself* and make him act *against himself*, they transgress the structure of consciousness and decompose it'.[206] This is the result Sade means to achieve and this is the state that endlessly fascinates Klossowski. How is one to avoid the depletion of these forces? This is a question that is all the more difficult given that there are not two different kinds of forces. The force as solvent energy and ego destroyer is one and the same. Developing these forces is tantamount to running the risk of them swinging back to create moral conscience; to develop these forces is simultaneously to produce the very thing that switches them around: the unity of the ego that is indispensable to the survival of the species. Klossowski speaks of 'contradictory simultaneity'.[207] Sade does not give in, however. Apathy is called back. Apathetic reiteration must empty the act of its 'sensuous'[208] dimension: the jouissance obtained by transgressing the norms.

> The Being cast *outside of oneself* [...] is in practice equivalent to a disintegration of the conscience of the subject by means of thought. Thought must re-establish the primitive version of the impulsive forces, which the conscience of the subject has inverted.[209]

The consequence is that

> for the disciple who will practice the doctrine [...] monstrosity is the zone of this being *outside of oneself, outside of conscience*; the monster can maintain himself in this zone only by the reiteration of the same act.[210]

206 *Ibid.*, p. 31.
207 *Ibid.*
208 *Ibid.*, p. 32.
209 *Ibid.*
210 *Ibid.*

The act becomes 'voluptuous harshness'.[211] It will no longer be inscribed in the field of the sensuous, producing an 'ecstasy of thought'.[212] Thought will be nourished by the representation of the reiteration of the same without the emergence of conscience; thinking will be organised by the tireless return of the same. The singularity thus achieved will have found its mental organisation, affording access to an act that, far from depleting the forces at stake, intensifies them without caesura. Apathy ruins temporal successiveness just as the perverse (sodomite) act had emptied all speech of its content. There reigns the pure silence of the act, as atemporal as myth.

The 1967 critique of the remarks on atheism made in 1947 may be summed up as follows:[213]

- *Rational atheism* merely reproduces the disputed monotheistic norms. The unitary economy of the soul, realising the unity and possession of the responsible ego, is upheld.
- This atheism promises man's sovereignty. Sade, on the contrary, pursues the disintegration of the unity of man since he is striving to put an end to the reign of the norms of reason.
- Because he thinks through rational atheism with the terms that were in common usage, Sade finds himself constrained, not without contradiction, to make atheism the *religion* of generalised perversion.
- This religion involves an asceticism, which is the supreme moment of its application: apathy. The apathetic reiteration of the perverse gesture signals the disappearance of God. Since atheism is insufficient, apathy as an effective practice must be assigned to it, thus cancelling out the time of the act and the locus of its realisation.
- Monstrosity conserves its divine character. It is realised through rites whose model is the sodomite gesture. These rites must be continually actualised so as to avoid their cessation, or even their cancellation. Priority is given to impulsive forces.

211 *Ibid.*

212 *Ibid*: '[…] an ecstasy here opposed to its functional analogue, orgasm'.

213 *Ibid.*, pp. 5–6.

– Atheism is not the cause of perversion. On the contrary, evil comes first. Whilst atheism must be derationalised, Sade tries to rationalise his perversion by founding it as a counter-generality. We see the efficacy of the chiasmus between reason and perversion.

The Metamorphosis of Bodies

In the section 'Homage to a Virgin' from his article 'Under the Mask of Atheism' (1947), Klossowski singled out an accursed virility that is exasperated by never being able to possess the inviolable virgin. Later, in *The Philosopher Villain*, Klossowski sharply critiques his old remarks and shows their limits. In order to think through this relation to virginity and sodomy in a different way, he takes up the *myth of the Androgyne*, separating it from its monotheist aspect, and showing its contemporary relevance in Sade's work.

Sade's pervert is represented by a man in so far as man is, by definition, the rational sex: he alone is 'called upon to give an account of reason'.[214] The female sex, from a misogynist point of view, represents an 'uncontrolled sensuous nature'.[215] This difference is a traditional one. What is interesting here is to see how a new connection is being introduced. The effect of the practice of integral monstrosity is 'the working of an exchange of the specific qualities of the sexes'.[216] When applied, it implies that the man, as pervert, presents himself as 'the assertion of sensuous nature'[217] and that the female character asserts reason.

214 *Ibid.*, p. 35.
215 *Ibid.*
216 *Ibid.*
217 *Ibid.*

Perversion corresponds to 'the expropriation of one's own body and the body of the other'.[218] The abolition of norms that integral atheism achieves has a fresh consequence: expropriation. For in suppressing the 'limits of the responsible and self-identical ego', one concomitantly abolishes the identity of one's own body.

> In itself the body is the concrete product of the individuation of the impulsive forces realised according to the norms of the species. [...] This body has only been restored to 'me' corrected in certain ways – certain forces have been pruned away, others subjugated by language. 'I' then do not possess 'my' body save in the name of institutions; the language in 'me' is just their overseer put in 'me'. Institutional language taught 'me' that this body in which 'I am' was 'mine'.[219]

The pervert's act is situated in these effects of transformation and metamorphosis: 'The greatest crime "I" can commit is not so much to take "his" body from the "other"; it is to break "my" body away from this "myself" instituted by language'.[220] Klossowski insists on this logic:

> The representation of having a body whose state is not that of one's own body is clearly specific to perversion. Although the pervert feels the alterity of the alien body, he feels much more the body of the other as being his own; and the body that normatively and institutionally is his he experiences as being really foreign to himself [...].[221]

By inhabiting the other's body the pervert strives to experience 'the irruption of an alien force within "himself." He is both within and without'.[222]

These remarks are extremely accurate for describing imaginary identification such as it is laid bare in perverse inter-subjectivity. The pervert, identified with his partner, tries to grasp this irruption of the solvent force in the other's body. For structural reasons he fails to do so. But this does not keep Klossowski from basing his analysis on this possibility. For him, the pervert obtains, albeit partially, the expropriation that would signal

218 *Ibid.*
219 *Ibid.*, p. 36.
220 *Ibid.*
221 *Ibid.*, p. 36.
222 *Ibid.*

the abolition of the ego's limits and its external guarantor: institutional language and universalising reason. This expropriation of the body, disconnected from the 'myself,' is most accurately achieved through the figure of the androgyne. The Sadean pervert is able to behave as a woman with his partner and feel 'female passivity'[223] from the inside, transferring into his victim's body. The metamorphosis of beings would allow him to treat his fellow man as a woman and a woman as a boy.

The character of Juliette best embodies this model of the androgyne, in so far as she is a 'woman-man.'[224] As a woman, part of her is originally linked to the sensuous experience, and she is the one who sets forth reason, the prerogative of virile thought.

> [...] it is the Sadean heroine who carries atheism all the way to its integral affirmation, dissociating it from normative and anthropomorphic reason, freeing thought itself in the experimental sphere of monstrosity.[225]

The figure of the androgyne has the value of a myth in Sade's work because it is a synthesis of opposites, of what is irreconcilable in reason and in the sensuous. But it is a *simulacrum* of synthesis. The development of perverse thought or practice only demonstrates the impossibility of a conjunction of opposites. Hence, the myth.

These are the principal remarks of *The Philosopher Villain* – to be understood as a critique of the interpretations that were being worked out as early as 1933 and systematised in 1947 in *Sade My Neighbor*. Klossowski has changed his line of attack. He has moved from a commentary on Sadean thought to a questioning of Sadism. There remains one last point which concludes his work of 1967: 'How does Sade's experience render his conventional form of communication "unreadable?"'[226] What does this mean? By way of writing, Sade gives an interpretation of his experience. The process is twofold: first, to give a representation of the (incommunicable) sensuous

223 *Ibid.*, p. 37.
224 *Ibid.*
225 *Ibid.*, pp. 37–8.
226 *Ibid.*, p. 39.

nature in an aberrant act (i.e. the perverse gesture); next, to provide a described representation (i.e. given-to-be-seen in the theatre of fiction). Communicating the personal experience (i.e. the singular way of feeling) is impossible and cannot be rationally accounted for. However, Sade does choose to give a translation of it – an interpretation – in the classic form of logical communication:

> Then the conventional communication becomes 'unreadable' each time the incommunicable experience asserts itself; but it becomes all the more readable when this experience disappears again.[227]

Taken literally, Sade's text bears the trace of what cannot be written therein. The presence of the singular experience makes the forms of its transmission indeterminate. In fiction we find this unreadable point where the incommunicable perverse gesture is written in negative.

When it comes to his reader, what is our author aiming at? His goal is didactic:

> [He] seems to represent his reader as someone he must continually keep gasping with the promise of yet another shock. Yet what the reader is seeking in the end at the expense of his reading is a sort of lapse of attention at the moment when the whole of the text wants sustained attention [...].[228]

Faced with the unreadable aspect of the text, the reader switches off – but this movement simply conveys the fact that he is approaching an incommunicable experience that is driving him towards ecstasy.

> In actualising the act, writing works up the ecstasy of thought; reiterated on the level of language, this ecstasy coincides with the transgression reiterated by fictitious characters. Thus the logically structured language with which Sade expresses himself becomes for him the terrain of outrage, as it is the terrain of norms.[229]

227 *Ibid.*

228 *Ibid.*

229 *Ibid.*, p. 40.

The veil is lifted on writing in its function. Writing or reading becomes identical to the apathetic reiteration of the act. The same process 'inscribes the presence of *nonlanguage* in language; it inscribes a foreclosure of language by language'.[230] Let us hold on to this word *foreclosure*, which Klossowksi defines as something that remains on the outside. That which remains outside language is 'the act to be done. The less it is perpetrated the more it raps at the door […] of literary vacuity'.[231] This interplay between inside and outside, between reason and the aberrant act, defines the literary arena of the Marquis: 'What gives Sade's text its disturbing originality is that through him this outside comes to be commented on as something produced within thought'.[232] The outside is shown to be internal to thought; the outside is thought's internal limit, its excluded part delineated. This outside is not the outer world, but what thought, in its roundabout way, defines as its own impossible – its specified real that proceeds from what it develops through reason.

> This outside is not at all the interior of the 'bedroom' where one would philosophise; it is the inwardness of thought which *nothing* separates from the 'bedroom'. In fact, the term *bedroom* is a riddle; it designates the bloody cave of the Cyclops, whose one eye is that of voracious thought.[233]

Sade forces us to think about the relationships between the text and its so-called outside. A fresh connection emerges:

> […] a set of tales, discourses, then a series of tableaux that slyly invite the reader to see outside what does not seem to lie in the text – whereas nothing is visible anywhere except in the text. His work then is like the vast layout of an urban showroom at the heart of a city, one with the city, where without noticing it one passes from the objects exhibited to objects that exhibit themselves fortuitously without being exhibitable. At length one recognises that it is to these that the corridors of the exhibition lead.[234]

230 *Ibid.*, p. 41.
231 *Ibid.*
232 *Ibid.*, p. 42.
233 *Ibid.*
234 *Ibid.*

These objects that are exhibited without being exhibitable form the unreadable aspect of the text where, clouding over the reference points of communication, the inassimilable aspect of a perverse experience is written in negative, actualising the solvent forces.

Perversion and the Industrial World

In 1970, Klossowski published the article, 'Sade and Fourier'. In it, he asks in what way Sade's oeuvre may 'enlighten us on the pathological behaviour of our industrial world, in so far as this is foreshadowed by his description.'[235] Let's take note, on one hand, of the term *pathological* to designate our world, and on the other, the conceptual place granted to the Marquis' thought. This will allow us to grasp the logic of the industrial system at the end of the twentieth century. Sade would have us grasp what is pathological in our world in a way that perhaps no other author permits – with the exception of Nietzsche, to whom Klossowski attributes the same power of spelling out something of our current social-economic state.

The point of departure would be the present-day economy, which he knows Marxist thinking sees, in the final analysis, as a determinant of the world's functioning. Without saying so, and not without playing with his reader, Klossowski would pit Sade – and likewise the utopian Fourier – *against* Marx. Let's come straight out with the thesis he presents: in the end, it is the impulsive forces that are decisive, and not economic ones. These impulsive forces are what perversion, *de facto*, actualises in the strongest possible way:

> [...] how does the economy, independently, but perhaps by the very law of supply and demand that governs exchange, reveal itself to be a mode of expression, representation and self-interpretation of the affective life?[236]

235 Klossowski, P., 'The Phantasms of Perversion: Sade and Fourier', *op. cit.*, p. 22.
236 *Ibid.*

What does this mean? There is a combat between the affects and the repressive forces, between what is singular in emotion and what is universal in institutional reason. Sade is a seer; he could 'divine'[237] and thus be witness to what no one else could see. On one hand there is the metamorphosis of the affects in their combat against the repressive forces. On the other, there are the modifications of these same censuring forces in their desire to destroy singular impulsions.

> But if this conflict gives rise to a reciprocal metamorphosis of the contending forces, it is because sexual impulses, and in particular the forms of voluptuous emotion, are directly affected by the norms of the economy at the time.[238]

This thesis was taken up, at the same time in the 1970s, by philosophers – and not by the least of them. They used these new remarks to develop 'Libidinal Economy'[239] as an approach to the psychical and social-political reality of the world today.

The first force of repression, acting on the goalless, shapeless affects, 'is the *formation of the organic and psychic unity of the agent*.'[240] The wording is dense, but the logic has already been developed, notably in *The Philosopher Villain*. But there is something new here. Beyond that which supports the agent as a unity there is a value system that takes the form of a 'hierarchy of needs'.[241] This hierarchy, where the market economy is to be found,

> is the economic form of repression imposed by institutions, by and through the consciousness of the agent, on the imponderable forces of his psychic life. Thanks to his acquired organic and moral unity, the individual defines his impulses to himself [...] only as a set of material and moral needs [...].[242]

237 *Ibid.*
238 *Ibid.*
239 Title of a book by Jean-François Lyotard, Indiana University Press, 1993.
240 Klossowski, P., 'The Phantasms of Perversion: Sade and Fourier', *op. cit.*, p. 22.
241 *Ibid.*
242 *Ibid.*

What consequence can be deduced from this? Objects that are possessed, conserved, produced, exchanged, consumed, received, etc., prevail and reign. Voluptuous emotion is transformed into an object caught in a logic of frenzied commodification. Such a formulation could portray a retrograde, obsolete or nostalgic view – a veritable pastoral for liberated affects. This is not where Klossowski wants to lead us. Our author is not out to liberate suppressed emotions. He is not a utopian announcing future happiness, nor is he the hero of positivity. 'The forms of voluptuous emotion might then reveal a connection, at once secret and tragic, with the anthropomorphous phenomenon of the economy and exchange'.[243] We can hear the radicalness of his position. Commodification does not lie beyond affects – it constitutes their centre.

For his demonstration, Klossowski returns to Sadean perversion, which is understood as a first reaction, or interpretation, from '*the impulses themselves such as to decompose what is genetically embraced by the term "sexuality"* [...]'.[244] Perversion separates voluptuous emotion from the instinct of propagation. In ever seeking out new sensations, it would hold the procreative function in indefinite suspension. Both simple and complicated passions are 'ruses'[245] of interpretation on the part of the original emotion. For Sade, it is not a matter of excluding the force at work in the instinct of procreation that ensures the survival of the species. He must retrieve the energy that is manifested there and use it in a different way. The pervert is a *diverter* of accumulated energies.

> The instinctual forces thus *deducted* then form the *material for a phantasm* that *emotion interprets*, phantasm here having *the role of 'fabricated' object*; it is the use of this *phantasm* by an instinctual force that *gives value to the emotion*, which in turn *only occurs with this use. The use of a phantasm in perversion to procure emotion requires, precisely, that the phantasm be unexchangeable.*[246]

243 *Ibid.*, p. 23.
244 *Ibid.*
245 *Ibid.*
246 *Ibid.*

The phantasm – this is the new contribution of 'Sade and Fourier' – constitutes a new modality of enciphering the extracted, stored up energy on the basis of the instinct of procreation. Strictly speaking, emotion does not interpret the impulse; it interprets the enigmatic encryption in the phantasm. This phantasm is unexchangeable. It can be neither transmitted nor understood. Hence the equally incomprehensible character of emotion when it emerges for the subject in the guise of a particular feeling. The felt intensity is unexchangeable, inscribed in the monetary system of exchange as 'priceless'.[247] At the heart of market economy dwells a *pricelessness* that constitutes its base.

As in *Living Currency*, the reference to phantasm constitutes the central concept in this article:

> Since the impulses always exceed individual unity in one's own phantasms, rendering it *capable* [...] of associating with other impulses in other unities, *the law of exchange* (supply and demand) *must involve psychically affirmed subjects, and not those economically determined by institutions*; *the true producer or true consumer is not the purely fictional unity of individuals, but their phantasmatic impulses: as things stand, their supposed abnormality*.[248]

The sodomite gesture finds its place again as the key sign of perverse practice since it stands in opposition to the law of the propagation of the species and brings about the metamorphosis of beings in favour of a new phantasmatic economy. The perverse propensity is fundamentally unproductive in a market economy that is legitimised on the outside by the hierarchy of needs. On the other hand, it is duly productive as a promoter of impulses.

The Marquis' aim (and this will be Fourier's aim too, but in different terms) is to base the possibility of psychical exchanges on the perverted model of the exchange of goods in the market economy.

> At issue is the sharing of the 'psychic goods' or wealth offered by the polymorphous perverse and the mechanics of this division of goods through exchange, which presupposes that to be exchangeable this kind of wealth is 'communicable'.[249]

247 *Ibid.*
248 *Ibid.*, p. 27.
249 *Ibid.*

How is one to communicate the incommunicable, exchange the unexchangeable? We should not be surprised to be coming across this question again. It is Klossowski's question – the very same that conditions his entire oeuvre and his life as a whole. In itself incommunicable, the phantasm gives rise to the creation of simulacra – and we know that the sodomite gesture, as well as the androgyne, are simulacra with which he tries to spell out or show what always eludes reason, words, and forms of expression.

> For a simulacrum to exist, there has to be a real, irreducible basis, inseparable from the *phantasm which* governs the reality of a particular behaviour. If someone is driven to *kill*, to *torture*, or to less radical forms of violence, the *phantasm* acting in the organism and its reflexes remain *ineradicable*.[250]

This is what Sade asserts – which Fourier moreover contests. Klossowski reuses the terms 'economy' and 'value' to pursue his own examination of the phantasm.

If the phantasm is incommunicable, then communication can only be a simulacrum. This simulacrum is constituted on the model of the universal equivalence of money. This

> simulacrum [...] excludes any intelligibility of what a person *momentarily represents* to the one who enjoys him, unless it be in fact his body or that *thing* his expropriated body may be *worth* for and in the phantasm of the other.[251]

In perverse practice, such as sodomy,

> the expropriated body is recovered as a phantasmatic domain such that it becomes merely the equivalent of the phantasm. But it will only really be the simulacrum of the phantasm provided it is produced under the sign of value or price.[252]

The body, disconnected from myself (i.e. from its agency of appropriation which fixes it down and names it as an individuated unity) becomes the equivalent of the phantasm; like the phantasm, it enciphers the impulses

250 *Ibid.*, p. 28.

251 *Ibid.*, p. 29.

252 *Ibid.*, p. 30.

in silence. If this same expropriated body is integrated into a psychical economy of exchange then, because it is taken up in the field of value, it is constructed as a simulacrum of this same mute phantasm. The simulacrum, for its part, can be exchanged.

> It falls to Sade to become the first modern thinker to insist on the close relationship between the phantasm and its commercial valorisation, thus on the role of money as a sign of the phantasm's inestimable value. Money is an integral part of the representative mode of perversion. Because the perverse phantasm is inherently unintelligible and unexchangeable, money constitutes (by its abstract character) its universally intelligible equivalent.[253]

This is '*the mediating function of money* between the closed world of abnormalities and the world of institutional norms'.[254] Language and money occupy the same structural space.

> Money, the equivalent of scarce wealth, [...] must signify the re-diversion of this wealth in favour of the perverse phantasm. If the phantasm requires a *determinate expenditure*, the equivalence of the phantasm thus concretised will be expressed by as much wealth as represents the purchasing power of this money. [...] That which does not exist according to the norms, hence the abnormalities only negatively stated in language as an absence of these norms, is positively stated by *the money unspent, thus denied to what exists.*[255]

Value and scarcity find their rightful place, but in a negative form. This Sadean dilemma can be expressed as '*either communication through the exchange of bodies, or prostitution under the sign of money*'.[256] The veil is lifted on the effect of such a dilemma: how can one assess in abstract monetary terms the non-assessable wealth of the phantasm? Here is the answer provided by the oeuvre of the Marquis, freshly transcribed by Klossowski: 'Abolish money and you will have universal communication between

253 *Ibid.*
254 *Ibid.*
255 *Ibid.*, pp. 30–1.
256 *Ibid.*, p. 31.

beings'.[257] The metamorphosis of beings would operate under the pressure of forces that circulate hither and thither, enciphered in and through the phantasm.

> Sade proves by this kind of challenge that the notion of value and price is inscribed at the very base of voluptuous emotions, and that nothing is more contrary to jouissance than gratuity.[258]

On this score, Sade cannot be reduced to the positive utopian Fourier.

The 1970 contribution of 'Sade and Fourier' enables us to grasp how and why, for the Marquis as read by Klossowski, the 'imponderable forces of affects' constitute the base of the present-day normative institutions, without, for all that, creating their own. Among these institutions, Klossowski examines the authority of the market (the market agency) and the universal value that governs its functioning – money. His thesis is that money lies at the heart of perversion since the question arises for Sade as to how to make a bond (i.e. exchange) with that which breaks any bond, that which breaks off any communication, namely, the phantasm. This does not mean that voluptuous emotion is one good amongst others, that it has a price. On the contrary, it is priceless. Its price is such that no monetary quantity could appropriate it. What needs to be understood here is that the motor of market exchange is situated, in relation to money which regulates it, as what is impossible in it – this impossible aspect is precisely voluptuous emotion. In being priceless, it is the condition of possibility of objects having a price. Sade's modernity is pertinent today. He imparts to us the rationale behind the un-thought of our industrial societies, societies that are teeming with objects and needs that are indissolubly linked. Sade's oeuvre, and its promotion of would-be integral perversion, instructs us on the pathological dimension of our industrial world today.

257 *Ibid.*, p. 33.

258 *Ibid.*, pp. 33–4 [Where the translation gives '... nothing is more contrary to sexual pleasure ...'].

Nietzsche: The Same, The *Stimmung*

There is a long-standing and insistent presence of 'Nietzsche's thought'[1] in Pierre Klossowski's work. His first published articles on the philosopher date from the mid-1950s.[2] His principal text is *Nietzsche and the Vicious Circle*. Dated 1969 (Klossowski was sixty-four), it is dedicated to Gilles Deleuze who in 1962 had published *Nietzsche and Philosophy*.[3] In this book Deleuze examines not the philosophy of Nietzsche *per se* but in what way the philosophical oeuvre constitutes a rupture in the sphere of thought: what kind of philosophy is still possible after Nietzsche?

Klossowski comes back to this rupture, but in no way does he question it in relation to the history or the main stakes of philosophy. In what way was the analysis of the Nietzschean rupture to allow him to make a pause in his own work and think about it differently? Klossowski was to

1 Klossowski, P., *Nietzsche and the Vicious Circle*, Continuum, London, 2009, trans. Daniel W. Smith, The Athlone Press, London, 1997, p. xiii.

2 In 1956: 'On Some Fundamental Themes of Nietzsche's *Gaya Scienza*' (published in 1963 in *Un si funeste désir*, Éditions Gallimard, Paris, and trans. Russell Ford in *Such a Deathly Desire*, State University of New York Press, Albany, 2007). In 1957: 'Nietzsche, Polytheism and Parody' (Lecture delivered to the Collège de Philosophie, published in *Such a Deathly Desire*, *op. cit.* In 1964: Klossowski would present papers at the Royaumont Colloquium ('Forgetting and Anamnesis in the Lived Experience of the Eternal Return of the Same', *Nietzsche and the Vicious Circle*, *op. cit.*, pp. 44–52) and the Cerisy Colloquium ('*Circulus vitiosus deus*', *Nietzsche*, Collection 10/18, Paris, 1973). One may also consult: Maurice Blanchot, 'L'exigence du retour', in *Klossowski*, *L'Arc* journal, 43, Aix-en Provence, 1970; Brice Parain, 'Son Nietzsche' in *L'Arc*, 43, *op. cit.*; Jean Decottinges, 'Nietzsche ironisé', in *Pierre Klossowski, Cahiers pour un temps*, Centre Georges Pompidou, Paris, 1985; Michel Balzamo, 'Klossowski et le "cas Nietzsche"', in *Klossowski*, *Revue des Sciences Humaines*, 197, Lille, 1985.

3 Deleuze, G., *Nietzsche and Philosophy*, Continuum, London, 1986.

say that his was a '*false* study'[4] showing an 'unusual ignorance'[5] of other works, notably academic ones. Only the German edition[6] of the 1880–8 posthumous fragments[7] would underlie his reading. In *Nietzsche and the Vicious Circle*, he comments on these fragments and their points of articulation, using long quotations in each chapter. The text to which this gives rise is repetitive, taking up Nietzsche's sentences directly. Some passages verge on the unreadable.[8] The reader soon wonders whether he is reading a book on Nietzsche or a narrative by Klossowski whose main character is Nietzsche.

Klossowski does not comment on the philosopher's work in general, only on the scraps that Nietzsche wrote over the ten years of his life that were tormented by madness and delusion. These fragments are essential for they are inseparable from the life of the subject Nietzsche and the madness that engulfed him. The posthumous fragments, unlike the philosopher's completed texts, examine the relationships between intimate experience and creation: what does Nietzsche tell us, at this time when he is falling into madness, about the creation, the writing, and the thought of he who devotes his life to creating, writing and thinking – to the point of dying from it? What relationships are there between an oeuvre and biographical data? This is what orients Klossowski's essay. It is less the philosopher's theory that interests him than the way subject and writing, life and creation, tie in.

This examination is Klossowski's own. It was to remain nameless and formless in Nietzsche's oeuvre. The oeuvre provides a name for, and allows for, a subjective experience that is incommunicable. This experience is certainly felt, though it is impossible to forge a social bond from it. The

4 Klossowski, P., *Nietzsche and the Vicious Circle, op. cit.*, p. xiii.

5 *Ibid.*

6 It was Klossowski himself who translated the posthumous fragments into French as *Fragments posthumes* for the *Œuvres Complètes* in 1976. He also translated (1954–64) *Le Gai Savoir* and the 1880–2 *Fragments posthumes*, as well as Heidegger's *Nietzsche* published by Gallimard, Paris, 1971.

7 Published by Gallimard under this title in Nietzsche's *Œuvres philosophiques complètes*.

8 The form should not be an obstacle to the content: silence should be present in this writing. The unreadable writes this silence, circumscribing it as un-transmittable.

oeuvre forms a social bond and constructs this experience. It inscribes a desire to know. Its success will be measured against its capacity to produce a new knowledge.

How do these posthumous fragments from 1880–8 constitute and refine the subject Nietzsche's experience that leaves his reason in tatters? What new knowledge is set down in these scraps of text? If the philosopher is mad, what guarantee is to be found in what he wrote? The fragments respond to this question precisely because it is the object of their investigation. Let us read Nietzsche's letters:

> My nervous system is splendid in view of the immense work it has to do: it is quite sensitive but very strong, a source of astonishment to me. Even the long and severe maladies, an occupation which did not suit me, and a dead wrong treatment have not harmed it [the nervous system] basically. Indeed, within the past year it has become stronger and owing to it I have produced one of the most daring, the sublimest and deepest of books ever spawned by a human brain and heart. Even had I committed suicide [...], a man would have died who was the most indomitable, and absolutely superior, not one who had given up in despair.[9]

The fragments endlessly list the effects of the subjective experience (the invasive madness) on the work of thinking and writing, which henceforth can be noted only fragmentarily! For eight years, Nietzsche was to reflect on the constantly shifting substratum of his pathos. Instead of trying to master this subterranean transformation, he tried to conform to it. These last writings investigate a question that Klossowski recognises as his own. In this respect, our author makes a 'parody'[10] of the thought of the posthumous fragments and plays out[11] his own question: what relationship

9 Nietzsche quoted by Klossowski in *Nietzsche and the Vicious Circle, op. cit.*, p. 17.

10 Klossowski, P., 'Nietzsche, Polytheism and Parody', *Such a Deathly Desire, op. cit.*, p. 99.

11 Klossowski recognises this: '[...] by playing on these words, I will not escape the reproach, under the pretext of showing the meaning of parody in Nietzsche, of making a parody of myself and thus of parodying Nietzsche. [...] we cannot avoid being the victim of a sort of ruse, nor can we avoid falling into the trap inherent in Nietzsche's own experience and thought. [...] the moment we try to elucidate Nietzsche's thought, he is always made to say more than he says and less than he says.

is there between my life (which is incommunicable) and my work (to be communicated)?

For Klossowski, there is a contemporary pertinence to Nietzsche's thought: the future the philosopher described, in a premonitory and fractured form, has become our everyday life. To read him is to return to his convulsive interrogations and to rethink what is specific to our lives today. The 'Nietzschean conspiracy'[12] was that of an isolated individual who used the means of his own social class in his fight against it, to the point of calling into question the 'existing forms of the human species as a whole'.[13] On this point, Nietzsche is comparable to Sade and his work on the destruction of an established order. But what singles out Nietzsche, in his passage from a strictly speculative realm of thought to conspiracy, is 'the irresistible attraction that Chaos [...] exerted on him'.[14] This is what distinguishes Nietzsche from Sade. The Marquis – a great aristocrat plotting against an aristocracy coming to the end of its total hegemony – thinks of destruction in terms of reason. Nietzsche on the other hand loses reason, and his oeuvre, at its end, translates his attraction for the 'chasm'[15] – the chasm of his subjective experience. At the start, Nietzsche fought this irresistible attraction of Chaos. Later, by probing the phenomenon of thought, he drew closer to this chasm. The fragments from this period do not cover over the chasm; they are constructed as a new creation that tells of this approach to the chasm. This creation becomes dissociated from reason: it is no longer a rational oeuvre of philosophy. The introduction of Chaos makes Nietzsche's 1880–8 texts contemporarily pertinent, a modern creation. Unlike Sade, Nietzsche examines the very 'act of thinking'.[16] Can one will the destruction of the world without thought (which elaborates this destruction) destroying

[...] In assimilating Nietzsche, we make him say more than he says, while in rejecting or altering him, we make him say less than he says [...]', *ibid.*, pp. 99–100.

12 Klossowski, P., *Nietzsche and the Vicious Circle*, *op. cit.*, p. xiv.

13 *Ibid.*

14 *Ibid.*

15 *Ibid.*

16 *Ibid.*, p. xv.

itself? Can one destroy the outside and still preserve the inside, which is the means of this destruction, perfectly intact?

Questioning the very act of thinking amounts to asking oneself: '*What is lucid* and *what is unconscious* in our thought and in our actions?'[17] The notion of lucidity is worthwhile 'only to the degree that total obscurity continued to be envisioned, and thus affirmed.'[18] In other words:

> At every moment chaos is still pursuing its work in our minds: concepts, images, feelings are therefore juxtaposed *fortuitously*, thrown together pell-mell. In this way relations that *astonish* the mind are created [...].[19]

What kind of thought is able to communicate the point at which the function of thinking, confronted with the emergence of Chaos, is shattered? Doesn't the irruption of this real, beyond the signifying foothold, immediately engender delusion – an attempt to give meaning to this edgeless hole? Does saying that Nietzsche is delusional, that he is mad, mean that the philosopher's work loses all its value because it is outside reason? Klossowski replies in the negative: for him Nietzsche's madness is the consequence of his attempt to avoid drawing back from this chasm, to make it the heart of his creation – '[...] *his thought revolved around delirium as its axis*'.[20]

Proceeding in this way, Nietzsche called into question:

- on the inside of thought, the identity principle on which language (the code of everyday signs) depends,[21] and the reality principle that gives the world its objectivity;
- on the outside, the competent institutional authorities: historians, philosophers, psychiatrists, etc., who assert the identity principle and the reality principle so as to know nothing of Chaos;
- science and its experimentations: the demarcations between the inside and the outside, between thought and the world, might be displaced.

17 *Ibid.*
18 *Ibid.*
19 *Ibid.*
20 *Ibid.*, p. xiv.
21 *Ibid.*, p. xv, see the section in this chapter 'The birth of signs'.

The work of destruction that was brought into play here was total. It left nothing beyond its scope, including the very thought that conceived it.

Thought, in wanting to accomplish such a task – and even upon itself – turns into the '*movement of a declarative mood*'.[22] It is no longer knowledge that is being transmitted, but the 'soul's tonality',[23] in its singularity. Saying that this experience is singular in no way signifies that it must be kept secret by he who experiences it. On the contrary, it must be communicated. But not in the manner of rational thought. The soul's tonality and the movement of the mood – the fact of transmitting a pure singularity – must become contagious.[24] To communicate them is to attack the identity principle and the reality principle head-on. Nietzsche was not developing a philosophy.

> [...] outside of the framework of the university, Nietzsche developed variations on a personal theme. [...] in the midst of the greatest intellectual isolation, Nietzsche was thereby abandoned, in the most auspicious manner, to listen to himself alone [*à la seule audition*].[25]

He is speaking to himself, to the thinker he was before.

This tonality of the soul is mute. Mood neither speaks nor designates. Both are pure 'muteness'.[26] This is the crux of the lesson: to introduce into thought what is wordless, what is pure silence – the real. 'This thought spoke to itself of an *obstacle* that the *intention* to teach would stumble over at the outset'.[27]

The specificity of this obstacle is that of being both *intensity* and *resistance* trapped in muteness: 'Muteness on the inside was merely *speech* on the

22 *Ibid.*, p. xvi.

23 *Ibid.*, p. xvii.

24 *Ibid.*, p. xvi.

25 Klossowski, P., 'Nietzsche, Polytheism and Parody', *Such a Deathly Desire*, *op. cit.*, p. 100.

26 Klossowski, P., *Nietzsche and the Vicious Circle*, *op. cit.*, p. xvi.

27 *Ibid.*

outside'.[28] The muteness of mood is projected onto thought. The subject Nietzsche identifies with this '*mute obstacle* of the mood'.[29] The result of the process is not limited to the field of speculation; it has effects on our philosopher, destroying his identity – there is no more subject Nietzsche – as well as that of the speaking agencies. Subject and language are destroyed in tandem. Nietzsche's declarations 'were directed to *an outside* that he had *reduced to the silence* of his own moods'.[30] Our subject goes mad, but he will have managed to reduce the speaking agencies to silence with his declarative mood. In this regard, that which produces noise and is transmitted, constituting culture (the sum total of different forms of knowledge), is 'the obverse of the soul's tonality, its intensity, which can be neither taught nor learnt'.[31] The muteness of Nietzsche's declaration becomes an issue: the more culture accumulates, the more the tonality of the soul grows. Language/culture and silence/muteness are like the two faces of a coin. The more the silencing pole of overlay (language and culture) intensifies, the more insistently urgent it is for the soul's tonality to find its place. The aphasia of Nietzsche the subject at the end of his life is none other than that of culture and science, which continually calculate 'so as not to have to speak, for fear of falling back into the nothingness'.[32] This muteness is the proof that discourse does not want to know. The philosopher's aphasia is an identification with the mute chasm; however, the aphasia of rational discourse marks the *not wanting to know anything about it* proper to the subterranean movement that causes this aphasia, wordlessly. The Nietzschean rupture substitutes declaration for demonstration, mood for institutional language, non-teaching for teaching, the soul's tonality for speculation, muteness for discourse, and intensity for resistance.[33] This is what Klossowski examines in his oeuvre. Nietzsche is his 'neighbour' – like him, he will endeavour to introduce muteness into the noise of culture and knowledge. But unlike

28 *Ibid.*, p. xvii.
29 *Ibid.*
30 *Ibid.*
31 *Ibid.*
32 *Ibid.*
33 *Ibid.*, pp. xiii–xvii.

the philosopher, he will not proceed via madness,[34] orienting himself differently: he will stop writing narratives to devote himself exclusively to painting – indeed we may call his painting his 'muteness'.[35] This reading of the late Nietzsche is essential for grasping Klossowski's step forward with regard to creation and his oeuvre.

A Semiotics of Impulses

Over the years 1880–8, Nietzsche is unwell. Working, thinking and writing are a torture. He can only accomplish any intellectual task for a few hours each month. In his rare moments of lucidity, Nietzsche scrutinises 'the forces that had been revealed through the disturbances of his organism'.[36] This term 'forces' is one to be singled out: illness confronts forces that daily life, in the periods of good health, conceals and nullifies. Illness has this revelatory function:[37] originally, there are forces that, when manifested, break up the subject's reason and attack his organism. Nietzsche first endeavours to consign and submit these forces to his vocabulary. Armed with a little jotter, he takes notes. He attempts to translate these forces of subterranean movement into words, images, reasoning, even rational refutations. This fight is in vain: his thinking gets muddled and his ideas become obscure. 'The writing stopped, the words were effaced, and a new and terrifying

34 'One doesn't go mad from wanting to!' as Lacan reminds us. Klossowski will speak of his 'eluded madness' and will give the following description of his experience: '[...] I jump into the void. [...] Just at the moment I jumped – how did I remain suspended over the bottomless void? – a hand pulled me back roughly by the hair [...]', [translated from] the 'Postface' of *Les lois de l'hospitalité*, *op. cit.*, pp. 336 and 349.

35 'La mutation', *L'Âne*, No. 28, Paris, 1986, pp. I to IV. [Republished in English at the end of this edition.]

36 Klossowski, P., *Nietzsche and the Vicious Circle*, *op. cit.*, p. 12.

37 '[...] we cannot do without sickness [...]. We *need* the abnormal, we give life a tremendous *choc* by these great sicknesses' affirms Nietzsche, *ibid.*, p. 69.

aggression exerted itself on Nietzsche's brain'.[38] This suffering strikes his cerebral organ periodically. Nietzsche goes on long walks in the forest to calm himself. The thoughts resurface and he immediately starts jotting down notes. Back home, he tries to develop them. During this work, terrible migraines set in, which put a stop to the elaboration.

That is his experience of illness. What does Nietzsche make of this state? He develops his own therapy, refusing to suffer for nothing; he will be his own doctor. Once he recovers his faculties he must describe this 'suspension of thought',[39] and specify its 'cerebral functioning in relation to other organic functions, [...] to distrust his own brain'.[40] The act of thinking becomes identical with suffering. Thought is suffering. The suffering, in its intensity, makes thought impossible. It will then be up to our subject to think 'suffering [...] as the *impossibility of thinking* [...]'.[41] This is for him the 'highest joy',[42] a jouissance that will not leave him be. How to isolate it, how to know what is doing the enjoying? Does 'thought really have the power to *actualize itself* without itself suffering [...]'?[43] Or: 'Does thought itself suffer from its own inability to actualize itself?'[44] The question is not a secondary one; answering it allows us to know who suffers, who enjoys, and thereby adopt a strategy for therapy: can the brain enjoy the suffering that attacks the body? Can the body delight in the pain that makes the supreme organ unusable? This reference to the body is essential, and constitutes one of the key lines of force throughout the posthumous fragments.

The body, with its concrete character as a living organism, concerns 'our most immediate forces, as those which [...] are the most distant [...]'.[45] Our body becomes a teller of our 'destiny'.[46] It is to be deciphered.

38 *Ibid.*, p. 12.
39 *Ibid.*, p. 18.
40 *Ibid.*
41 *Ibid.*
42 *Ibid.*
43 *Ibid.*
44 *Ibid.*
45 *Ibid.*
46 *Ibid.*, p. 19.

> Perhaps the entire evolution of the spirit is a question of the body; it is the *history* of the development of a *higher body* that emerges into our *sensibility*. [...] hundreds of thousands of experiments are made to change [...] the body; consciousness and evaluations of the body, all kinds of pleasure and displeasure, *are signs of these changes and experiments. In the long run, it is not a question of man at all: he is to be overcome.*[47]

The migraine is an attack on the brain. This attack does not come from without: it is within. The root of the evil (the migraine) comes from the organism itself. Nietzsche reads it as testifying to a defence, an effort: it is the 'physical self [...] attacking in order to *defend* itself against a dissolution'.[48] 'Active forces'[49] exist in Living body. They are 'organic [...] functions'[50] which, because they assert a function, seek to break with this servitude. This will passes through the brain. It becomes, for this particular case, a battle site[51] between the forces that ensure its coherence enabling it to think, and the solvent forces that threaten it with the impossibility of thinking. There is a confrontation between the solvent somatic forces and the unifying spiritual forces (of the brain); between the (dominant) active forces and the (dominated) reactive forces. Nietzsche takes sides in this combat: he opts for the body and its solvent forces – for activity. 'If the body is presently in pain, if the brain is sending nothing but distress signals, it is because a *language* is trying to make itself heard at the price of reason'.[52] The consequences of hearing and transcribing this language

47 *Ibid.*, p. 26.

48 *Ibid.*, p. 19.

49 *Ibid.*

50 *Ibid.*

51 The term 'force' is a central one in Nietzsche's thought and is inseparable from a philosophy of will. See Deleuze, G., *Nietzsche and Philosophy*, *op. cit.*, p. 6: 'Nietzsche's concept of force is therefore that of a force which is related to another force: in this form, a force is called will. The will (will to power) is the differential element of force. A new conception of the philosophy of the will follows from this. For the will is not exercised mysteriously on muscles or nerves, still less on "matter in general", but is necessarily exercised on another will. The real problem is not that of the relation of will to the involuntary but rather of a relation of a will that commands to a will that obeys – that obeys to a greater or lesser extent'.

52 Klossowski, P., *Nietzsche and the Vicious Circle*, *op. cit.*, p. 19.

will be the loss of reason and the destruction of the person as a conscious and reasonable unity. This is the price to pay for bringing these forces into being, and for finding a locus of effectuation for them. Nietzsche wishes to elaborate 'a mode of intelligence which he wanted to submit to exclusively physical criteria.'[53] The suffering that attacks is energy, and, most of all, becomes an unbound jouissance – a 'voluptuous lucidity'[54] that either destroys thought, or leads it to delirium. Rational thought and jouissance are mutually exclusive. Jouissance is the effect of the unbinding of unified forces, whereas reason implies the binding of energies.

> The body wants to make itself understood through the intermediary of a language of signs that is fallaciously deciphered by consciousness. Consciousness itself *constitutes this code of signs* that inverts, falsifies and filters what is expressed through the body.[55]

These 'libidinal forces'[56] distinguish themselves in the form of impulses transmitting messages. Consciousness enciphers these messages, i.e. it distorts and transforms them in the service of coherence. But in order to preserve himself Nietzsche will take the path that leads in the opposite direction: deciphering these messages is 'an inversion of the message, which is now attributed to the individual.'[57] He speaks for these 'corporeal *states* as the authentic data that consciousness must conjure away in order to be an individual.'[58] Choosing the states of the body amounts to opting, at the risk of evil's furious assaults, for the 'forces of the unspoken,'[59] forever silent, acting in their purity. 'Purity' means that which lies outside language. The body is not an attribute of the person whom consciousness thinks of as a coherent unity. It is, on the contrary, 'the locus where a group of individuated impulses confront each other so as to produce this interval that constitutes a *human life*, impulses *whose sole ambition is to de-individuate*

53 *Ibid.*, p. 20.
54 *Ibid.*
55 *Ibid.*
56 *Ibid.*, p. 71.
57 *Ibid.*, p. 21.
58 *Ibid.*
59 *Ibid.*, p. 13.

themselves'.[60] It will fall to the subject Nietzsche not to oppose this de-individualisation by means of the forces that are fortuitously balanced in a human life. Living body is the chance association of impulses. It is the locus of this opacity produced by the ebb and flow of these intensities.

Grasped by consciousness, this body '*dissociates itself* from the impulses that flow through it, and which, having come together fortuitously, continue to sustain the body in an equally fortuitous manner'.[61] Cerebral activity comes into play to select these forces: '[...] the body adopts only those *reflexes* that allow it to *maintain* itself *for* this cerebral activity, just as the latter henceforth *adopts the body as its own product*'.[62] It is reduced to the instrument of the person. It is through thought – brain activity – that this disjunction between the body and the impulses is obtained. Thought attempts to empty the body of its impulses, which do not disappear but are fought back and temporarily dominated, energetically reduced. As soon as cerebral activity has subsided, the body alone is present and the person – the human life to which thought attributes a fixed body – absents itself. The more these bodily manifestations assert themselves, 'the more the return of the "person" seems to be delayed'.[63] The reconstitution of the person is only possible (after the event) by virtue of forgetting that this 'body is only the *fortuitous encounter* of contradictory impulses, temporarily reconciled'.[64] Klossowski specifies:

> *I* am sick in a body that does not belong to me. *My* suffering is only an interpretation of the struggle between certain functions or impulses that have been subjugated by the organism, and are now rivals: those which depend on me and those which escape my control. Conversely, the physical agent of my self [*le suppôt physique de moi-même*] seems to reject any thoughts I have that no longer ensure its own cohesion, thoughts that proceed from a state that is *foreign* or *contrary* to that required by the physical agent [...].[65]

60 *Ibid.*, p. 21.
61 *Ibid.*
62 *Ibid.*
63 *Ibid.*, p. 22.
64 *Ibid.*
65 *Ibid.*, pp. 22–3.

The *I* is an illusion. It takes as its product that which does not come from it, that which is and will remain heterogeneous to it: the body as a locus of impulses. The *I* rejects that which stands in opposition to its pretended mastery. What needs to be done is to bring about these rejected forces – thus breaking apart the identity that says *I*.

The demonstration continues: what about the ego's identity? It is called for, through the irreversible history of the body, in the name of the rational chain of causes and effects. With a unique and continuous ego, the body seems unique and continuous. Surely there is just one body, the same concrete living reality that thought considers as identical to itself? The ego makes one forget that there is not one body alone, that the body is discontinuity: in fact 'this body *dies* and is *reborn* numerous times – deaths and rebirths that the self pretends to survive in its illusory cohesion'.[66]

To say that the body is discontinuity is to say that there is a plurality of 'impulsive movements that form and deform it, and finally tend to abandon it'.[67] These genuine impulsive metamorphoses are a threat to the cohesion of thought. Hence this ego that endlessly covers over these movements – the Chaos – with a continuity, an identity.

These impulses are both the body's resources and threats to its cohesion: the ego's identity is posited as being irreversible. '[...] [B]ecause the ego, as a product of the body, attributes this body to itself as its *own*, and is *unable* to create another, the ego too has its own *irreversible* history'.[68] What allows for this coincidence between the ego and one's body is the creation of a meaning: a life's irreversible course. This direction or meaning is experienced as an eternity: it is there once and for all! Such is the notion of fatality – the *fatum* of the Romans: it is thus and may not be otherwise.

A supposition: meaning – its principle – is dismantled.

> From this point on, Nietzsche would no longer be concerned with the body as a *property of the ego*, but with the body as the locus of impulses, the locus of their

66 *Ibid.*, p. 23.

67 *Ibid.*

68 *Ibid.* [Where the translation gives: '... because the *self* [...] is *unable* to create another, the self too ...'].

> confrontation. Since it is a product of the impulses, the body becomes *fortuitous* [...][69] it is neither reversible nor irreversible, because its only history is that of the impulses. These impulses *come and go* [...].[70]

In other words, 'there is no individual, there is no species, there is no identity – nothing but the highs and lows of intensity'[71] – and Nietzsche adds: 'I recognised *active force*, created out of the fortuitous! – the fortuitous case itself is only the mutual collision of creative impulses [...]'.[72]

Disconnecting the body from the ego is only possible under pressure from a subjective experience that annuls meaning, continuity of thought, and identity. This experience is the emergence in thought of a stopping point, of what thought cannot grasp despite its efforts: jouissance, or ecstasy, as Nietzsche names it. An emergence that is signalled by the terrible migraines: the brain, as the seat of meaning, is afflicted. With each onset of illness, the body separates a little more from its faltering agent. '[...] the brain was forced to approach the *boundaries* that separated it from these somatic forces [...]'.[73] Such a task brings up a question: how will the body be able to remove the cerebral activity from the ego's control? Nietzsche's answer accentuates muteness: it is thanks to the body's muteness that we can appropriate it. Restoring thought to the 'corporealising' forces[74] amounts

69 Nietzsche develops a genuine theory of the fortuitous case. He states it thus in aphoristic style: '1. My endeavour to oppose decadence and the increasing weakness of personality. I sought a new *centre*. 2. Impossibility of this endeavour recognised. 3. Thereupon I advanced further down the road of dissolution – where I found new sources of strength for individuals. We have to be destroyers! ... I perceived that the state of dissolution, in which individual natures can perfect themselves as never before, is an image and isolated example (*cas singulier)* of existence in general. Theory of the *fortuitous case*, the soul, a being that selects and nourishes itself, strong, crafty, and creative – continually [...]', *ibid.*, p. 168.

70 *Ibid.*, p. 24. [Where the translation gives: '... the body as a *property of the self*.]

71 [Translated from] Klossowski, P., *Nietzsche et le cercle vicieux*, Mercure de France, Paris, 1969, p. 137.

72 Klossowski, P., *Nietzsche and the Vicious Circle*, *op. cit.*, p. 168.

73 *Ibid.*, p. 24.

74 *Ibid.*, p. 25.

to an expropriation of the agent, the ego. The lucidity thus obtained must enable it to penetrate the shadows.

Klossowski asks the following question:

> [...] how can one remain lucid if one destroys the locus of lucidity, namely the ego? What would this consciousness be without an agent? [...] How can we remember as a being that can remember everything except himself?[75]

In Nietzsche there is reference to physiological and biological research: it is a matter of re-creating the self beyond one's own ego, of liberating the forces that underlie the conditions of consciousness.

How does Nietzsche construct his demonstration? For our philosopher the body is the *Selbst*, the Self, as a 'force, unconscious to the cerebral consciousness, which obeys a hidden reason'.[76] It resides within the body and expresses itself through the body. That which the brain refuses has the distinctive feature of staying hidden away in the life of the body. Suffering can thus be understood as a 'quarrel between the body's multiplicity, with its millions of vague impulses, and the interpretative stubbornness of the meaning bestowed on it by the brain'.[77] The creative forces arise from the Self. Nietzsche insists: the Self, when it comes to manifest itself in the body in the form of impulses, is only a '*prolonged* extremity of *Chaos*'.[78] The impulses that are felt take on an organic and individualised form when delegated by Chaos. They are the representatives of Chaos and it is in this capacity that they become Nietzsche's interlocutors. Atop the 'cerebral citadel',[79] these impulses have a meaning – that of being stripped of meaning, of being insane. For the brain, Chaos is madness manifest. Since the body is the product of impulses – subjected, organised, and hierarchised impluses – its cohesion with the ego is only fortuitous. From this fortuitousness there results a decisive consequence: the impulses may serve a new body! Let's be sure to hear what Nietzschean reason leads to, and what Klossowski

75 *Ibid.* [Where the translation gives: '... namely the self'.]
76 *Ibid.*, p. 26.
77 *Ibid.*
78 *Ibid.*
79 *Ibid.*

singles out, by insisting: the forces of non-speech manifest themselves in and through a body that they thereby produce. But these forces pre-exist any individualised agent. First there is Chaos, which then and only then finds a locus of effectuation: the agent precisely. It confronts contrary forces – forces that bind, forces of mastery: cerebral activity ordered by meaning, by goal, and by causality. To free these impulses from the body is to give them fresh force and intensity in order to use them differently. These forces are not the product of the body, they are what constitute it as such.

The philosopher has the task of being a man 'of experiments'[80] with the forces that he can understand only through corporeal experiences. It is only through his body that the philosopher is able to gain access to the delegation from Chaos. Based on his own experience the philosopher founds a theory of the particular that is legitimated by the thought he discovers in the fortuitousness of his ego's cohesion with the body. The universal is no more; more exactly, the universal is reduced to the affirmation that all there is, always and everywhere, is the particular. Philosophy is no longer a part of institutionalised culture and knowledge. It is sent back to a semiotics of impulses – the semiotics of the subject who utters it. Such a philosophy – one that is experimental and specific to the drive – has a revelatory effect with regard to the un-said of philosophy: its truth is neither its history of doctrines nor its method, but rather the Chaos that constitutes a body with he who speaks. 'The philosopher is sent back to his "own" truth that his impulsive life has imposed on him'[81] and which is thus understood. This

80 '[...] the philosophers of the future [... with] just as much right one could call them critics: and certainly they will be men of experiments. With the name in which I dared to baptise them I have already stressed expressly their attempts and delight in attempts: was this done because as critics in body and soul they like to employ experiments in a new, perhaps wider, perhaps more dangerous sense? Does their passion for knowledge force them to go further with audacious and painful experiments than the softhearted and effeminate taste of a democratic century could approve? No doubt, these coming philosophers will be least able to dispense with [...] the certainty of value standards, the deliberate employment of a unity of method, a shrewd courage, the ability to stand alone and give an account of themselves', Nietzsche, F., *Beyond Good and Evil*, Vintage Books, New York, 1966, p. 134.

81 [Translated from] Balzamo, M., 'Klossowski et "le cas Nietzsche"', *op. cit.*, p. 24.

would be Nietzsche's 'treachery' – of which he is 'guilty with regard to the perennial principles of philosophy [...]'.[82]

Klossowski writes: the philosophers 'claim that it would be a question of "the truth" – when, at bottom, it is only a question of themselves'.[83] He adds: '[...] every coherent system of a philosopher demonstrates that *one* impulse directs it, that *there is a fixed hierarchy in it*'.[84] The remark is valid for all thought:

> One should not conceal and corrupt the *fact* that our thoughts come to us in a fortuitous fashion. The profoundest and least exhausted books will probably also have something of the aphoristic and *unexpected* character of Pascal's *Pensées*. The driving forces and the evaluations lay below the surface a long time; what comes out is effect.[85]

So writes our philosopher. Hence the following consequence: '[Nietzsche] made fun of himself for not being a philosopher [... he] here acted ruthlessly, disruptively, and wound up, one might say, bringing the house down'.[86] From within philosophy, Nietzsche tries to bring down the house of philosophy[87] – likewise, from within thought, he wants to destroy thought; from within the body, he wants to destroy it to bring out the impulses that do not belong to any agent and that are able to pass into new bodies. The fact of affirming Chaos produces effects for both philosophical discourse and philosopher-subjects confronted with their cause: subterranean energies. Such a discovery is not a paralysing one. It opens the way for creative and unprecedented experiments. The philosopher is no longer confined

82 *Ibid.*

83 Klossowski, P., *Nietzsche and the Vicious Circle*, *op. cit.*, p. 2.

84 *Ibid.*

85 Nietzsche quoted by Klossowski, *ibid.*, p. 196.

86 *Ibid.*, pp. 3–4 [Where the translation gives: '... wound up achieving, one might say, a "smashing" success (*il "casse la baraque"*)'].

87 It is because he effects this undermining of philosophy within philosophy that we are continuing, in our text, to designate F. Nietzsche as a philosopher. He is the philosopher of an Other philosophy, and he thereby counts on himself becoming an Other philosopher.

to his study, but is open to an act that transforms the world! It is within him – in his impulsive life – that he finds the strength for acts, and not in any exterior doctrine.

This demonstration of Nietzschean thought leaves a question: should such creative action come about, what will become of consciousness and cerebral activity? It is a matter of providing the subject with 'the *knowledge* of this illusory perspective, the "consciousness" of this "unconscious" [...]'.[88] The conditions of a new creative liberty would thus be created. The consciousness of unconsciousness would consist in 'retranslating the "*conscious*" *semiotic* into the *semiotic of the impulses*'.[89] Why such a retranslation? It is so as to recover an authentic spontaneity. The intellectual organ

> must in turn be treated as a simple automaton [...]. By consequence, as a spectator of itself, the automaton finds its freedom only *in the spectacle* that moves from intensity to intention, and from the latter to intensity.[90]

The automaton is not a unity posited as one intellectual totality. It is the locus in which the combat and impulsive spontaneity would be maintained. Subjects would manage to overcome their servitude because they would know they are not free. They would know that the impulses are in command. In the last analysis it is Chaos that is decisive.[91] Economics come second. From this moment on, creation would find its rightful place and assert its full rights.

This step forward in Nietzsche's thought, which designates a state and delimits the forms of its means, allows one to grasp in what way it intrigues Pierre Klossowski. It furnishes him with an answer to the possibility of creation, developed on the basis of what constitutes an enigma for the subject. The subject's own content does not signify anything, for the impulses have neither goal nor meaning: they lie outside of all signification. '[...] [T]he terms "coherence" and "incoherence" are inapplicable to the activity of the

88 Klossowski, P., *Nietzsche and the Vicious Circle*, *op. cit.*, p. 39.

89 *Ibid.*

90 *Ibid.*

91 Klossowski was always pitting Nietzsche against Marx.

impulses [...]'.[92] The liberation of these forces obtained by disconnecting the ego from the body, and the reduction of the subject to an automaton that no longer annuls what happens to him, are modalities for replying to this enigma. They allow one to avoid paralysis and they open onto creation. This is what Klossowski retains from the posthumous fragments. In his 'Postface' to the *Roberte* trilogy, *Les lois de l'hospitalité*, he notes:

> Is it to say that the thinking subject would lose his identity starting from the moment that his own coherent thought is foreign to him? [...] With every word I can wonder if it is I who is thinking or if others are thinking in me, or even that they are thinking before I really think myself that they are thinking.[93]

These formulations would be incomprehensible without reference to Klossowski's reading of Nietzsche. Literary creation has the function of telling, of transcribing experience: multiple interplays of the ebb and flow of intensities that destroy the thinking unity and the ego. Writing will carry a trace of this experience where thought loses its coherence, where the artist is transformed into an automaton. Through reading and commenting the 1880–8 fragments, Nietzsche's question becomes Klossowski's when confronted with his own creation.

Values

Attentive observation of his own 'valetudinary'[94] states of illness leads our philosopher to call into question both psychological prejudice (the identity of the thinking ego) and sensuous prejudice (the reality of the world). Nietzsche does not stay at the level of these general remarks. Observing his illness leads him to describe how this deconstruction operates. What

92 Klossowski, P., *Nietzsche and the Vicious Circle*, *op. cit.*, p. 198.

93 'Postface' to *Les lois de l'hospitalité*, *op. cit.*, p. 337.

94 Chapters 2 and 4 of *ibid.*

signifiers does he use to recount his observations? From the outset he is pre-occupied with the contrary notions of 'healthy' and 'morbid', indispensably articulated with another couple: 'singular' and 'gregarious'. With these four terms, Nietzsche sets out to grasp the mainspring of a 'growing perplexity concerning what, in his own experience, would be *valuable* or not [...]'.[95] A '*fault line*'[96] ran through his mental effort, threatening to render futile his attempt at thinking what is nameless – Chaos. 'What if the *act of thinking*, in the end, were nothing but a symptom of total impotence?'[97] What if that which he holds to be most precious were identical to what he is fighting against? What if that which he pinpoints as his power – 'the source of every active [...] value'[98] – were only decadence and unproductivity? His entire attempt would be reduced to a failure. He would discover inside himself what he had been combating on the outside: 'The voice of the censor, which he sometimes called the *tyrant*, was ceaselessly insinuating itself: [...] this is a weakness [*velléité morbide*], it reveals an incapacity for living'.[99] Nietzsche will go so far as to invert Parmenides' statement: '*What is thinkable is real and what is real is thinkable*' into its 'opposite: *What is thinkable is unreal*'.[100]

He is, however, wary of his own elaboration. He thinks against himself. Nietzsche knows that he, too, thinks with the words and ideas of the thought of the Other he is fighting against! Hence his wariness, his doubt and his perplexity push him to specify his subjective experience in precise terms. He will reckon the for and against. 'Nietzsche's own reflections never took shape without first *reflecting* in themselves the perspective that was opposed to his own',[101] remarks Klossowski. The 'against' that could be used by the adversary is introduced by Nietzsche himself – he makes it his own. He is not for all that a dialectician. Taking into account the for and against is not enough to found a dialectical reasoning: everything depends on the

95 *Ibid.*, p. 59.
96 *Ibid.*
97 *Ibid.*
98 *Ibid.*
99 *Ibid.*
100 *Ibid.*
101 *Ibid.*, p. 151.

function attributed to the negative in the relation of contradictory elements. With our philosopher there is no negative: he reasons exclusively in terms of forces, and the waxing and waning of the intensities that constitute them. We do not meet a force and its contrary (i.e. its negative) which would permit a dialectics. All that is present and active are non-homogeneous forces, or the differences between forces – their pluses and minuses of intensity. Such force has its value only in its pure difference in intensity from the others (and not from one other). The forces are hierarchised, or ordered in terms of the power they develop. In this hierarchy, it is quality that marks the difference between quantities. Force is affirmation. This is how it is lived by the subject: '[…] the secret experience remained an experience whose only evidence lay in its intensity'[102] – there is no working of the negative in this thought. This anti-dialectics can be found in Klossowski's oeuvre. Like Nietzsche, he thinks – and 'dreams up'[103] – forces, powers, but also demons, pure spirits, undesirable thoughts, hypostatic unions, and makes his characters evolve within this mental context.

Pairs of opposites – which he uses to build his experience of the chasm (which is approached from the angle of illness) – fall into two series:[104]

First series:

decadence	vigour
morbid	healthy
weak	powerful

Second Series:

singular	gregarious
degenerate type	successful type
unexchangeable	exchangeable
unintelligible	comprehensible
muteness	communication
non-language	language

102 *Ibid.*, p. 73.

103 See for example 'The Denunciation' in *Roberte Ce Soir*, trans. A. Wainhouse, Marion Boyars Press, New York/London, 1989, pp. 17–43.

104 Klossowski, P., *Nietzsche and the Vicious Circle*, *op. cit.*, p. 59.

From these traditional oppositions a question arises: 'How can the attributes of power, health and sovereignty be restored to the singular, to the unexchangeable, to muteness [...]?'[105] A formulation like this one disarticulates the two contrasting series by combining the contradictory terms, by saying *and* where usually there is an *exclusive or*, by activating the combat between the forces that underlie these designations. This project leads to an attack on the forms of instituted morality 'since language, communication, and exchange have attributed what is healthy, powerful and sovereign to *gregarious conformity*'.[106] Gregariousness presupposes exchange, '*being equivalent to something else*'.[107] It is a question of establishing values, based on power – but a power that is expressed in terms that the pervading morality defines as its opposite: weakness. Power, for Nietzsche, is incompatible with all that an interpretation would make of it: a pure and simple conquest to the profit of arrogant political forces.[108] What steers our philosopher is quite different: does one want to 'become happier or more indifferent to happiness and unhappiness?', does one want to be 'more contented with oneself or more exacting and inexorable?', does one want to 'become softer, more yielding, more human, or more "inhuman"?', does one want to 'become tyrant or seducer or shepherd or herd animal?'[109] Nietzsche's desire to articulate what has never been said (the for and against, the struggle between competing forces) makes his formulations astonishing. He employs terms – power, weakness, health, illness – from which he constructs new acceptations, which can even contradict those in common use.

A new moral problematic arises from these acceptations:

Is all that is healthy and powerful necessarily a product of gregariousness, namely, of the species' instinct for survival? Is everything that is singular ('excluded from what we call the *norm*'[110]) condemned to disappear?

105 *Ibid.*
106 *Ibid.*, pp. 59–60.
107 *Ibid.*, p. 60.
108 Klossowski clarifies this point in 'On Some Fundamental Themes in Nietzsche's *Gaya Scienza*' *op. cit.*, pp. 1–2.
109 Klossowski, P., *Nietzsche and the Vicious Circle*, *op. cit.*, p. 61.
110 *Ibid.*, p. 60.

In subjective experience, what refers to the singular, and what belongs to the order of gregarious propensities?

These remarks convey the fact that 'the way Nietzsche questioned Western culture, whose metaphysics and traditional morality he was combating, was merely one aspect of the way he interrogated himself'.[111] To say that the opposition between healthy and morbid stems from the opposition between gregariousness and singularity, is to posit that the 'two schemata [are] interchangeable and convertible'.[112] For instance, in order to speak of the singular, language – which falls under gregariousness and thus apparently under the opposite schema – will have to 'circumscribe the *singular muteness*, and what it contains that is *un*intelligible to the species, with respect to the intelligibility required by gregarious institutions'.[113] The singular is anachronistic for language. But in circumscribing the impossible of language – what can be neither said nor explained – it comes to exist as a presence without a name. This mute singularity, occupying a hollow place in discourse, reverses the process: it is language, the gregarious and the communicable that become anachronistic. The singular takes on the value of denunciation. It accuses. Identifying with muteness – which is what Nietzsche does – has an active function: the subject is driven to action.

Our philosopher goes on: from the perspective of traditional morality, '*it is an "evil" for the agent to be unable to resist its impulses* (to resist harmful invasions)'.[114] Nietzsche names this lack of resistance 'resignation' and 'humility'. It comes from weakness. Thus, one point of view is substituted for another: 'strength consist[s] in resisting harmful invasions' becomes '*weakness ha[s] to give way to the will to power*'.[115] Traditional morality is reduced to the negation of life.

Running counter to this morality is power. '*Power resists everything*, except that it cannot *resist itself*. It must act – as long as it is not reacting,

111 *Ibid.*
112 *Ibid.*, p. 62.
113 *Ibid.*
114 *Ibid.*, p. 64.
115 *Ibid.*, p. 65.

it must provoke in order not to be provoked'.[116] The risk is that real power might be confused with morbidity. Nietzsche then examines the expression 'will to power'.[117] Is there not a contradiction between willing – which has a goal, and power – a force without coherence?

> The will merely concerns the *agent*. Power, which belongs to life, to the cosmos – which represents a degree of accumulated and accumulating force – produces the agent, in accordance with its *rises and falls*. Thus whenever there would be a will to power, the agent would be sick or healthy: if it is sick, it succumbs to the impulse; if it is healthy, it succumbs to its *over-fullness*, but all the same it succumbs to the movement of a *power* that it confuses with its own will.[118]

This is an important remark because it allows for a way out of the healthy/morbid opposition, and for our subject's perplexity to be relieved. It is of little importance whether the subject is sick or sane, since the will to power manifests itself in both cases. The agent succumbs and thereby accepts as a force what the combated morality names weakness. The goal has been reached: the agent cannot resist 'the invading and uncontrolled forces'.[119] Through this reasoning, Nietzsche tries to free himself from the haunting question: what if what I am feeling is the effect of morbidity, thus of a degenerative debility? It is of little importance, he replies, the subterranean forces will be able to operate nevertheless.

The philosopher hesitates in his thinking and goes back on what was said: what becomes of the unity of one's '"personal" life'?[120] Must it be liquidated, considered obsolete since it has disappeared under pressure from the solvent forces? Quite rightly, Klossowski notes accents worthy of Goethe in this questioning. This juxtaposition makes for the pertinence

116 *Ibid.*, p. 68.

117 'The will to power is the element from which derive both the quantitative difference of related forces and the quality that devolves into each force in this relation. [...] Force is what can, will to power is what wills', in 'What is the Will to Power?', Deleuze, G., *Nietzsche and Philosophy*, *op. cit.*, pp. 46–7.

118 Klossowski, P., *Nietzsche and the Vicious Circle*, *op. cit.*, p. 68.

119 *Ibid.*

120 *Ibid.*, p. 70.

of the posthumous fragments today. It translates the combat between an agent and the libidinal forces; this is when the presence of a subjectivity is confronted with the intermediary moment when the new is still part of the combated old. To put it in our commentator's terms: this coexistence translates the idea that 'the meaning of the affects lies in their hierarchical unity'.[121] Practically speaking:

> What Nietzsche applauds is this movement towards cohesion in its *efficacy*, which he classifies as health. *What he fears most is exactly what he sees deep in himself: a mutual antagonism* of the passions, a multiplicity of souls in one breast, which points to an internal ruin.[122]

The internal ruin, whose effects he is starting to feel, makes the unity of his soul all the more present to him – for the first appearances of madness are starting to crack it apart. A base unity needs to exist in order to be deconstructed, in order for a chasm to be formed there. Nietzsche both praises plurality and opposes the co-presence 'of different passionate states'[123] in his sick body and brain. He comes to distinguish between 'changing' and 'becoming'. Chameleon-subjects 'change', but do not really bear witness to any contradictory tension. They 'merely offer a simulacrum of it'.[124] 'Becoming' on the other hand brings about the fact that 'only the intensity of an all-consuming passion metamorphoses into a "unity"'.[125] Nietzsche is the breeding ground of this combat between forces.

Our philosopher does not, however, care to serve as a model. That would be 'the most dangerous misunderstanding'.[126] He fears that one might confuse 'exhaustion' with 'richness', sickness with health. He would become the object of a cult, the fool: the 'buffoon of eternities'.[127]

121 *Ibid.*
122 *Ibid.*
123 *Ibid.*
124 *Ibid.*
125 *Ibid.*
126 *Ibid.*, p. 66.
127 *Ibid.*, p. 67.

To insist on Nietzsche's fears is to emphasise his subjective position. There is the risk that his valetudinary states might lead him into a dead end. Not to point out his misunderstanding would be to reduce Nietzsche to an accomplished thought. The base of this thought is a singular, shifting, progressive experience. Isolating it as such allows Klossowski to ascertain the forms of this combat – which is also his own struggle, in as much as he is a creator. The combat leads to the 'conquest of a new possibility of living!'[128] In this 'merciless war' that Nietzsche wages against 'everything that wants to smother the *continually possible* in man',[129] it was indispensable to locate the forms of the impossible that reveal themselves there. Klossowski's reading, far from being hagiographic, shows us the cutting side of a poignant experience, as well as Nietzsche's failure to record it all, to write it all down. The *remainder* that does not bend to the word is what Klossowski examines. The question of our writer and painter reasserts itself: if 'our pathos knows', but, if 'we cannot share in its mode of knowing',[130] then how, in spite of everything, are we not to remain helpless faced with the impossible? How can one create an oeuvre; how can one form something that is equivalent to, that stands in for, that which is nameless? The response is that an oeuvre (literary or art) is in fact nourished by this misunderstanding, which, as such, must be located in order to be opposed.

The Return of the Same

Nietzsche develops a semiotics of impulses where the forms of instituted knowledge and the unity of the ego are abolished. But the ego's unity, in its dimension of an individual creative life, continues to make itself heard. In

128 Klossowski, P., 'On Some Fundamental Themes in Nietzsche's *Gaya Scienza*' *op. cit.*, p. 2.
129 *Ibid.*, p. 6.
130 Klossowski, P., 'Nietzsche, Polytheism and Parody', *Such a Deathly Desire*, *op. cit.*, p. 109.

this subjective, in-between period when these subterranean forces attack what still constitutes a unity and a centring, what place is there for a power that is singular, what value is to be given to the realisation of a creative life? These questions account for Nietzsche's hesitations in developing a new morality.

Such remarks leave the nature of the experience Nietzsche found himself confronted with intact. What occurred for our philosopher? How did Chaos, with its libidinal forces, manifest itself? The shift that occurs for the subject Nietzsche is twofold: at one and the same time the forces of non-speech manifest themselves – they break into his thought – and in their manifestation, they reveal to thought the truth that governs them. Nietzsche's experience is not purely passive: he can glimpse the logic[131] to what is happening to him. The experience becomes a revelation. Our subject is admittedly mad. But to see in his writings only the forms of a delusion taking shape would be to forget the stakes his work carries. Besides, Klossowski sticks to his guns: Nietzsche is mad because he refused to provide an equivalent to his experience. This is why this ordeal has an intensity that so fascinates its commentator.

Nietzsche might not provide an equivalent to his experience (neither in language nor in art) but he does not for all that stay mute: he will describe it and, above all, what it has revealed to him. First of all, he gives it a name: 'the experience of the Eternal Return'. Next, he describes the effects, for a subject, of this encounter with the 'circular movement': the vicious circle, a description to which Klossowski devotes the greater part of his essay. 'The Eternal Return of the Same' becomes the form of the thought in which Klossowski testifies to his calling as a writer and to the impossibility of its realisation.[132] In this respect his reading is not just academic. It speaks of his experience of literature, with all its torments, and even its madness lying close by for whosoever should endeavour to practice it.

131 Unknown to the rational logic of the Cartesian ego.

132 Klossowski, P., 'Postface' to *Les lois de l'hospitalité*, *op. cit.*

'The thought of the Eternal Return of the Same'[133] surprises Nietzsche at Sils-Maria – it is an abrupt awakening in the midst of a 'certain tonality of the soul' – a *Stimmung*.[134] It would have been an error to mistake this *Stimmung* for a thought. In the strictest sense, the Eternal Return of the Same is a 'revelation', a '*sudden unveiling*'.[135] It breaks off from the associative chain of thought and imposes itself through an ecstatic presence. The Eternal Return is inseparable from forgetting. Forgetting is the source and the necessary condition 'not only for the revelation of the Eternal Return, but also for *the sudden transformation of the identity* of the person to whom it is revealed [...]'.[136] Why? Because only forgetting can allow one not to be attached any longer to the illusory unity of the ego. Identity must be forgotten in order for the revelation of the Eternal Return to be potentially introduced as a singular experience in the blank spaces of thought. Forgetting is a necessary condition for the wording of the doctrine that opens onto the act:

> [...] act as though you had to relive your life innumerable times and will to relive it innumerable times – for in one way or another, you must recommence and relive it.[137]

Nietzsche specifies: there is, in opposition to forgetting, anamnesis. Anamnesis coincides with the revelation of the Eternal Return. Without it, the experience could not come to pass:

> Not only do I learn that I [...] have been brought back to the crucial moment in which the eternity of the circle culminates, the moment to which the truth of its necessary return is revealed to me; but at the same time I learn that I was *other* than I am *now* for having forgotten this truth, and thus that I have become another by learning it.[138]

133 Klossowski, P., *Nietzsche and the Vicious Circle*, *op. cit.*, p. 44.
134 *Ibid*. *Hohe Stimmung* = high tonality of the soul.
135 *Ibid.*
136 *Ibid.*
137 *Ibid.*
138 *Ibid.*

The revelation teaches me something: *I'm not the same anymore!* I was other, and even this other I am no longer, because the revelation has transformed me. I learn that I had an identity at the very moment I lose it under pressure from the *Stimmung* of Eternal Return, which makes me other, and so on and so forth. Forgetting is prolonged and can be formulated not by an: 'I know I am an identity', but by an: 'I know I was an identity because I have lost it absolutely'. This loss is crucial.

A contradiction arises: the Eternal Return is a 'necessity that must be willed'.[139] Now, will presupposes a responsible subject – but a subject whom the law of the Circle abolishes. '[...] only he who I am now can will the necessity of my return and all the events that have led to what I am [...]'.[140] How to resolve this paradox between a goal to reach (being as multiple), and the means to get there which are opposed to it (will, and thus being as a unity)? Nietzsche's answer is a novelty:

> [...] I deactualise my present ego in order to will myself *in all the other egos whose entire series must be passed through* so that, in accordance with the circular movement, I once again become what I am at the moment I discover the Law of the Eternal Return.[141]

At the very instant – a veritable bolt of lightning – of the revelation of the Eternal Return, '[...] I cease to be myself *hic et nunc* and am susceptible to becoming innumerable others, knowing that I shall forget this revelation once I am outside the memory of myself [...]'.[142] There is a loss of consciousness because my consciousness is established in the 'forgetting of my other possible identities'.[143] This formula encapsulates the logic of the Circle: it is impossible to stop its movement; it is impossible to turn this revelation into a new content, a new form of thought that could form the basis of the ego's reflexive identity. The Circle is movement. No point of equilibrium can last. Consciousness and memory are no longer reflexive positions from

139 *Ibid.*, p. 45.

140 *Ibid.*

141 *Ibid.* [Where the translation gives: 'I deactualise my present self in order to will myself *in all the other selves ...*'.]

142 *Ibid.*

143 *Ibid.*

which the ego as such can become autonomous. As soon as they appear it is clear they have no object, no fixed bearings. The outcome of the paradox is that the subject must will himself as a fortuitous moment, a fortuity that signals the necessity of the return of innumerable possible identities.

> All that remains, then, is for me to re-will myself, no longer as the outcome of these prior possibilities, no longer as one realisation among thousands, but as a fortuitous moment whose very fortuity implies the necessity of the integral return of the whole series.[144]

What does this declaration entail for the subject caught in the *Stimmung*?

> [...] to re-will oneself as a fortuitous moment is to renounce being oneself *once and for all*; for it is not 'once and for all' that I have renounced being myself and had to will this renunciation; I am not even this fortuitous moment *once and for all* so long as I have to re-will this moment ... *one more time*! For nothing? For myself. Nothing here is the Circle *once and for all*.[145]

The essential thing to note is the disappearance of the 'once and for all' that perpetually characterises the unique identity. There is no more 'once and for all', or more exactly: only the Circle is 'once and for all'. But the circle cancels out the possibility of a 'once and for all'. Nietzsche posits that the present moment is transformation, movement, and metamorphosis. Consciousness and identity are conjugated in the future perfect: that which will have been fixed – but never 'once and for all', since the revelation opens up the series of possibles. The circular movement is endless:

> [...] this revelation did not come to me as a reminiscence – nor as an experience of *déjà vu*. Everything would stop *for me* if I *remembered* a previous identical revelation – even if I were continually to proclaim the necessity of the return – for it would serve to keep me within myself, and thus outside the truth that I am teaching. It was therefore necessary for me to forget this revelation in order for it *to be true*![146]

144 *Ibid.*, pp. 45–6.
145 *Ibid.*, p. 46.
146 *Ibid.*

The revelation cannot be taken as a memory. It is unmediated experience. To remember it would be to falsify it. It would no longer be a revelation, a pure experience, but one thought amongst others submitted to reason. Revelation and the forgetting of this revelation are inseparable. On the other hand, revelation creates anamnesis.

> Within the series that I suddenly glimpse – the series that I must live through in order to be brought back to the same point – the revelation of the Eternal Return of the Same implies that *the same revelation* could just as well have occurred at *any other moment* of the circular movement. Indeed it must be thus: for in order to receive this revelation, I am *nothing* except this capacity to receive this revelation at *all the other moments* of the circular movement: nowhere in particular for me alone, but always in the movement as a whole.[147]

For our philosopher the Eternal Return of the Same will become a supreme thought, but also a supreme feeling – the 'highest feeling'.[148] Let's listen to him:

> My doctrine teaches: live in such a way that you must desire to live again, this is your duty – you will live again in any case! He for whom striving procures the highest feeling, let him strive; he for whom repose procures the highest feeling, let him rest; he for whom belonging, following, and obeying procures the highest feeling, let him obey. Provided that he becomes aware of what procures the highest feeling and that he shrinks back from nothing. Eternity depends upon it![149]

In a word, it is best not to resist necessity because eternity is at stake. These formulations leave a question in suspense: 'How can a tonality of the soul, a *Stimmung*, become a thought, and how can the highest feeling – [...] namely the Eternal Return – become the supreme thought?'[150] Nietzsche is constantly examining the emergence of the high tonality of the soul. What effect does it produce upon thought? What can it mean to teach

147 *Ibid.*, pp. 46–7.
148 *Ibid.*, p. 47.
149 *Ibid.*
150 *Ibid.*

the Return of the Same? How can a silent experience be turned into the content of a doctrine?

The tonality of the soul, he affirms, is not a thought: it is first and foremost 'a fluctuation of intensity'[151] – it appears as excess, a surplus force, a libidinal rise. In this capacity of being pure singularity thus neither representable nor communicable, it lies beyond the symbolic. But to speak of doctrine implies that it has to be rendered communicable.

Nietzsche responds: the thought of the Eternal Return is the undeniably necessary form that imposes itself upon the subject when the *Stimmung* arises. The thought of the Eternal Return is not the *Stimmung* – it is the effect of this *Stimmung* in thought. They have the same cause (Chaos) but take on different, incomparable forms: one is silent, the other is taken up in significations and semblables.[152] But there is only one self-same intensity; Nietzsche deploys both the for and the against – no longer to contrast their forms but to combine them.

This intensity succumbs to a shifting Chaos with neither beginning nor end – a perpetual movement. Nothing can anchor it. It ruins any form of unity and coherence. '[...] in each person, apparently as their own possession, there moves an intensity, its flux and reflux forming significant or insignificant fluctuations of a thought that in fact belongs to no one [...].'[153] If thought is merely a translation of intensity – just one of its partly unintensified forms – then it has no owner. It is no longer the thought of such and such a person who produced it. Thought is fortuitously associated with an agent. It can invest itself elsewhere and metamorphose because such is the destiny of the energies of Chaos: unbound and free, they assemble according to the will of chance and transitory unities. The ego's error is to mistake the unity that it constitutes for a halt to the fluctuations; the movement does not for all that come to a stop. Its error is to confuse intensity with its resumption of, or its return to, its designation. 'Everything is led back

151 *Ibid.*

152 [TN, We follow B. Fink in leaving *semblable* as 'semblable' for the reasons he puts forward on pp. 763–4 of his translation of J. Lacan's *Écrits, The First Edition in English, op. cit.*]

153 Klossowski, P., *Nietzsche and the Vicious Circle, op. cit.*, pp. 48–9.

to a single discourse, namely, to fluctuations of intensity that correspond to the thought of everyone and no one'.[154]

Nietzsche insists: what becomes of my own coherence at the moment intensity arises, which breaks my thought apart?

> The Circle opens me to inanity, and encloses me in the following alternative: *either* everything returns because nothing has ever had any meaning whatsoever, *or else* nothing has ever had a meaning except through the return of all things, without beginning or end.[155]

What fascinates Nietzsche is not the fact of being-there, but of returning to that which returns. What is the status of the subject when he returns to the law of the Vicious Circle?

> Here is a sign in which I myself am nothing, a sign to which I always return – for nothing. What is my part in this circular movement in relation to which I am incoherent, or in relation to this thought that is so perfectly coherent that it excludes me *at the very moment* I *think* it?[156]

The subject is excluded as incoherence from this absolute coherence of the Circle: the Circle can cover over itself entirely, without any loss. It is in this respect that it is a revelation, that it cannot be caught in a dialectical movement of thought. The subject loses his illusory coherence – the coherence promulgated by the thinking ego – because he is confronted with pure coherence. The Circle takes the subject outside of himself by expropriating him.[157] In the strictest sense, it makes him lose his reason, his bearings, and his principles, which form the basis of his unique identity. The Circle sets down the psychological, sensuous and radical critique of presuppositions – along with their foundation: causality.[158] Nietzsche's

154 *Ibid.*, p. 49.

155 *Ibid.*, p. 50.

156 *Ibid.*

157 Klossowski, P., 'On Some Fundamental Themes in Nietzsche's *Gaya Scienza*' *op. cit.*

158 See Nietzsche, F., *Beyond Good and Evil*, *op. cit.*, p. 29: 'In the "itself" there is nothing of "causal connections", of "necessity", or of "psychological non-freedom"; there the effect does *not* follow the cause, there is no "rule of law". It is *we* alone

discovery is a mighty frontal attack on the different forms of philosophical thought and culture: '[...] the true essence of things is a fabulation of being that represents things, and without which being could not be represented at all [...]'.[159] Klossowski reaches a conclusion on Nietzsche's progressive thought with the words:

> The high tonality of the soul in which Nietzsche experienced the vertigo of Eternal Return created the sign of the Vicious Circle. What was instantaneously actualised in this sign was both the highest intensity of thought, self-enclosed in its own coherence, and the absence of any corresponding intensity of the everyday designations; by the same token, the designation of the ego, to which everything had heretofore led, was itself emptied.[160]

Nietzsche will become the 'dance of gods',[161] or that which makes us comprehend, in the style of Zarathustra's mythic vision, the ebb and flow of the intensities of Chaos.

The Vicious Circle becomes the reference point for all experiences and revelations realised at any point on the circular trajectory – is not each point of the circle equidistant from the centre?

> [...] with the sign of the *Vicious Circle* as the definition of the *Eternal Return of the Same,* a sign befalls Nietzsche's thought as *an event that stands for everything that can ever happen,* for everything that has ever happened, for everything that could ever happen in the world – and indeed, in thought itself.[162]

The sign of the circle does not stand in opposition to that to which it gives name and image in the experience of the *hohe Stimmung*. The ever-present difference between an experience and its designation is reduced to

---

who have devised cause, sequence, for-each-other, relativity, constraint, number, law, freedom, motive, and purpose; [...] we act once more as we have always acted – mythologically.' On the critique of the *causa sui* see chapters 21, 22 and 23, pp. 28–32.

159 Klossowski, P., *Nietzsche and the Vicious Circle, op. cit.*, p. 51. [Where the translation gives: '... designation of the self'.]

160 *Ibid.*, pp. 51–2.

161 *Ibid.*, p. 51.

162 *Ibid.*, p. 52.

a minimum. The Vicious Circle has the function of a general equivalent, of a systematic stand-in for all experience. Nietzsche almost managed to superimpose the Eternal Return and the sign of the Vicious Circle. The result is twofold: the subject is expropriated from himself because coherence is no longer part of him but rather outside of him in the sign of the Vicious Circle; and thought is a stand-in for everything that must happen and that is only movement and metamorphosis.

There we have it for the results of Nietzsche's elaboration! But in a chapter entitled: 'The Elaboration of the Experience of the Eternal Return as Communicable Thought',[163] Klossowski pursues an opposition that haunts him: experience/transmission. Our commentator comes back to the revelation that occurred at Sils-Maria. What happened there?

Nietzsche describes his Sils-Maria experience as a hallucination: in and of itself, it is unintelligible. At the very instant it emerges in the real, it reveals in a flash to our philosopher something from which, after the event, he would never stop learning – something with great consequences.

The instant is multiplied. It is no longer one instant but many. It 'reflects in a *flash* [*échappée*] of mirrors'.[164] Time is no longer diachronic, but is broken apart, multiplied, and infinitely divided. Temporal bearings are lost and time lapses into eternity, frozen in a specular multiplication. At the moment of his hallucination, Nietzsche intuits the abolition of time – which he will translate as an unprecedented experience of eternity. He sinks into the time of myth, namely a temporality in which all the elements are co-present and in no way ordered by duration. Seized in this immobilised moment, the subject will discover that he has been there for all eternity. Nietzsche is in this instant for eternity, and no matter what he thinks or does, he will be drawn back there inexorably, for all eternity. Caught in this instant he cannot escape the law of the Eternal Return of the Same. Nietzsche leaves worldly time and plunges, henceforth alone, into the nameless time of myth, which is eternity: no beginning, no end, just the pure circularity of the Same.

163 *Ibid.* pp. 52–6.
164 *Ibid.*, p. 52.

> [...] the world exits historical time in order to re-enter the time of myth, that is, eternity: [...] it means that the vision of the world is an apprehension of eternity.[165]

Nietzsche's contribution is to postulate that the Same is not the same; it is not identical to itself: '[...] the ego [...] awakens to an infinite multiplication of *itself* and its own life [...]'.[166] This remark might seem surprising – yet this is the novelty of our philosopher's thought. The ego breaks apart because time is annulled. The scene is certainly freeze-framed but the characters have not been transformed into statues – on the contrary, a Brownian movement of multiple lives and identities is realised. The loss of time and the loss of the ego are concomitant losses. Certainly, in clinical terms this experience bears a name: the failure of the Name-of-the-Father[167] projects the subject onto the imaginary axis where there is no anchorage to stop him; from the lack of a settling, fixing metaphor, the subject's experience is metonymic. But Nietzsche's advance remains (including the fascination it exerts on Klossowski): hypostasising time destroys the ego and establishes multiplicity. For Nietzsche, the Sils-Maria hallucination was imposed upon him from without – from beyond temporality. Here, Klossowski finds the possibility of creating an oeuvre that reveals the experience that causes it, rather than masking it. It presupposes a demon – like the genie in the Arabian tales – who will say to the subject: 'You will have to live this life once more, and innumerable times more'.[168] If the subject submits to this, the expected consequence can take place: *if this thought is true, then you shall be an other.*

This effective loss of the ego's identity, provoked by the revelation of Eternal Return, has an absolute precondition: the death of God as the divine Other who would be the guarantor of the unity of the responsible ego. An exterior God would be the guarantee of the interior ego. This

165 Klossowski, P., 'Nietzsche, Polytheism and Parody', *Such a Deathly Desire, op. cit.*, p. 103.

166 Klossowski, P., *Nietzsche and the Vicious Circle, op. cit.*, p. 52.

167 [TN, See Lacan, J., *The Seminar Book III, The Psychoses*, trans. Russell Grigg, Norton New York/London, 1993.]

168 Klossowski, P., *Nietzsche and the Vicious Circle, op. cit.*, p. 52.

articulation between God and ego unity is one of the most novel contributions Klossowski brings in his commentary on Nietzsche – a contribution recognised as such by his critics.[169] It is a question that runs through all of his essays, notably those dedicated to Sade and perversion as we have seen. God's death would make possible 'the successive realisations of all possible identities'.[170] Nietzsche will go so far as to proclaim: 'at bottom every name of history is I'.[171] One of Klossowski's theses is that from the moment God is dead, 'everything is possible'. He experiences its anticipated yet unheard of effects: *Being could be multiform!* This is what Nietzsche's revelation corroborates in exemplary fashion.

By becoming an other, and yet an other, you shall carry out, in your metamorphosis, the death of God as the guarantor of what had made you a unity. If you can live and re-live, if the thought of the Circle is true, then God is dead. For the subject this death entails the loss of all limits between the inside and the outside. Nietzsche will even say that, following this experience, from now on two gods coexist in him: Dionysus and The Crucified One. 'Let us distance ourselves from all questions of pathology, and retain this declaration as a valid judgement of its own apprehension of existence'.[172] What is this apprehension? It perpetrates the death of God. This would be one of the points of his doctrine: to teach the death of God and to show that everyone might carry out this teaching within him; by tirelessly becoming an other, each individual might act out the death of the divine Other.

> The substitution of the divine names for that of 'Nietzsche' immediately touches upon the problem of the identity of the person in relation to a *single* God, who is the truth, and to the existence of many gods, in so far as they are the explication of being, on the one hand, and an expression of the plurality within a single individual, on the other.[173]

169 See the discussion following Klossowski's lecture at the Royaumont Conference, *Nietzsche*, Éditions de Minuit, Paris, 1968.

170 Klossowski, P., *Nietzsche and the Vicious Circle*, *op. cit.*, p. 45.

171 *Ibid.*

172 Klossowski, P., 'Nietzsche, Polytheism and Parody', *Such a Deathly Desire*, *op. cit.*, p. 117.

173 *Ibid.*

Let us take note of this identification of God with truth: 'a single God, who is the truth'. The death of this one sole God annuls truth. Truth is an effect of God's uniqueness, and exists only because there is an instauration of an absolute Other.

> *God is dead* does not mean that divinity ceases to act as a clarification of existence, but rather that the absolute guarantee of the identity of the responsible ego vanishes from the horizon of Nietzsche's consciousness, which in turn merges with this disappearance. If the concept of identity vanishes, at first sight all that remains is the fortuitousness that befalls consciousness. [...] identity is a fortuitous case arbitrarily maintained as necessary [...].[174]

From such an operation only the being of fortuitousness subsists, and not the ego in as much as it stands in opposition to the fortuitous. His consciousness enumerates

> like so many drawings in a lottery, the different possibilities of being that, taken together, would be being itself. These different possibilities make use of the momentary success that is named Nietzsche, but who, as a success, winds up abdicating himself for a more generous demonstration of being. [...] Existence as the eternal return of all things is produced in the physiognomies of as many multiple gods as it has possible manifestations in the souls of men.[175]

In other words: '[...] *the only being guaranteed to us is being that represents itself, and is therefore changing, non-identical to itself, completely relative*'.[176]

Klossowski insists so firmly on this Nietzschean theme of the dissolution of identity as being conditioned by the death of God, because his own reading is inseparable from a theological question: how to demonstrate the inexistence of God? This remark may seem surprising because theologians strive rather to demonstrate God's existence and its consequences. Klossowski employs a theological method to prove the contrary of what theology affirms. Klossowski reads Nietzsche theologically. Admittedly, our commentator is a particular kind of theologian – apophatic, a theologian

174 *Ibid.*, pp. 117–18 [Where the translation gives: 'the identity of the responsible self'.]
175 *Ibid.*, p. 118.
176 Klossowski, P., *Nietzsche and the Vicious Circle, op. cit.*, p. 101.

of the obscure, of darkness, of the non-communicable. But a theologian nevertheless. His reading of Nietzsche consists in demonstrating that his ecstatic experience at Sils-Maria (as well as the doctrine that arose from it: the Eternal Return of the Same) translates the death of God. Klossowski tracks down the proof in Nietzsche's writings of the death of the guarantor of the ego, of thought, and of law. He is looking for what destroys the semblants: what lies beyond the veil upheld by God the Father? What is there beyond (or shy of) language, the responsible ego and rational thought? The chasm Nietzsche encountered is where semblants are ripped apart, where the imposture of divine law is revealed. The law of the Eternal Return of the Same is the unmistakable proof of the imposture of the law of unity. In reading Nietzsche, Klossowski identifies the despotic authority of the law of the father as God, language, and the Cartesian ego.

This theological demonstration gives rise to the oeuvre's possibility – one that will actualise this discovery of God's death, that will substitute for the 'tyranny of a unique truth'[177] the creation of multiple truths that parody any thought and practice of the monotheistic *one*. Klossowski draws three conclusions from this theological revelation: the philosopher (as well as the creator) is an impostor; the function of the philosopher-creator is to fight against existing culture; such a practice implies a new conception of the stand-in and, above all, of language posited as the original simulacrum.

The Imposter-Philosopher

In an attempt to counter delirium, Nietzsche feels the necessity of acting outwardly, of transforming the exterior world. This will be the role of the creator:

177 Klossowski, P., 'Nietzsche, Polytheism and Parody', *Such a Deathly Desire*, *op. cit.*, p. 118.

> Every creator is at once someone who tempts others and who *experiments on (tempts) himself and others* in order to create something that *does not yet exist*: a set of forces capable of *acting upon* and *modifying that which exists*.[178]

The task of the creator shall be to liberate the powers of Chaos by becoming pure fortuitousness wherein these powers are transitorily realised. The use of these liberated forces will be experimental:

> [...] *to create* is to *do violence* to what exists, and thus to the integrity of beings. Every creation of a new type must provoke a state of *insecurity*: creation ceases to be a game at the margins of reality; henceforth, the creator will not re-produce, but will itself produce the *real*.[179]

How does the creator go about transforming the real? '*Let us be the deceivers and embellishers of humanity!*' proclaims Nietzsche.[180] It is not a matter of representing the world, but of making it move. The notion of the false lies at the root of artistic creation. The false, in its accepted positive sense as extended to every problem raised by existence, points to mystification. But it is in no way a matter of reducing creation to a conjuring trick. The very ground of existence itself is mystification: it has no meaning, while all cultures and philosophies, ever dependent on theological thought, claim that there is one. It would be a matter of affirming mystification in a new practice, but one that would present itself as such, no longer bearing the insignia of immutable truth. Such a mystification is thus, above all, a demystification: it shows what mystification is, and it will have the function of revealing the mystifications already in place, starting with the one that states: God is truth, eternal and immutable,

> [...] *demystifying in order to mystify better* (no longer simply to *exploit* but to *favour these obscure forces* as creative and fecund) [...] The remedy would thus be a *remystification* that would generate new conditions of life, that would validate the creative force of the impulses.[181]

178 Klossowski, P., *Nietzsche and the Vicious Circle*, *op. cit.*, p. 97.

179 *Ibid.*, p. 99.

180 Nietzsche quoted by Klossowski, *ibid.*, p. 100.

181 *Ibid.*, p. 101.

The subterranean forces are inaccessible, yet they relentlessly produce effects; they run through the corporeal agents, they are the cause of all reflexivity. Their inaccessibility is absolute and cannot be annulled; attempting to do so would be absurd and would result in impotence. The philosopher-creator affirms, however, that any statement, any representation, covers over this Chaos.

To describe creation, Klossowski chooses Nietzsche's term *Trugbild*, which he translates as 'simulacrum'.[182] This is his key concept.[183] *Trugbild* synthesises the scattered definitions of imposture, falsehood mystification, cover-up, representation, etc.

If the existence of Being as a unity can no longer be guaranteed because of God's death, then art must establish a 'praxis of the simulacrum'.[184] Why? We have to come back to the tying-in between impulses and the agent, between forces and intellect. The terms 'coherence' and 'incoherence' cannot be applied to impulsive activity. In return, 'when the impulse exerts its constraint on the agent, *a coherence is established between the impulse and the agent agitated by its activity*'.[185] If there is a constraint, it is because a '*repressive* force'[186] is opposed to the impulsive discharge: the emergence of libidinal forces is a danger – a threat to the agent and its unity. At this point in his reasoning, Klossowski makes reference to the phantasm – which he always writes with a *ph*. The phantasm enciphers the fortuitous coherence between the nameless, plural impulse and the agent in so far as he is *one*:

182 *Trug* = guile, trickery, imposture, deception; figuratively = error, illusion. *Trugbild* = illusion, simulacrum, phantom. *Trug-gestalt* = phantom. *Trug-gewebe* = tissue of lies. *Trug-schluss* = false conclusion, paralogism, sophism. Translated from *Dictionnaire Allemand-Français*, Denis, J., Garnier, Paris.

183 Anne-Marie Lugan-Dardigna artfully entitled one of her essays, 'Klossowski, L'homme aux simulacres', Navarin, Paris, 1987, and Jean-Pol Madou wrote *Démons et simulacres dans l'œuvre de Pierre Klossowski, Connaissances du XXeme siècle*, Méridiens, Klincksieck, Paris, 1987.

184 Klossowski, P., *Nietzsche and the Vicious Circle, op. cit.*, p. 101.

185 *Ibid.*, p. 198.

186 *Ibid.*

> The phantasm – the phantasmic coherence of the agent with a determined impulse – is thus produced at the *limit point* where this impulse is turned *into a thought* (of this impulse), as a *repulsion* against the *adulterous coherence* – precisely so that it can appear at the level of the intellect, no longer as a *threat to the agent's coherence with itself*, but on the contrary as a legitimate coherence. In this way, it can retain its *thinkable character* for another intellect.[187]

The phantasm is willed by the impulses, but the subject can only ignore why the impulses have willed it so. Here we are at the heart of one's own fundamental unintelligibility: the phantasm has a constraining role that the subject does not understand. By specifying the impulses, the phantasm reveals their presence in the agent. It designates the moment at which the libidinal forces inhabit a body – this one, and not some other one. The 'phantasm is what makes each of us a singular case'.[188] It endorses a mute declaration that the subject makes to himself in an attempt to know what this strange impulse might want.

The simulacrum has the function of simulating what it is that may be willed by the impulse, which is enigmatically enciphered by the phantasm in all its constraint.[189] Once realised, it provides an equivalent to this enigma; it is a stand-in for muteness. The philosopher-imposter must know that man's phantasms are externalised, take on shape and name in simulacra. The philosopher does not necessarily create the simulacra – some are already there: existing, agonising ones because they no longer manage to give an intelligible presence to the subterranean forces. The intellect and the phantasm of the impulses degenerate, finding themselves in a desperate face-off. The philosopher's function will be to create new simulacra: 'The inability to invent simulacra is therefore merely a symptom of degeneration'.[190] The simulacrum must not be taken for the product of the phantasm. It is 'its skilful reproduction, by which humanity can *produce* itself, through

187 *Ibid.*, p. 200.

188 *Ibid.*, p. 201.

189 Klossowski sometimes describes this constraint as 'obsessional', emphasising its burdensome, repetitive and inevitable character. No will power can get around it; the subject cannot escape it.

190 Klossowski, P., *Nietzsche and the Vicious Circle*, *op. cit.*, p. 102.

forces that are thereby exorcised and dominated by the impulse'.[191] Our author adds: 'In the hands of the "imposter" philosopher, the *Trugbild* – the simulacrum – becomes the *willed* reproduction of non-willed phantasms, born from the life of the impulses'.[192] To invent is no longer to refuse the presence of impulses, but to produce simulacra: interpretations of phantasms that make us singular.

In turn, the simulacrum exerts its own constraint – it responds to the necessity of the phantasm. Saying that the simulacrum is constraining amounts to positing it as an active entity: it is not a passive stand-in. For it to succeed, it must carry within it that which it testifies to through an equivalence. The process of constituting the simulacrum is twofold: it allows the subject to act, to be a creator, to respond to the interplay of the forces it meets; and without it, the phantasm would remain an enigma. Any social bond, any communication would be impossible. There is no way out save autism.[193] Klossowski insists:

> If the impulse already 'interprets' something for itself, the phantasm remains unintelligible, below the level of consciousness; it is merely the intellect's *ossified incomprehension* of a *state of life*.[194]

It is ossified because the impulse's intensity – or better still, the 'difference' between the intensities of the opposing forces – is enciphered. The difference that the phantasm enciphers is meaningless – at most, for the intellect, it is unreason. So as not to lapse into unreason – which Nietzsche always thinks of as a disintegration of meaning under pressure from the enigmatic 'state of life'[195] – the intellect must construct or elaborate 'what

191 *Ibid.*

192 *Ibid.*

193 'No doubt, *certitude* is what drives one insane [...]' writes Nietzsche in *Ecce Homo*. 'Certitude takes on the offensive characteristic of delirium. [...] What kind of certainty is in question here? It is the certainty of the irreducible depth whose muteness has no equivalence', *ibid.*, pp. 155–6.

194 *Ibid.*, p. 102.

195 *Ibid.*

the phantasm wants to "say"'.[196] The intellect can neither say nor apply this construction/elaboration to the intensities themselves, as they are shifting and ungraspable. For Nietzsche, there is no possible equilibrium of forces, i.e. no moment at which they can be stabilised.[197] Only the phantasm is graspable, although still incomprehensible. The interpretation bears on the phantasm – it is an invention, and thus a 'deformation'. '[...] [A]s such, the phantasm cannot have any meaning outside the time of the intellect, outside its dimensions: something monstrous that takes shape only through a delimitation of the non-comprehensible'.[198] It is not that the simulacrum renders the phantasm comprehensible; rather, the simulacrum allows the phantasm to be present as something non-comprehensible. Because, in its relation to the intellect, the phantasm acquires a presence, a value, a weight no doubt, which are defined, ascertained and grasped only negatively. In this respect, the simulacrum introduces some continuity where pure discontinuity reigns: the abolition of the principle of causality, and consequently, of the principle of '(so-called) reality'.[199]

> What for the intellect is a function of continuity – from cause to effect – is for the phantasm something without any preconditions: a gesture, an action, an event of which the phantasm is the residue, having at the same time the value of a gesture, an action, an event already accomplished or yet to come.[200]

The binomial simulacrum-phantasm constitutes one of Klossowski's freshest theological contributions, not only with which to read Nietzsche, but also to grasp the contemporary pertinence of his own oeuvre, and to understand the motivation behind his vocation as a creator. Klossowski sticks to his opinion: 'Nothing exists apart from *impulses* that are essentially

196 *Ibid.*

197 'That the world is not *striving* toward a *stable condition* is *the only thing that has been proved*. Consequently one *must* conceive its climactic condition in such a way that it is not a condition of equilibrium [...]', *ibid.*, p. 83.

198 *Ibid.*, p. 102.

199 *Ibid.*, p. 103.

200 *Ibid.*, p. 102.

generative of *phantasms*',[201] which are then translated by simulacra. This is his thesis reduced to its bare bones.

And what of art? It indicates a way out of madness, out of an autism considered to be the apotheosis of atomist thought, out of the incomprehensibility of the state of life:

> [...] there is only one mediator that can say what a phantasm 'wills': through its conventional procedures, *art* essentially reconstitutes in its own figures the conditions that have constituted the phantasm, namely, the intensities of the impulses. The simulacrum, in relation to the intellect, is the licence that the latter concedes to art: a *ludic* suspension of the reality principle.[202]

For Klossowski, via Nietzsche, art is not the only simulacrum: all signs in language, all representations are a simulacrum in as much as it is equivalent to the phantasm. These simulacra are weak, empty, and degenerative. They are sterile in that they affirm the reality principle and force belief in the ego. They are operators of censorship on behalf of current morality. However, the simulacra of the artist-impostor can modify human behaviour when it is confronted with the real, since they are accorded 'a *ludic* suspension of the reality principle'.[203] Admittedly, like any simulacrum, they still fix a goal and give a meaning, but they do this in order to obtain the opposite of what morality stifles. They orient Living forces and elicit 'new centres of forces'.[204] The function of the simulacrum as creator becomes clearer: '[...] this is what the simulacrum does: a simulacrum of goal, [...] of meaning – *which must be invented*!'[205] It is not that the simulacrum is stripped of its goal or meaning; rather, its goal and meaning are parodied – and in fact oriented by the lack of any goal or specific meaning in the libidinal forces.

201 *Ibid.*
202 *Ibid.*, p. 102.
203 *Ibid.*
204 *Ibid.*, p. 103.
205 *Ibid.*

The function of art as 'praxis of the simulacrum' has a dual direction:

- The simulacrum as creator must favour the 'will to power', namely activate the differences between the intensities to make them more active. Art does not have a calming, Apollonian role. On the contrary, it is in the service of the 'violence of the absurd'[206] that destroys pseudo-equilibriums and affirms the singular case. Artistic creation is in no way disinterested. Nietzsche cannot find words strong enough to condemn 'art for art's sake'. In his own way, an artist is similar to a criminal – like him, although with a different goal, he diverts the aggressive and (non-gregarious) asocial forces in favour of representation. Art must reproduce violence and attest to the presence of a surplus force. Art as simulacrum is active – not reactive. It is Dionysian, a source of 'creative bliss',[207] an 'exuberance'.[208]
- Emphasising the notion of the simulacrum results in promoting what is false and illusory, in a critique of a unique truth. Art lies: its object – power – can be neither said nor shown. But this lie does not make it powerless. Art is not reactive (dominated) in the face of forces. It accumulates untruths, distortions, parodies, and buffooneries. It is a '*willed error*'[209] that gives value to lies and their derivatives. It shows and proves that the idea of a unique truth, legitimised by a monotheistic theology, is imposture par excellence. Art has a decisive role in affirming plurality and multifariousness because God is dead and there is no (more) monadic truth: 'Art is with us in order that we may not perish through truth,' affirms Nietzsche,[210] who adds, '*The simulacra are ours!*'[211]

206 *Ibid.*

207 *Ibid.*, p. 155.

208 *Ibid.*

209 Klossowski, P., 'Nietzsche, Polytheism and Parody', *Such a Deathly Desire, op. cit.*, p. 116.

210 Nietzsche, F., *The Will to Power,* trans. A.M. Ludovici, Digireads.com Publishing, 2010, p. 309.

211 Klossowski, P., *Nietzsche and the Vicious Circle, op. cit.*, p. 100.

The Challenge of Culture

'Is the "philosopher" still possible today?'[212] Nietzsche asks. How will he manage with the forms of bourgeois culture he is subjected to? To be a spectator is discrediting: he sees, notices and describes, but cannot do anything. Ought he to be a critic, and thus explore in detail and in depth the mainsprings of culture? In so doing, ought he to play the naysayer? Nietzsche is not committed to a logic of the negative and does not acknowledge the value of dialectical reasoning between a thought and its negation. He thus rejects the position of the intellectual's commitment. To critique culture is still 'legitimating it in "human" terms'.[213] Instead of criticising bourgeois culture from the inside, Nietzsche shall counter it. Why? Because, for the philosopher, there is no more culture. All historical society is 'founded on the *ideological disavowal of the external constraints* it necessarily exerts'.[214] This disavowal bears a name: the concept of culture.

It is because 'lived culture'[215] has disappeared that the concept of culture has emerged, designating an activity separated from life. Culture that has become abstract has a function of legitimisation with regard to reactive forces that have regrouped in social organisations. Historical society is the paradigm of the triumph of reactive forces over active forces. Communities are flocks subjected to gregariousness. In such societies, culture is what keeps the flock together and the reactive forces tethered and sterile. It exists so that societies continue not to want to perish. The goal of such societies, as well as that of history, is to produce men who are like animals: gregarious, sick, obedient, and broken-in.

212 *Ibid.*, p. 1.
213 *Ibid.*, p. 6.
214 *Ibid.*
215 *Ibid.*

> History thus appears as the act by which reactive forces take possession of culture or divert its course in their favour. The triumph of reactive forces is not an accident in history but the principle and meaning of 'universal history'.'[216]

This ideological disavowal, evident in Christian morality and its ersatz, makes culture an equivalent of equality: culture must be extended to all and sundry! This position, a veritable ideal of western democracy, is refused – and to demonstrate this Nietzsche will become anti-Hegelian. Hegel's thesis is that culture is the slave's – he has succeeded in producing it through his fight against the master. He has become its conscious master. Nietzsche refutes this because it assumes a reciprocity of consciousnesses: the struggle between the autonomous consciousness of the master and the dependent consciousness of the slave. Hegel's thesis assumes that a transmission takes place between the two – and that a way out is possible, which that culture attests to. By becoming a separate category, culture marks the objectification of servile consciousness, and is thus inseparable from the mastery of consciousness that is the realisation of an autonomous ego. Criticising culture serves only to reinforce it.

On the other hand, to assert that lived culture 'can never have a gregarious foundation'[217] is to do away with the concept of culture. It is to substitute lived culture – which has never been realised historically – for abstract culture. Lived culture is 'the *fact* of the particular case – and thus, from the viewpoint of the bourgeois concept of culture, a monstrosity'.[218] Culture no longer affirms equality and distributive justice in terms of its access and its realisation. Quite the contrary, it 'restores the *servitude* that the concept of culture conjures away'[219] – it is fundamentally non-egalitarian. This position coheres perfectly with Nietzsche's thesis on the source of what makes the world. Culture implies servitude and inequality because there is no possible equilibrium of forces: any body – whether physical, living, or social – is a hierarchy of forces, a fight between the forever enduring active and reactive

216 Deleuze, G., *Nietzsche and Philosophy*, *op. cit.*, p. 130.

217 Klossowski, P., *Nietzsche and the Vicious Circle*, *op. cit.*, p. 6.

218 *Ibid.*

219 *Ibid.*, p. 7.

forces. It includes the conflicting, shifting relationship between these 'two powers: the *levelling* power of gregarious thought and the *erectile* power of particular cases'.[220] Culture has no sense because the doctrine that accounts for it forgets the mainspring of its own constitution: the 'initial Desire',[221] namely, the will to power that is functioning here. Culture is structurally non-egalitarian because there is 'inequality and struggle (between different groups of affects)'.[222] This inequality is what makes culture possible. For the philosopher, this is the challenge of culture: to intervene in this struggle of forces. Questions still remain: who is dominating? Who is dominated? Where are the active forces – and the reactive?

These formulations might imply that active forces are always dominant while the reactive ones are always dominated. Were this the case the philosopher's action would be limited: he would be favouring the play of forces, nothing more. The term 'challenge' for culture would then have no meaning; it would be merely a locus for the effectuation of relationships between forces. For Nietzsche – and history demonstrates this – reactive forces can be dominant. They can occupy centre stage. How do they proceed? They disconnect an active force from what it is able to do, they disengage it from its power – the active force is drawn towards the void, nihilism, the will to nothingness. The reactive forces attract the active ones emptied of their power: slaves who remain slaves replace the masters. One could say that between the two forces there is a mirror: that which is active is, according to the optical principle of the reversed image, an opposition, a danger and a threat to the reactive forces. The yea of the active reverses into a nay for the reactive.

The philosopher's work will be twofold: on the one hand, he will have to favour the active forces. On the other hand, in order to understand these forces he must choose an angle from which to observe them, thus positioning himself from the point of view of the yea, of the active. Should he forget to take this viewpoint, the creator runs the risk of error;

220 *Ibid.*, p. 5.
221 *Ibid.*, p. 9.
222 *Ibid.*, p. 8.

he could unknowingly support the reactive forces by positioning himself on their side. It is in this respect that culture is a challenge, that it necessitates a double action, that it implies some tact when it comes to choosing the point of view. In playing the genealogist, the philosopher cannot treat the forces as an abstraction: there are no general laws. It is within a precise, case-by-case dynamic that he must ascertain the stakes of the specific moment at which he intervenes.

In concrete terms, he is defying culture. This defiance will amount to a yea, to a veritable 'for' in favour of the subjected forces. '*To assume the crime of the combat against culture*' will become '*to assume culture's "crime" against existing misery* [...]'.[223] To fight against bourgeois culture – its reactive manifestations of breaking-in and selecting forces – is to admit '*a feeling of bourgeois guilt*'.[224] To affirm culture against the existing misery (of which cultural forms make up an integral part) is, on the other hand, to invent a culture that is both lived and criminal. Our philosopher 'would side with the "criminal" as an *irretrievable force*, virtually superior to an order of things that excludes it'.[225] He 'undertook his own *combat against culture* – in the name of a culture of the affects – which would be built on the ruins of the hypostases of consciousness and its antinomies [...]'.[226]

A culture of the affects has never historically existed. Should it come into being, it would affirm inequality, for affects are dominant, strong, and moving quantities of energy. To arrive at such an affirmation, Nietzsche called into question the concepts of consciousness and the categories that stem from them – in other words, he fought against the Hegelian positions and rejected dialectic. Consciousness is just an individual form, thanks to which the ego imagines that it is *one*, continuous, and autonomous. For Nietzsche, there is no '*consciousness for itself mediated by another consciousness*',[227] because one's emotion does not enter into dialectic – there is no possible transmission, only '*the sovereignty of an incommunicable*

223 *Ibid.*, pp. 7–8.
224 *Ibid.*, p. 8.
225 *Ibid.*
226 *Ibid.*, p. 10.
227 Hegel quoted by Klossowski, *ibid.*, p. 9.

emotion'.[228] The forces result from pathos – the pathos that the agent fortuitously presentifies.

The challenge of culture is crucial: it is the locus in which a creative action is possible, a creation that, once accomplished, dislocates culture. As a lived culture, the concept of culture is annulled, seen for what it is: a sterile mystification of life forces. There is nothing to be expected from the present culture where selection and hierarchy are reversed. Were it to be put right again, it would burst under the pressure of the Eternal Return of the Same: it would be Other. Intervening in the field of culture delimits a point of attack in order to bring about on the outside what Nietzsche first experienced inside his organism. As soon as Nietzsche no longer confines himself to an experience of intensity that destroys his brain and his reason, he encounters culture. It is unto culture that he will first brandish the sword in the combat of forces. It is not just a question of defence but of counter-attack. The philosopher-creator becomes a singular case. He appears as a '[...] *kind of occasion and chance through which the impulse is finally able to speak*'.[229] For the singular case, this 'ability to speak' is surprising, for it will happen without a word: the act will be in the form of a gesture. The philosopher, in silence, shall mime out his counter-attack on culture 'in accordance with the gestural semiotic of the Soothsayers and Prophets [...]'.[230]

The Birth of Signs

For Nietzsche, 'The culture of *affects* will be possible only after a progressive dislocation of the *substructures* that are elaborated in language'.[231] Language occupies a key place. It is the archetypal substructure – the one from which

228 *Ibid.*
229 *Ibid.*, p. 3.
230 *Ibid.*
231 *Ibid.*, p. 10.

all others originate: societies, states, religions, etc. Language is the first simulacrum.

Nietzsche will develop a theory of the birth of language, which is to say, a theory of the simulacrum. What is 'the function of the signs of language?' '[...] how and *where* are signs born?', he asks.[232] First, in the inorganic world there is no '*misunderstanding*, communication seems to be perfect'.[233] There is nothing to mediate the relationship between forces: 'there is no possible *disagreement* between what is strong and what is weak'.[234] Here, the will to power is pure. Next, the organic world is constituted where there is assimilation and exchange. Error begins, misunderstanding becomes possible. Why? Because

> exchange and assimilation take place only through interpretation: from trial and error to certainty [...]. The latter can be obtained only after a long experimentation with the similar and the dissimilar, and thus with identity. Only then can points of reference, repetition and comparison appear – and finally, comparable signs.[235]

From the moment there is displacement, movement, exchange and transformation, mediation occurs. The notions of others as identical to oneself, of the consistent whole that masks itself, and of the non-chronological time of eternity disappear. Mediation brings forth goal, direction, and orientation of the play of force. In the organic world, each power is not teasing out its last consequence at every moment. Power is oriented from the outside by a goal that wants to give it a meaning.

And what of the signs of language? They constitute the most evolved system of interpretation of the play of forces. This is the form that mediation takes on – and that which subsumes all other mediations. The code of signs inaugurally creates a necessary illusion for the thinking subject that ensures his survival. It posits the 'conditions of existence'[236] as a necessity, whereas in fact it is but pure chance. For Nietzsche, organic life is a fortuitous case,

232 *Ibid.*, p. 34.
233 *Ibid.*, p. 35.
234 *Ibid.*
235 *Ibid.*
236 *Ibid.*

a 'possible "*error*" in the cosmic economy'.[237] But in order to maintain the conditions of existence one must believe that life has its logic, that it is neither chance nor error. Thus '[truth] *is the kind of error without which a certain species of life could not live*'.[238] The code of signs holds together the illusion that bears the name of truth. Without this simulacrum, life is not possible, the agent cannot exist.

From this standpoint, the code of signs is seen as an '*abbreviation of the (impulsive) movements of gestures in signs*'.[239] What are the signs of the impulsive movements? Forces affect one another. The sign of the impulse is the name that the quality of the relationships between forces takes on: who dominates? Who is dominated? The sign describes the state of forces at a given time: '[...] the combat of the impulses takes place through a mutual interpretation of their respective intensities, which implies their own "code"'.[240] For example, the impulse reacts to excitations. Also, impulse and repulsion are already interpretative since a quality is introduced: a differentiation of intensities in regard to their relative power. There exists a coding prior to the code of language: the will to power is one name for this anterior impulsive code. 'Every living being interprets according to a code of signs, responding to variations in *excited* or *excitable* states'.[241]

And what of the abbreviations of signs? Nietzsche posits that the '*contradiction is not between the "true" and the "false" but between "abbreviations of signs" and the "signs" themselves*'.[242] Klossowski explains that:

> [...] the impulses – which confront and interpret each other through their fluctuations of intensity and, at the level of organised beings, through *gestures* – create *forms* out of these movements and gestures, and cannot be distinguished from this invention of signs, which stabilises them through *abbreviation*.[243]

237 *Ibid.*
238 *Ibid.*
239 *Ibid.*
240 *Ibid.*, p. 36.
241 *Ibid.*
242 Nietzsche quoted by Klossowski, *ibid.*, p. 37.
243 *Ibid.*

Impulses are mistaken for signs for two reasons: first, because signs give meaning to that which does not have any meaning – power is unto itself its own unique reference; second, because signs are merely abbreviations of a whole – the general state of the forces that make up a (chemical, living, human) body. There is a loss from the start:[244] that of the reduction to abbreviations in relation to the full set of the signs of the impulses. Language substitutes fixity for movement, sense for non-sense, the aim for the aimless, the partial for the whole, misunderstanding for no possible disagreement, unity for multiformity, and finally continuity for discontinuity. '[...] *we have no language to express what is in becoming*,' remarks Nietzsche.[245] Language is the operator of consciousness, the original instrument of the thinking ego that considers itself to be a unity.

> [...] these *abbreviations of signs* (words) are in effect the *sole* vestiges of its continuity, that is to say, they are invented in a sphere where the 'true' and the 'false' necessitate the erroneous representation that something can *endure* or remain *identical* (and thus, that there can be an agreement between the *invented signs* and what they are supposed to designate). Moreover, this is why the impulses themselves must now signify a coherent 'unity', and their similarity or dissimilarity can be assessed only in relation to a *primary unity*. This unity will henceforth be the *soul* of the agent, or its *conscience*, or its *intellect*.[246]

Klossowski, through Nietzsche, shows that language has the function of founding the unity of the *I* as a subject of all grammatical propositions. Language is thus reduced to being merely something the subject uses – language is a means. When a subject uses language in all its fixity, he himself becomes a fixed unity that can think of himself as such: *to be*

244 Klossowski insists: 'A word, once it signifies an emotion, passes itself off as identical to the experienced emotion, which in turn had strength only when it had no word. A signified emotion is weaker than an insignificant emotion. Whenever a communicative designation intervenes in an exchange of words with other (subjects), there is therefore a discrepancy between what was experienced and what was expressed', *ibid.*, p. 166.

245 *Ibid.*, p. 38.

246 *Ibid.*, p. 37.

conscious is to use language.[247] Language is the condition of consciousness. That which is not conscious cannot be articulated through language. The unconscious, made up of forces, is the prolongation of Chaos in a fortuitously constituted agent. The Nietzschean unconscious is pure muteness: it is fluctuations of mood.

Passions (the effect of the forces that affect the subject) are interpreted thanks to the signs of language: they become propensities, tendencies, inclinations, etc., 'terms that always concern the representation of an enduring *unity*, a fixity, a "summit" that necessarily has "slopes"'.[248] The Nietzschean subject is the grammatical subject:[249]

> [...] the *system of 'signs' abbreviates* the gestures of the impulsive constraint, and leads it back to the coherent *unity* (of the agent), which forms the grammatical 'subject' in a series of propositions and declarations about everything that happens to it, whether from without of from within.[250]

One can better grasp how and why language's system of signs plays a key role for both Nietzsche and Klossowski. This system makes possible everything that hinders the movement of forces; it produces the ego, time, the individuated agent, passions, and thought. To examine the birth of signs is to ascertain the modalities of the elaboration and realisation of a simulacrum. Signs are the operators of the subject's fiction. They bring about the conditions of psychological prejudices (the ego), sensuous prejudices (the reality principle) and logical prejudices (principle of causalist reduction). It is in this regard that, for Nietzsche, God and language are one. The monotheistic God states *I am that I am* – and it is because he merges with the principle of the grammatical *I* that he is an absolute and tyrannical identity. God is one of the names of the *I* of grammar and logic – his name as a tyrant as the One, as an *atomon*:

247 *Ibid.*, pp. 40–2.

248 *Ibid.*, pp. 37–8.

249 Nietzsche, F., *Beyond Good and Evil*, *op. cit.*, p. 27.

250 Klossowski, P., *Nietzsche and the Vicious Circle*, *op. cit.*, p. 38.

> […] without accepting the fictions of logic, without measuring reality against the purely invented world of the unconditional and self-identical, without a constant falsification of the world by means of numbers, man could not live […].[251]

God is also a name of the linguistic sign. There is an arbitrary power that binds a thing (*res*) to the sign that names it. Nietzsche questions this in terms of intensity and fixation:

- To be interpreted, an intensity must take itself as an object. It must effect a return, a repetition, a mediation, thus creating a before and an after – something that the intensity, in and of itself, cannot know since its only time is that of its drive as force.
- In this turning back to the trace it leaves behind, the intensity interprets itself. How does it do this? Nietzsche's answer includes the logic of forces. The intensity becomes 'a counterweight to itself'.[252] To manage this it has to separate, to divide, to become double. Now, this separation is brought about by the fluctuation in intensities. The force is never constant – always differential – there is no possible equilibrium. This ebb and flow, the very structure of intensity, conditions the possibility of interpretation.
- Rise and fall have no meaning. Force is no more than a part of activity. Hence the questions: 'What is a meaning? And how can it be constituted? What is the agent of meaning?'[253] For Nietzsche, the agent of meaning is intensity. The intensity's turning back on itself – the construction of a new fluctuation – creates meaning. 'By turning back on itself, by repeating and, as it were, imitating itself, it becomes a sign'.[254] It returns to its own trace and thus produces a repetition between the thing and its imitation: its sign. The movement of force – like the waves of the tide – bears the sign. It is supposed

251 Nietzsche, F., *Beyond Good and Evil*, *op. cit.*, p. 12. See also 'What is Religious', pp. 58–76.

252 Klossowski, P., *Nietzsche and the Vicious Circle*, *op. cit.*, p. 47.

253 *Ibid.*, p. 48.

254 *Ibid.*

that what is without mediation introduces a sign of itself on being reproduced.

- The sign is a trace, the mark of a fluctuation of intensity. How does a sign retain its meaning? When 'the degree of intensity coincides with it; it signifies only through a new afflux of intensity, which in a certain manner joins up with its first trace'.[255]

However, a sign can signify something other than the trace of a fluctuation: it can also signify its absence. To do so a new afflux of intensity is necessary – it replaces the flaw in the previous intensity. The sign of presence can be called attention, will, or memory. The sign of absence is indifference, relaxation, or forgetting. In other words 'it is always a question of the same intensity, no different from the moving waves of the incoming tide. "*You and I*," Nietzsche said to them, "*we are of the same origin! the same race.*"'[256]

To Nietzsche's credit, although he is sometimes reproached for his conceptual imprecision, he always maintained his original hypothesis on the state of forces in presence. For him, this hypothesis is what was revealed to him, what ruined his life and his brain, and from which he deduced his theory of language as the paradigm of all simulacra in that it masks the initial Chaos. Language '*can never absolutely disengage itself* from the moving chasms it masks'.[257]

From this remark, Klossowski deduces two consequences concerning his work as an inventor of new simulacra:

What becomes of being once it is taken up in this code of signs? What becomes of the singular case once it is referred to gregarious language? The response is direct: being is lost, the fortuitous case is excluded. There is a

> fraudulent exchange between the *singular case* and the *gregarious* generality. [...] The singular case *disappears* as such as soon as it *signifies* what it is for *itself*. In the individual there is only *a particular case of the species* that assures its intelligibility.[258]

255 *Ibid.*

256 *Ibid.*

257 *Ibid.*

258 *Ibid.*, p. 201.

We approach the unbearable: being is lost, the singular case is annulled in favour of its representation in the logic of the gregarious. Our author is justly pointing out the inherent alienation in the process of signifying: there is an intolerable loss due to the logic of masking over. This loss is horror (*Grauen*[259]). If Being is lost, if the singular case disappears, then Chaos is distanced, the real escapes and jouissance becomes ungraspable. The exteriority of institutional language is substituted for the uncontrollable interiority (of the agent) – whose unpredictability knows no bounds.[260] This is a fine demonstration, showing that its domain can only be that of simulacra, especially of this primary simulacrum which is language.

In this context, what effect can be expected from language? What can the writer expect from what he writes?[261] This question lies at the heart of Klossowski's writing in two respects: not only does the writer Klossowski ask it, but it is also the question that moves the characters in his narratives. His answer is precise: language has the function of bringing the other (the partner, the interlocutor, the reader) to the moment at which arises the intensity that is silently enciphered by his phantasm. Indeed, if the degree of intensity coincides with the sign of language, it will be up to the user of the words to keep on bringing this intensity into being. The words become the means to titillate the jouissance that constitutes the core of each and every subject. The use of words is active, not passive. Klossowski recognises this explicitly: the conspiracy of silence

259 Term from Freud, S. (1923), 'The Infantile Genital Organization (An Interpolation into the Theory of Sexuality)', *The Standard Edition of the Complete Psychological Works of Sigmund Freud, Volume XIX (1923–5): The Ego and the Id and Other Works*, trans. J. Strachey, Hogarth Press, London, 1958, pp. 139–46.

260 Klossowski, P., *Nietzsche and the Vicious Circle*, *op. cit.*, p 41. 'Language is thus the stranger inside us'. Klossowski, P., 'Language, Silence and Communism,' *Such a Deathly Desire*, *op. cit.*, p. 76.

261 Blanchot, M., 'Laughter of the Gods', in *Friendship*, trans. E. Rotenberg, Stanford University Press, 1997 and in *Decadence of the Nude*, trans. P. Buck and C. Petit, Black Dog, London, 2004. In his book *Le corps impie*, Collection 10/18, Paris, 1979, Daniel Wilhem investigates textuality in Klossowski's work.

> is woven under Roberte's[262] skin as much as it is in my syntax. Thus, it disputes my writing, it refuses it the right to speak. However, Roberte's skin could not so much as quiver without my syntax that is only the wrong side [*l'envers*], while the conspiracy of silence pretends to be the right side [*l'endroit*].[263]

The same thing happens in the scenes where the character Octave manages, with words, to put his wife Roberte, the partner of his (pornographic) devices, beside herself. The other halts and becomes mechanical much like an automaton, a frozen, silent body. Speech is replaced by a declamatory gesture that translates the agitation of the impulse that is finally freed from what was masking it. Words serve to bring the other out of his frozen identity, to cause the ever-present jouissance to tremble. They produce in the other – whether ritual partner or reader (is there a difference?) – the intensity of the libidinal forces of non-speech.

When Klossowski abandons fiction for non-speculative specularity – for painting – it is in order to devote himself henceforth entirely to revealing the moment at which the other is divested of his identity, when, frozen, he silently confronts the Chaos of the forces. Painting will show what words strive to say: that instant at which the signs of language are interrupted and gestures take their place.

We can grasp here the importance that Nietzsche's thought had for Klossowski. It supplied him with the rich vocabulary that he used to describe his own confrontation with the incommunicable powers that marked his essence. It brought him specific concepts that enabled him to account for the tying-in between intensity and sign, between Chaos and simulacrum, and from which he created both a textual and art oeuvre. Nietzsche's thought is one of the elements that allow our writer to pass from the *speculative* to the *specular*, from words to muteness, from writing to painting. Klossowski's new, erudite, rigorous and provocative reading of Nietzsche is indispensable for understanding the development of his own oeuvre.

262 The heroine in Klossowski's stories.

263 Klossowski, P., *Les lois de l'hospitalité*, *op. cit.*, p. 9.

Body, Currency, Utopia

La Monnaie Vivante [*Living Currency*][1], published in December 1970, develops the principal theses put forward in the *Art and Text* article 'The Phantasms of Perversion, Sade and Fourier'. The numerous commentaries on 'the semiotics of impulses', previously seen in *Nietzsche and the Vicious Circle*, are here fully established, and shown to be implemented by the insane philosopher in both his physical and mental life. Along with this theoretical aspect, the work proposes the construction of a counter-utopia whose name becomes the book's title. *Living Currency* is an invented (and ideal) society where the present-day economy of needs is replaced by a Brownian circulation of emotional impulses freed from their straight-jacket, and ordered into diverse unities: the ego, rational and logical language, market structures, and so on. It would be naïve to give credence to this counter-utopia, as if it were something that could be brought about in a not so distant future. *Living Currency* uses irony, semblance, the *as if*, and provocation in a parody of the classic utopian text. In spite of this, it is not a vain text to be simply filed away as one of the author's amusements. On the contrary, this essay, which is frequently cited though seldom commented on at the level of its demonstrations and conceptual articulations, is to be taken seriously – to the letter.

1 The quotes in this chapter are taken from the original 1970 Éric Losfield publication of *La Monnaie Vivante*. This edition was published without page numbers, and with untitled photos taken by Pierre Zucca. The photos show Roberte in diverse positions that are related to the themes developed in the *Roberte* trilogy, *Les lois de l'hospitalité*, but without captions the photos are incomprehensible. The chasm between the written text and the images shown beside it makes this edition of *La Monnaie Vivante* particularly unusual. [TN, Although no English-language translation of the book is as yet available, we have taken the step of translating the title in the text below, where it features heavily.]

From the moment it first appeared, the text produced a good many effects on some of its readers. Michel Foucault, who tended not to be very forthcoming with his compliments, wrote:

> Dear Pierre,
> [...] of course I was already speechless. [...] Now, from having reread it several times, I know that it is the greatest book of our time. We have the impression that everything that has ever mattered in one way or another [...] has been insidiously bringing us to this: but there you have it, it's been said now, and from on high, so high that I draw back and feel only half a man. It is this that had to be thought. [...] You have spelt out and volatilised our fatality; we don't know where it is, but we know that it's right where you've said it. What you have done for all of us goes beyond thanks and acknowledgement.[2]

This dithyrambic praise might seem surprising and excessive; if *Living Currency* provokes this kind of effect, it is because when it takes aim, it hits the target.

Use and Uselessness

From what question does Klossowski set off? He gives a picture of how things stand: industrial civilisation has wrought devastation whose consequences have been felt in 'affective life'. How has industrial production become so powerful? How is it that the manufacture of 'objects to be used as utensils' has completely modified the production of 'objects of use' – 'those produced by art, "useless" for subsistence?' The source of the logic of our economy and market can be grasped from the standpoint of manufactured objects – those artificially 'needed' by the individual who has now become a consumer. Since the creator (the writer, the

2 [Translated from] Foucault, M., 'Lettre à Pierre Klossowski,' 1970, in Klossowski, P., *La Monnaie Vivante*, Éditions Joëlle Losfeld, Paris, 1994 (this edition is without Pierre Zucca's photographs), p. 7.

painter) is also a producer of objects, we can see a rivalry between industrial logic and the logic of art. What will the effects be of the production of objects that do not serve a utilitarian purpose? Of the work of art in the age of the widespread reproduction of objects whose only reason for being produced is their utility? Klossowski dares raise the question: what relationship is there between a utensil reduced to its purely functional use and the simulacrum which is, by definition, a useless object – the work of art?

Klossowski answers these questions – wholly in keeping with his keen analyses of Sade and Nietzsche – by engaging in a theory of the genesis of the value and use of manufactured objects. As surprising as his references might seem (they are always strongly asserted, although sometimes without following the demonstration through) they are to be read attentively. 'Goods of use are originally inseparable from the customary sense of use'. Custom is always a ritual, an organisation in which the same gestures are repeated, thereby setting an 'immutable' meaning that stems from a dogmatic theology, even if it is not mentioned by name. The Mass – and the Eucharistic mystery – is the paradigm thereof. In this case, goods are unexchangeable. They are intrinsically linked to the ritual that realises them under the watchful gaze of the eternalised Other, the guarantor of the immutable. Klossowski's particular contribution is to introduce the individual's 'own body' into this theological system – not Christ's body, but Living body that has been wrought through and intensified by voluptuous emotion – by 'affective life' as he says with ironic reserve.

What custom is possible when it comes to an encounter between bodies, especially the 'way of putting one's body at the disposal of the body of another [...]?' Does the body have an alienable or inalienable character? It all depends on custom, answers Klossowski, referring to Sade and Nietzsche. Yes, if custom so requires, the body can be alienated by the other, by the partner. Besides, to assert that it is inalienable would be a masquerade. There are no inalienable living goods because the body itself is constituted through a combat where impulses, in their relationship with the present forces, have been duly alienated. Any custom is revocable or transformable by whosoever has the courage, the strength, or the genius to do so.

> As the act of manufacturing becomes more complicated and diversified, the manufactured object [...] relatively loses its fabricated character. Diversified in accordance with its progressive complexity, the act of manufacturing substitutes the efficient utilisation of objects for the use of goods [...].

In an economy of measurable, quantifiable profit, which has become the general reference, the customary use of goods 'is found to be sterile'. This is to say that the 'the use, [...] the enjoyment thereof, is sterile in as much as these goods are judged to be unproductive in the circuit of manufactured efficiency'. Its effects on the body are revealed at the end of this rationale on production:

> In the industrial era, utensil manufacture breaks off definitively from the world of sterile uses, and installs the world of fabricated efficiency according to which all natural or cultivated goods – the human body as much as the earth – are in turn evaluable.

Klossowski is attempting to grasp how, in the customary ritual, the product is equivalent to what is unexchangeable, to what is *priceless*: the phantasm. On the other hand, once it is fabricated as a utensil, the object is uprooted from all custom: everything has to be capable of being evaluated via market accounting, all the more so given that the object produced is rendered abstract through the logic of a quantifiable profit. The product, like the custom that gives it its immutable meaning, is quality; the utensil is pure quantity.

The manufacture of utensils is no stranger to sterility, i.e. the unexpected appearance of inefficacy. This is the fault inherent to willed, functional utilitarianism, and the only weapon there is to fight against this flaw is 'waste'.

> The experience of manufacturing when it has an eye to making a profit amounts to eliminating the risk of the product's being sterile in favour of wasting materials and human force (the cost price).

In order to evacuate inefficiency, it is incumbent upon the industry of utensils to waste time and money. Now this 'wasteful experience' is peculiar to 'the phantasm that voluptuous emotion procures'. For Klossowski, it is not that there is waste associated with the phantasm on one side, and lossless efficiency linked to the utensil on the other. Rather, there is waste within the logic of the utensil. A new question arises: how does wasteful experimentation operate within the production of a simulacrum? The act of manufacture, within the logic of the utensil, 'produces waste only so as to express itself through the act of constructing, destroying and reconstructing indefinitely'; as for the creation of the simulacrum, it 'constructs only in order to express itself through waste'. Waste is present in both logics, but its place is inverted. There follows a somewhat surprising example: the nuclear bomb

> has no other use besides anguishing the world of sterile uses. Nevertheless, the callipygian Venus is nothing other than the laughing face of the bomb, meeting utility with derision.

To say that there is an articulation between the two logics of utensil and waste has a consequence: in both cases, any possible act confronts and manipulates the same forces.

To imagine that the utensil does not have its wasteful side is to forget that any utensil is a simulacrum. Admittedly, it is a particular simulacrum, but a simulacrum nonetheless, in that it functions as an equivalent to the unexchangeability of the phantasm itself. The logic of the utensil claims to be based on a production without loss, sustainable only through market accounting. But this is not at all the case: the utensil is rather a way of disguising the incommunicability of the forces in presence. This remark is an important one: it affirms that the utensil is a simulacrum, but unaware of this, and it does everything to annul what has constituted it as such.

However, this is not the decisive point in Klossowski's analysis; a second consequence is to be drawn from his thesis on the genesis of value. There is a 'purely mercantile character to the life of impulses in individuals [...]'. Not only is there a failure to recognise the useless waste in the utensil, but also and above all 'the disguises of pathological utility' in the customary product are entirely ignored. Certainly, there is uselessness in the utensil in order to arrive at its construction, but also (and especially?) there is usefulness in the pathological dimension as a locus (*topos*) of the play of forces.

This is why Klossowski cannot find words harsh enough to oppose a conception of gratuitous or pure art. On the contrary, he insists on the 'accounting capacity' of the impulse's pathos. And what is its irrefutable proof?

> [...] in that regard, it is in the most emancipated domains, such as the economic applications of science, that this force has developed its most ingenious invention, because it was the last one ever imaginable: the industrial regime.

If the industrial regime is the most 'ingenious invention' of this force, it is because this force is, as such, already keeping the accounts. Certainly the accounting in question has nothing to do with the accounting of utensils, but (and here we find Nietzsche's lesson) it is an accounting in as much as the forces can be grasped as such only in their combat, their hierarchy, and in their limited and relative movements and stabilisations.

Impulses as Infrastructures

We thus come to Klossowski's fundamental thesis in *La Monnaie Vivante*:

> Do not the economic norms in turn form a substructure of affects, rather than the ultimate infrastructure, and if there were an ultimate infrastructure, would it not be constituted by the behaviour of affects and impulsions? Responding affirmatively amounts to saying that economic norms are a mode of expression and representation of impulsive forces. The way they express themselves in the economy, and ultimately in our industrial world, corresponds to the way they have been treated by the economy of governing institutions. That this original and ultimate infrastructure finds itself determined each time by its own reactions to previously existing substructures is undeniable, but the forces in presence are those that pursue the same combat of infrastructures in substructures. So, if these forces specifically express themselves first in accordance with economic norms, they themselves create their own suppression, as well as the means of breaking the suppression they are subjected to in varying degrees. And this is how it remains as long as there is a combat of impulses, which, in a given organism, is engaged both for and against the formation of the agent, for and against its psychical and bodily unity. There, indeed, the first schemes of a 'production' and a 'consumption' will be drawn up, the first signs of compensation and bartering.

These formulations are extremely precise and constitute a compass from which our author takes his bearings in our world economy – in this case, an economy inseparable from theology[3] and his vision of a negative utopia (i.e. counter-utopia). The basis of the Klossowskian economy is that which is initially played out, actualised, and 'represented' as he says, in the (provisional) unity of the agent. This economy is what forms the pathos of being – where the first operations in an 'economy' of energy fluxes are played out: production and consumption.

This is not an economy that reconciles or ensures the surpassing of contradictory or opposing terms. Klossowski's thought is not dialectical; a notable characteristic of his economical flux of impulses is that it is not Hegelian or Marxist. Contradictory terms are, however, modified under pressure from the intensities that they encipher – they respond to one another, communicate, interpenetrate, but are never resolved in a third term which, being new, would constitute an advance. A dialectical advance. It is in this respect that Klossowski has strong leanings towards Gilles Deleuze and the empiricism that governs his philosophy – an empiricism that stands in opposition to dialectic and transcendence.[4]

Klossowski brings these remarks up to date by posing a new question: how is one to consolidate 'the possible relationship between the perverse elaboration of the phantasm, on the one hand, and the manufacture of the object of use on the other?' Such a question allows his previous remarks and reflections (which went via Sade and Nietzsche) on the phantasm's enciphering of impulses to be tied in with his considerations on the functioning of the industrial world. Again, there is reference to the artificial unity of Living agent. What does this mean? Linked intrinsically to the impulses of which it is a 'product,' the phantasm is thus a threat to the unity of the ego that has been constituted by the strict censorship of these

3 See Arnaud, A., *Pierre Klossowski*, Les contemporains, *op. cit.*, especially Chapter 3: 'L'économie du pathos'.

4 Mengue, Ph., *Gilles Deleuze ou le système du multiple*, Editions Kimé, Paris, 1994, especially Chapter 1, 'L'immanence et l'image deleuzienne de la pensée'. Following Nietzsche, Deleuze took up the themes of a Heraclitism of fluxes, a differential pluralism, and immanence.

impulses. On the other hand, the utensil 'presupposes the individual's stability' – all the more so given that, thanks to these manufactured objects, the individual finds himself endowed with needs that must be satisfied by these objects that stand ready for consumption. The hierarchy of needs holds up the individual's unity from the outside – much like scaffolding or prosthesis. Klossowski sums up as follows the distinction at the level of the consequences of the production of objects:

> The phantasm wants to last, at the expense of individual unity; the manufactured object has to serve this unity; its production and its use imply exteriority, delimitation with regard to milieu, and therefore with regard to other unities as well.

The logic of the utensil rules out an exchange of impulses because it isolates and divides: each unity in its place! Hence the economic subject.

Is one to conclude that the phantasm rules out use? Not at all, because the use of the phantasm '[...] merges with the use of jouissance or suffering'. In using the phantasm, our individual is immediately confronted with a new 'constraint' due to his unity. The phantasm becomes an operator of the unity's own dissolution (i.e. the free circulation of impulsive fluxes) to which what lies behind the centring of the agent's unity is opposed. An exchange is created, to wit, a veritable economic matrix:

> [...] for there to be exchange, there has to be an equivalent, namely a stand-in for something, as much within the sphere of the phantasm elaborated at the expense of the individual's unity as at the level of the individual, in the outer sphere, of the manufactured object.

Therefore, what is important for Klossowski is the heterogeneity of the phantasm and the unity, along with the modalities of their encounter. Non-dialectical communications exist between the 'two circuits'. But the individual confronted with this communication finds himself in a most difficult position.

> Any equivalent at the level of the organic unity of the individual consequently represents a double sanction: an internal constraint as well as an affirmation of the outer self; hence the dilemma: enjoy without affirming yourself, or affirm yourself without enjoying simply in order to exist.

This is what our agent is faced with – a combat between the logic of objects and needs, and the logic of impulses. It is at this point that work and utensil manufacture are tied in. Why?

> Accounting for these two sanctions is only possible if we form the equivalent not of the internal constraint, but of its renunciation. The equivalent of this renunciation is what working conditions are founded on, along with the specific act of manufacture.

To work and to manufacture is not a choice to affirm the outer self. It is to renounce – and thus to censor and annihilate – the internal impulses, which, as a consequence, is an affirmation of the external logic of needs and their objects.

What is the creator translating, he who decides to produce objects without use, namely, simulacra? What function, in the broad sense of the term, does the artist fulfil? Klossowski's answer does not beat around the bush: the artist divulges his own phantasms, explicitly giving 'an equivalent to the state of his impulses'. We can see how this stands in contrast to the producer of useful objects: he divulges nothing, or, rather, shows that he has stopped submitting himself to his impulsive states in favour of the pure subsistence of the unity of the economic subject. Whereas the creator of simulacra of sterile uses 'claims to enrich knowledge through the sensations he procures,' the producer – and the worker in general – merely set in motion the metonymic series of the 'need for other objects coming from existing objects: namely, the perfected use of an object that always prescribes and limits one to this exclusive use'. The creator produces sensations that divide his ego's unity as well as that of the viewer; the worker produces objects debased to the level of instruments. Our author reminds us that

> [...] the instrument understands its object and its effect differently and better [...] because it has been designed in accordance with the explorable and manufacturable object, and because this object – whether inanimate or living – is only defined in relation to what is explorable or manufacturable about it.

Klossowski's goal is not only to show the existence of two heterogeneous circuits; his keenest aim is to discern the passage of one circuit into the other, and then to ascertain the effects. There is – and this confirms the circuits' heterogeneity – neither the slightest coincidence nor analogy 'between the act of manufacturing a utensil and the act of divulging a *phantasm* through a simulacrum'. This analysis raises a new question: does not the simulacrum reveal only the presence of an impulsive 'phantasm', which has become partially freed of its censorship? No, it also divulges the logic of what the system of production censors. In this capacity, the simulacrum of art provides the reason for industrial logic. This means that affect, on being freed, gives the causal explanation of what organises our modern world.

> The world of utensils cannot in any way compensate for the overthrow of the impulsive state by productive activity, because this very activity is already a form of compensation. Thus only the simulacrum of art is capable of accounting for this reversal and, because it simulates, its products cannot be assimilated to objects of [productive] use.

Declining to play dialectician, Klossowski's merit is to have introduced a third phase that, rather than cancelling them out, turns the two preceding ones around to reveal their nether side – their *un-thought*. What does this mean? Let us read our commentator: the simulacra of art divulge an 'impulsive urgency'. By being manufactured, they become, paradoxically, 'utensils to be used by affects'. Utensils and simulacra no longer stand in opposition. They are still heterogeneous, yet no longer devoid of any possibility of knotting and relation. From this Klossowski deduces that utensils are also simulacra. Why? His reply conveys the cutting edge of his approach. Utensils simulate too – but what?

> [...] industrial tools, by nature the farthest things from simulacra in that they prescribe a rigorously restrained use by being only efficient (namely, that which circumscribes an irreversible operation in its effects and, as ramified as this operation may be, excludes any simulated result), will by this very fact be simulacra of non-simulation, thus of a *fait accompli*, thanks to which this part of the life of passions is extracted, and thus diverted for the manufacture of objects of use.

At this point in his demonstration, Klossowski comes back to the logic of the utensil that lies behind constructed simulacra: '[...] if the simulacrum of art is a utensil of the passions, then its simulation ought indeed to be an efficient operation too'. Otherwise, it would merely be a poor 'simulated simulacrum' and would fall short of its effect: to produce disorganising sensations for any centring unity.

> In the art product, the affect finds the expression of its 'phantasm': in the logic of the utensil where this expression is refused, the affect acts under cover of the utility of something where affect is of no use.

The affect is present as cause, as origin, in the logic of the utensil, but the specificity of its industrial realisation is its refusal to be expressed. Affect subsists, but under cover of a purely superficial utility.

The combat of forces continues, however, as affective urgency; the impulsive force always wants to manifest itself, to divulge itself. Two solutions emerge: either the simulacrum of art gives presence to a 'phantasm', or the utensil simulates its postponement. But in either case there is simulacrum.

> To postpone voluptuousness is to count on the future. [...] However, the impulses know no other limit to their urgency than their own, and voluptuousness as such means to be just as immediate as it is latent and unpredictable.

This particularity of the impulse has its consequence:

> If, when it comes to the utensil, voluptuousness is not urgent, it is still urgent for voluptuousness to be simulated by some means so that what is properly serious (since it is of unquestionable urgency) may not be simulated.

Klossowski concludes this description of the intrinsic logic of forces by insisting on the necessity of a living agent so that the combat can be realised:

> impulsive 'phantasm' – simulacrum; subsistence – utensil fabrication: two circuits which intersect within the individual unity, but which this same unity never manages to break, if only to postpone perpetually the urgency of one or the other circuit.

The two circuits affirm, each in their own way, that both voluptuous emotion and subsistence are impossible to simulate – in other words, all that remains are stand-ins for what always lies outside the circuit: the real of affect.

From these remarks, Klossowski summarises his analysis of price and gratuity, bringing us to the theme of counter-utopia properly speaking: what he called *Living Currency*.

'Nothing in impulsive life seems to be strictly free-of-charge'. Here we have the thesis reduced to its bare bones.

> As soon as an interpretation directs the process itself (the emotion's struggle to subsist despite the instinct of propagation), evaluation, and therefore price, intervene.

Price is the name our author gives to the evaluation of the differences in energy specific to the power of the forces in presence. It is the name of an initial difference in energy between emotion and the agency of survival that preserves the species and individual unity. Price indicates comparison. From price stems trafficking, negotiations, compromise, and so on, which create a dilemma for the subject: 'Either internal perversion – dissolution of the unity; or internal affirmation of the unity – external perversion'. This 1970 text most certainly portrays perversion in a radically different way from the medical and legal approach. Here, perversion is the name of the voluptuous emotion freed from the procreative instinct that channels it. Perversion is not only internal, it is also external. Affects are utilised by the economy of utensils. The hypertrophy of economic needs constitutes a perversion – albeit the opposite of internal perversion. In this capacity, perversion is the rationale behind economy. It would be necessary to know how to replace the perversion of needs with the perversion of affects. This is where price is to be found:

> Whosoever refuses to pay the price of voluptuous emotion and demands the instinct of propagation (thus of his own unity) free of charge, will pay this gratuitousness a hundredfold through the external perversion of the conditions in which the individual unity is called upon to affirm itself.

If it were otherwise, what would happen for the subject? The terms of a utopian aim start to take form:

> The day human beings will have overcome or reduced external perversion, i.e., the monstrosity of the hypertrophy of 'needs', and will consent, in return, to their internal perversion, i.e., to the dissolution of their fictive unity, a concordance will be struck between desire and the production of its objects in a rationally established economy, in accordance with its impulses.

This realisation, reconciling Fourier (to each passion its object) and Sade (to possess the object in order to destroy it unrelentingly), reconciles the irreconcilable. Effort becomes free of charge – it is removed from productive labour – thereby corresponding to 'the price of the irrational', i.e. to the price of affect that lies wide of norm and reason. To pay the price of what is priceless, to bankrupt oneself in order to possess what cannot be possessed: 'Here we find the "overdrawn account" of the individual unity'.

Free-of-Charge

In the chapter 'La gratuité et le prix', our author systematises his remarks, while at the same time replying – wilfully? – to *The Accursed Share* by Georges Bataille, a close friend of Klossowski's. His remarks are sharp.

- The free-of-charge '[...] boils down to enjoying something that is priceless, or according it jouissance without compensation'. Can such a basic definition be applied to voluptuous emotion? We already know that Klossowski does not think so, but in this chapter he pushes the structural reasoning behind his argument even further.
- The absolute owner – namely, 'the "divinity" or "inexhaustible life"' – is not part of a logic of exchange: for instance, the Dispensing Sun that gives without receiving (this reference is already present in Bataille).
- If this is the case for everyone, then there is no price. All is given and exchanged for free on the basis of an initial inexhaustibility.
- Klossowski insists on the consequence of this 'If [...]': the possibility of value is ruled out, and so too therefore is the price to pay.

> 'Life' beyond price, without price, that is given, received, and subjected for free, does not have a price in and of itself. It is worth nothing without voluptuousness. But voluptuousness, and the ability to experience it, is in turn given to one and all for free: it does not have any price either.

At this point we come to a contradiction. Klossowski was proposing to demonstrate that precisely 'nothing in the life of impulses seems to be properly free,' and yet the preceding remarks now affirm just the opposite: that the free-of-charge can be deduced from the original inexhaustibility, thus forgetting that the absolute owner is not a living agent, a separate unit, but is God or life itself. What about the individuated agent? A dissymmetry appears, a 'plus' emerges that is irreducible to endless quantity – just where the 'accursed share,' so dear to Bataille, is to be found. However, Klossowski's approach is based on different principles: '[...] each of us receives only according to our capacity to receive (first restriction)'. The capacity to receive varies from one agent to the next. If an agent is that which he really can receive, the possibility of value necessitates that he give what he did not receive – that he give 'more than what he is'. 'This is why no one can bear to receive more than he can give back'.

To give more than what has been received – how does the agent manage to effectuate this operation? This is the paradox: 'If he gives, he augments himself. But how is it that through giving he is augmented rather than diminished?' The answer is reminiscent of Marcel Mauss's studies, prefaced by Claude Lévi-Strauss, on sumptuary exchanges.

> He gives so as not to receive, and, because he can, he augments himself [...]. He has worth only in the eyes of the one who, being no more than what he has received, falls short. Thus, the price that one acquires with regard to the one who receives without being able to give back is expressed by a right to take back even more than has been given.

In other words, the mainspring of this affair is to be found in the dual inter-subjective logic wherein one of the partners finds himself reduced to 'the inability to give back, despite the capacity to receive [...]'. This logic is worthy of that detailed by Mauss, but the author quickly assumes a Sadean-sadistic point of view:

> Whosoever gives so as not to receive takes possession each time of whomsoever, having received in order to be, cannot give back; the latter has already given himself over entirely to the power that augments, rather than diminishes, by giving without receiving so as to take back more than he has given.

Giving in order not to receive so as to oblige the other is incomprehensible outside of a perverse subjective logic. At this moment, the agent, in being augmented, would also be immediately put beside himself – the exteriorisation of this 'plus' that expropriates him. And the submitted, indebted (unable to give back) partner is likewise put beside himself since he is at the mercy of his rival who is henceforth victor.

Klossowski breaks off his analysis at this point, but one cannot fail to see Sade behind this keen illustration of perverse logic. It is his proposed universal prostitution. Let us compare this prostitution to his demonstration of the inability to give back, which augments *he who gives in order not to receive*. We explicitly obtain the position of the libertine. According to the logic of universal prostitution,

> all men and women are called upon to sell themselves, or are put on sale; for each man and woman to be sellable, they must keep their moral ownership which constitutes the value of the individual put on sale [...] Sadean erotic emotion results from the rupture of this integrity, through this voluntary or forced prostitution.

The partner – who henceforth has the status of victim – can no longer give back but can only receive; at this point he falls apart as a unity.

> The 'quality' of prostitution depends on the upping of the price that the subject attributes to himself in proportion to his moral degradation; the more he is 'corrupted', the higher goes his price – like the character Juliette. Thus, to begin with, the voluptuous sensation is intensified not for free, but from the very fact that the object from which this sensation results deems itself sellable. This venality – according to the Sadean interpretation – is founded on the fact that beings can only communicate amongst themselves as tradable objects.

It is not poverty that drives one to sell oneself, just as it is not absence that drives one to steal, or abstinence that drives to sexual assaults. On the contrary, it is wealth that impels one to sell oneself. Likewise, it is possession that orients one towards theft, and it is libertine practice that obliges one to reiterate sexual crimes. This is Sade's logic. Why? Klossowski's remarks allow us to grasp its incitement. It is not a matter of filling a lack that is already there or occupying a previously noticed empty place. It is a matter of bringing about a 'plus', of systematically creating and deepening a discrepancy, a debt. The Sadean pervert does not manage a shortage; rather, he intensifies a world of wealth in order to extort, in the fraudulent exchanges that take place, a surplus, an increase of riches in which the partner finds himself impoverished and powerless. As we know, in 'Frenchmen, one more effort [...]', Sade will go so far as to recommend punishing not the robber but the robbed, 'so as to teach him to take care of his property'.

The Sadean world wonderfully illustrates this absence of the free-of-charge. It is also an absence of reversibility. This is not the law of a particular case, but a general rule that only perversion can explicitly realise. In other words, with regard to inter-subjectivity, the 'irreversible' always installs a dissymmetry, a discrepancy, thus creating value and esteem: price. This is why, in spite of his admiration for Fourier's utopia which promotes reciprocity in the free play of passions, Klossowski is far closer to Sade's counter-utopia founded on non-gratuitousness.

Either Currency or Living

Now that his key markers, which have the status of concepts, have been set out and developed, Klossowski introduces his utopia: *Living Currency*. The style of this fable is part of the writer's ruse. He presents this counter-utopia (devised against the backdrop of an absence of any positive content) in the manner of one of Fourier's tales of future bliss. In true Fourierian style, Klossowski authors a project that is directly aligned with Sade's objective: the absolute anteriority of evil. What is it all about? We are invited to picture a society that returns to reinitialising exchange based on custom, towards the reign of goods that only know use value. We are warned from the outset: such a 'regression [is] apparently impossible'. The point of this fable is not to show us a society that dates from before the industrial revolution. *Living Currency* is not a rural, rustic pastoral. On the contrary, Klossowski suggests that we picture our own industrial society, with all its prodigious development of *savoir-faire* and perfected, sophisticated objects. However, at its heart he places what it can only exclude: the reign of customary use. *Living Currency* is the ritual of custom transferred to modern industrial society. To carry out this 'impossible' project, our author makes a hypothesis:

> [...] namely, an industrial phase where producers have the means to demand, as payment, objects of sensation from the consumers. These objects are living beings.

What today appears to be impossible is here realised as a general functioning of this ideal society. Payment is no longer made by means of money as an abstract equivalent of market exchanges, but by virtue of 'living beings'. One's 'own body' finds itself implicated as such in this new means of payment, now established as the one and only means of making purchases.

> Following the example of barter, producers and consumers will come to constitute collections of 'persons' understood to be destined for pleasure, emotion and sensation.

Barter serves as payment – thus, in this sense, we see a historical regression. The exchanged object is not one's 'own body' as an isolated unit, but rather one's own body in as much as it is agitated by its basic impulses, in as much as it can produce – for both its agent and the one who is monopolised by him – pleasure, emotion and sensations. Klossowski stresses the givens on which he bases this new industrial phase:

> How can the human 'person' fulfil the function of currency? How ever will producers, instead of 'treating themselves' to women, get paid 'in women'? How will entrepreneurs and manufacturers pay their engineers and workers?

The answer is clearly stated: 'in women'. The inverse of this society is equally possible: 'Women practicing a profession will be paid "in boys"'. Here we may note the first contradiction in the conceptual presentation of the rules in the text: female currency is sustained by other women, virile currency by the owners of female currency – men. Men and woman are thus both owners not only of the natural wealth made up of living bodies, but also of the currency itself that is used in the barter. Virtually every man and woman is both possessor and the goods possessed. The possessor does not possess himself, but rather constitutes 'collections of "persons"' up for barter. This contradiction is not resolved by Klossowski's fable; on the contrary, it is put forward as the basis of the entire development that follows. *Living Currency* is founded on a logical impossibility; it is based on the interplay of logically contradictory terms and propositions. This is why *Living Currency* is not some other site, some other society, or some other economic organisation. It is a non-place, the 'no' of place – and in this respect one finds, to the letter, the etymology of the word 'utopia,' coined in 1516 by Sir Thomas More: *u-topos*, the negation of place in as much as it is observable in the *hic et nunc* of a description.

For a long time, commentaries on utopian texts were disparaged, despite, where some of them are concerned, of their seriousness or erudition. This most certainly changed with the 1973 publication of Louis Marin's magisterial study, *Utopics: The Semiological Play of Textual Spaces*. For Marin, the utopian text does not present a coherent structure in accordance with the readings that the said text proposes to construct, which can be put as follows: each time utopia (in its pertinent historical period) is summoned, it breaks down what it claims to construct, rendering inaccessible what it nevertheless shows to be present, existent, and therefore graspable. In other words, utopia reveals a process of occultation. In this capacity, in a text, utopia introduces the Other of place – and therefore the Other of society, of life, of the city. A textual operation brings about utopia, and produces it as a specific text: the neuter, which is to be understood as the neutralisation of opposites in the text. The neuter does not bring about the synthesis of co-present terms, it does not resolve a contradiction. On the contrary, it isolates the contradictory terms and separates them. In its way, it does not take sides. Here we find one of the notions of 'neutrality' – it does not opt for one or for the other, it is neither one nor the other, as is clearly seen in the Latin etymology of *ne-uter*. It is a term put in the position of a supplement, not a complement. How is the neuter inscribed into the text, precisely making it utopian? It is written as a blank space, as a flaw, as that point at which an affirmation cannot be made. Between yea and nay, between truth and falsehood, between here and elsewhere, between impulse and monetary equivalent, the neuter finds its niche. It conjoins these incompatible oppositions only to immediately disjoin them; it is a logical operator of conjunction/disjunction. It is at once *neither one nor the other*, and *both one and the other*. This 'between' is to be taken quite literally.

It is a blank 'space', a place devoid (because it has been emptied) of operations to come. At the heart of what is given-to-be-seen, the neuter hollows out the empty place of a nether side: a literal *non-lieu*, a firm negation of place. Neuter is the name of this empty place, forever void, delimited by the neutralisation of the elements of a contradiction, the parts of a visible topographical space. Marin will say that:

> The 'content' of utopia is the organisation of space as a text; the utopian text, its formal structuring and its operational processes, is the constitution of discourse as a space.[5]

The neuter is not a textual figure. It is a logical operation of production of which the text, called utopian, is the product, the effect. *Living Currency* is a utopian text produced by the logical operation of the neutralisation of opposites: the blanks in the narrative that describe this society. In this case, it is a counter-utopia: the structural impossibility of giving a positive form to perversion. Only by taking into account, literally, this chiasmus between the space-*in*-the-text (i.e. the space referred to and given-to-be-seen as realised) and the space-*of*-the-text (i.e. the textual operations) can we grasp the logic of this 'Living Currency'. The exploration and development of this chiasmus will guide us in our reading.

Let us continue reading the fable, keeping in mind the specificity of its starting hypothesis. Klossowski indicates to us that the process he is describing already exists overtly in our industrial economy.

> What we are saying here exists in fact [...]. All modern industry is supported by a barter mediatised by the sign of inert currency, neutralising the nature of exchanged objects, i.e. by a simulacrum of barter – a simulacrum in the shape of the resources of the workforce, and thus in the form of a living currency (not avowed as such) that already exists.

Our industry does not therefore exclude Living being, but is, on the contrary, nourished by it. Without it no economy would be possible; it is the workforce formed of the flesh and blood of those who sell it on the labour

5 [Translated from] Marin, L., *Utopiques: jeux d'espaces*, Collection Critique, Éditions de Minuit, Paris, 1973, p. 24. [*Cf*, *Utopics: Spatial Play*, trans. R.A. Valrath, Open Humanities Press, 1984].

market. However, once introduced into the monetary market of exchange, the worker is annulled as a living being, as unique. Even though he is pure quality, he is reduced to a measurable and purely quantitative dimension: to the time of work in exchange for money. Living is replaced by the inert. This is precisely what the logic of economics does not want to acknowledge: there is something alive in market exchange. Once again, Klossowski turns his analysis into a means to deconstruct the mistaken affirmations of the present system – a system he duly combats.

The question that arises from such affirmations concerns the comparability of these two heterogeneous entities: one's own body, which is alive and the source of emotions, and labour that is measured by its time in a quantitative logic. In other words, how is the time of labour (that which has a price) to be reconciled with emotion (that which has no price)? This question, constantly present in the theoretical analyses of *Living Currency*, is found again, unchanged, at the heart of this utopia.

> Eradicating wages in cash so as to pay the worker in living objects of sensation can only be practised if Living object is itself evaluated as labour provided [...].

In order, therefore, for this economic system to function, emotion needs to be quantifiable – which is impossible. How might one resolve this paradox that would bring down the utopia on account of the very means it had adopted?

> For an object of sensation to be worth a quantity of labour, this (living) object needs to constitute, beforehand, a value that from the start is equal if not superior to the work product. There is no common measure between the sensation that this living object is able to procure on its own and the quantity of work provided, equivalent to such and such a number of resources proper to the potential upkeep of this object of sensation.

The only solution would be to attribute a value to emotion, but arbitrarily, since the conditions of its production can be neither found nor deduced. This solution is incompatible with the starting hypothesis: to turn emotion into currency. The notion of currency presupposes a generalised equivalence valid for one and all. Yet if attributing value to emotion is arbitrary, it can only be carried out on a case-by-case basis. Emotion would be an element of barter, though variable from individual to individual. Since it has no universal equivalence, emotion cannot be a currency. What is to be done?

Search as we might, line by line through the text, the reply to this question is missing. The demonstration we had been waiting for is nowhere to be found. For there to be a reply, another state has to be supposed which has the particularity of never having existed, and which is even, properly speaking, unimaginable.

> In order for Living object (a source of rare emotion) simply to prevail as currency, there will be no denying that a psychical state must have been universally attained; that this state expressed itself in the form of undisputed practices and customs.

The difficulty lies in the following point: putting Living, impulsive body on the market as an element of barter should create new customs. From then on, the use of voluptuousness (the simulacrum of affects that have broken from their limits) should become commonplace and widespread. However, in order for these affects to become active again on the market, they would have to become part of new practices and customs – that are already there. '[...] [T]his custom would profoundly modify exchanges and their signification'. Thus, in this fiction, the realisation of living currency becomes immediately impossible and leads to a standstill: in order for affects to circulate, custom has to change, and yet in order for custom to change, affects must be introduced into exchange, and so on and so forth. A formula sums up this contradiction:

> But a living object, the source of voluptuous sensations, either shall be currency and erase the neutralising functions of money, or it shall found exchange value on the basis of the emotion procured.

Whichever solution is chosen, the ineluctable fact remains that:

> [...] within the context of the conditions of modern economy, the disproportion in nature then appears to be much greater between the quantity of work, taken as a norm of value, and Living object in the capacity of currency.

Moreover, the rest of the chapter shows that this contradiction cannot be resolved. The examples demonstrate that living currency is not, in fact, alive. For instance the 'movie star', even though his image circulates, is not living currency, but rather an 'industrial slave'. Our author goes on to recall the principal characteristics of living currency:

> It would ensure the quality of a sign of value whilst at the same time integrally constituting the value thereof, namely, the quality of the goods that correspond to the 'immediate' satisfaction, not of a need, but of the initial perversion.

We come to the following definition: living currency is 'both equivalent to wealth and wealth itself' – which, of course, in the norms of our economic system, is impossible: a contradiction in terms.

Let us examine these two terms, 'equivalent' and 'wealth', which Klossowski brings together, while leaving a little space between them which his fiction explores. If living currency is taken as an equivalent, then, in so far as it feels voluptuous emotion, the body is reified and abstracted in a logic of exchanges. It takes on a relative value determined by the play of coded differences. The body is annulled as a living entity; it is emptied of jouissance (of emotion, of impulses) in favour only of the inexistence contained within. This is how Sade defines the possible. Living body disappears in favour of what represents it in abstract equivalences. A mortified body, barren of jouissance, a circular clearing, scorched in the earth, as Lacan puts it.[6]

On the other hand, if Living body is taken as wealth itself, as only a substance of what is enjoyed, then all commercial economy disappears. The communication of beings through the exchange of their bodies becomes realisable, but it is a communication in the real – wordless, without distance or mediation. Economy is no more because the person can no longer be reduced to a discernable unity. The agent is destroyed in favour of the intensities that he suppresses and limits to his corporeal envelope. By introducing wealth itself – the real impulse – into economy, all that goes to make up a society, and which it sets in place, tends to become un-individualised – it tends to disappear.

6 Lacan, J., 'Remarks on Daniel Lagache's Presentation' in *Écrits, The First Complete Edition in English*, *op. cit.*, p. 558.

Living body, in as much as it is a support of Being and the associated jouissance that lies outside the symbolic, introduces the non-evaluable, the ungraspable, the useless and the arbitrary into market exchange. This means that the Other jouissance cannot be exchanged, nor can it be the basis of any market or social economy. A sheer supposition, this Other jouissance is not palpable; it cannot be hoarded in order to be given or taken. The realisation of Living being as currency is impossible: either, by becoming an equivalent, Living being is mortified (the paradigm of this productivist logic being labour) and the Other jouissance is evacuated and lost; or Living being is introduced as such into these exchanges, but then every equivalent, every symbolic mediation is destroyed and sexual relationship would become possible (in the real). In other words, there is either signifier or jouissance, either currency or living being.

Following Sade (and incidentally Charles Fourrier), here then is precisely what the fiction *La Monnaie Vivante* wanted to proclaim: the abolition of all the existing economic norms in favour of the only impulses that singular perverse practices bring about on a case by case basis. Klossowski's project was to turn impulses into a monetary value, marking the passage from a singular fixated practice (the pervert's) to a counter-generality of perversion as a principle of society, and legitimised through reason. The currency constituted by impulses establishes an integral economic monstrosity, i.e. an integral perversion. Klossowski – like Sade – does not manage to provide a positive formulation of perversion. It is always approached negatively, precisely because it shows that its target is unattainable – the Other jouissance, Living body of the Other. The negative at work in perversion is this negativised insistence of Other jouissance, supposed to exist beyond the logic of the phallic One. The impossibility of positively formulating perversion is not therefore contingent, but structural. Integral monstrosity and *Living Currency* can, effectively, only be counter-utopias.

Roberte: Exchanging the Unexchangeable

The trilogy of the 'Roberte' volumes, Klossowski's work of fiction, is composed of the narratives *Roberte ce soir* (1953), *La Révocation de l'Édit de Nantes* (1959) and *Le Souffleur* (1960). It was published by Gallimard in 1965 in a single volume entitled *Les lois de l'hospitalité*.[1]

Hospitality – The Challenges of a Reading

In the first two narratives, Klossowski's protagonist is the seventy-year-old Octave, an admirer of Marshall Pétain, a reactionary in every choice he makes, and an anachronistic professor in Canon Law and Scholastic Instruction at the Catholic Faculty in Paris. In *The Revocation*, Octave also turns out to be the well-informed and passionate collector of a nineteenth century painter, Frédéric Tonnerre (invented by Klossowski), whose (inexistent) canvases will be described in minute detail. In the third text, *Le Souffleur*, the central character is Théodore Lacase, a writer. Théodore is a double – the veritable Siamese twin – of both Octave and a certain K. who is none other than Pierre Klossowski himself; the author slips into the fiction he weaves. Klossowski was to confide that *Le Souffleur* is his most autobiographical narrative.

Octave, like Théodore, is married to Roberte, a pretty young woman around whom the plot of the trilogy turns. She is present and active in every paragraph. The movements of her body, her attire, her comings and goings,

1 [TN, In 1989, the first two novels were published together in English under the title *Roberte Ce Soir* and *The Revocation of the Edict of Nantes*, trans. Austryn Wainhouse, Marion Boyars Publishers, New York/London, 1989. No English version of *Le Souffleur* has as yet been published.]

her words, her intimate thoughts and above all her sexual practices and games are described at length. In the first two narratives, Roberte is both president of the Board of Censors at the Ministry and a radical-socialist deputy! In her everyday life, Octave/Théodore imposes a cleverly devised law on Roberte: *Hospitality*. The wife is 'lent'[2] by the husband to other men. He prostitutes her, or rather, he submits her to ritual adultery:

> She is not a fortuitous mistress that I exchange with mistresses of my friends; I lend them my wife. [...] One can never give the unexchangeable, but one can lend in order to better possess what one has.[3]

He adds:

> [...] I am only a primitive mentality. [...] So primitive that the transgression of a marriage is still for me as religious an act as marriage itself. [...] we cannot escape our essence; it is what guides us. [...] Universal prostitution cannot be practised if it does not presuppose the appeal to transgress marriage. The wife, prostituted by the husband, is no less a wife and the unexchangeable good of the husband, the priceless good whose value is given at the moment of consent when she yields to the lover chosen by her master. [...] If we take away marriage and the notions of conjugal loyalty, order, decency and chastity in their representative aspects that orient our wants and stimulate our desire – and the forbidden is only a dyke, a reservoir of energies – then all will be dispersed, degraded, nullified in total lifelessness. [...] [the suppression of the forbidden], under the auspices of an audacious innovation and turning a new leaf, is only aiming towards chaos and general deliquescense [...].[4]

Facing this adultery that has now turned into a picture, Octave himself becomes the gaze.

Once the characters have been presented, and the 'theatre society'[5] set up, the stories of the novels can unfurl and reveal the challenge: to exchange that which cannot be exchanged – the unexchangeable spouse. In light of

2 Klossowski, P., *Roberte Ce Soir* and *The Revocation of the Edict of Nantes*, *op. cit.*, p. 115.

3 [Translated from] Klossowski, P., 'Le Souffleur', *Les lois de l'hospitalité*, Gallimard, Paris, 1963, p. 302.

4 *Ibid.*, p. 304.

5 The subtitle chosen for *Le Souffleur.*

this impossibility, Klossowski doubles the stakes, intensifying the exchange to the point of producing a Brownian ritual. Since the object of exchange is unexchangeable, its impossibility is not overcome but rather confirmed as an absolute impossibility. The trap snaps shut on Octave – and on Théodore too. Both of them will give their lives absurdly demonstrating that the exchange of the unexchangeable spouse is possible, but that no living subject can achieve it.

To reduce these fictions to one person, Octave/Théodore, whose adventures as an old pervert the reader follows, is one way of avoiding reading Klossowski. Certainly the perverted set-ups and rituals of Octave/Théodore should be taken into account in all their detail, but this must be done by referring them to the conceptual markers that Klossowski's fiction develops. A back and forth between theoretical concepts and perverse set-ups is established, and it is up to the reader to delimit their trajectories and isolate what is at stake. There are no rituals without concepts, no concepts without practices; this is Klossowski's first lesson.

Octave practices the law of hospitality with Roberte. This law, by which our character prostitutes Roberte to his 'guests',[6] with her consent, is an attempt at cure. Octave is gravely ill. He '[…] suffered from his conjugal happiness as though from an illness, firm in the belief he would be cured of it, once he had made it contagious'.[7] It is an illness that is cured by being communicated and transmitted to others! Though Octave knows and feels himself to be ill, he does not know what he is suffering from. By making his misfortune hatch out in someone else, his suffering finds its expression – it thus becomes objectified by the other, in the other.

The happiness of our old professor is enigmatic, and this enigma is Roberte herself. Roberte is an enigma because she is 'equivocal',[8] presenting at once a particular characteristic and its opposite. She is pure and defiled, loyal and a whore. Failing to resolve himself to admit the contradictory attributes of his wife, Octave will be endlessly asking: who is Roberte? Who is she really? Is she pure or defiled; is she loyal or a whore? The equivocation

6 A term chosen by Octave.

7 Klossowski, P., *Roberte ce soir* and *The Revocation of the Edict of Nantes*, *op. cit.*, p. 9.

8 *Ibid.*

is deduced from an initial observation: 'Roberte's beauty was of that sober sort which so often conceals pronounced tendencies to frivolity'.[9] The word has been uttered: *conceal*. This concealment, imputed to his wife who herself is perhaps unaware of it, as attentive as she is to her husband, imposes itself upon him with all the characteristics of something obvious. It exists, never to be doubted or put into perspective. Octave will not budge when it comes to what he knows, and from which he will draw endless conclusions in his ritual practice of hospitality. What he knows is that *Roberte is frivolous*, her lightness does not have the status of a hypothesis – this is 'things as they are [*un fait accompli*]';[10] it is 'something that has been done'.[11] Octave's position is not a demonstration, even though his endless sophistic reasoning parodies theological and mediaeval scholastic arguments. Rather, his aim is to bring about a revelation of the 'fait accompli' which suffers no contestation because it is inscribed right where words can no longer be uttered. This *fait accompli*, like a silent oracle (no sentence can be articulated or communicated anymore), is where a gesture brings about the irrevocable.

Objectively, Octave is mistaken: Roberte is not an 'emancipated'[12] woman. On the contrary, she is modest, gentle, reserved and attentive to her husband. Roberte is the mistress of the house who pampers Octave, including sexually. Octave affirms his conjugal happiness without any possible contestation. Roberte was quick to realise that the equivocation lay in her husband's mind, whilst she '[...] had become much more rigid in her hostile attitude toward all his ideas'.[13] Roberte's opposition counts for nothing in the affair: '[...] the more she entrenched herself in this attitude, the more enigmatic [Octave] judged her to be'.[14] By positing what he constantly sees and observes, namely, Roberte's beauty, as a 'trap',[15] as a deceptive 'sign',[16]

9 *Ibid.*
10 *Ibid.*, p. 24.
11 *Ibid.*
12 *Ibid*, p. 9.
13 *Ibid.*
14 *Ibid.*
15 Klossowski, P., 'Le Souffleur', in *Les lois de l'hospitalité*, *op. cit.*, p. 187.
16 Klossowski, P., *Roberte Ce Soir* and *The Revocation of the Edict of Nantes*, *op. cit.*, p. 56.

Octave attributes to his wife, *de facto*, a hidden 'physiognomy',[17] a secret even she is not aware of, which he will track without respite. Our protagonist makes himself the voyeur of his young wife's soul. He admits that her soul, 'eluding him in every which way'[18] is the source of his illness. Proximity, banal daily life, the physiognomy of the couple, endlessly keep his wife's soul from his grasp, from his *contemplation* in the theological sense as a mode of God's vision. In Klossowski's novels, the husband (in the following quote it is Théodore) is confronted with a severe psychical difficulty:

> After blundering the portrait of a woman because she is close to me, yet her soul eludes me every which way, so much so that all I could talk about was suspicion, and all that I attempted to say about her concerned only the trap that was her body, her face [...] I will now try to evoke how I wanted to capture the physiognomy emanating from this woman that lives with me, and how her own life, although so simple, fought me, turned away from me – it is, in fact, the life we lead together.[19]

The image of a presence, the 'trap' of body and face, creates a screen. It reveals, only to straightaway hide again, the soul that lies ultimately behind, beyond, and remains Other. How, wonders the professor, '[...] to read the soul of the young widow I married'?[20] By making himself the voyeur of Roberte's hidden soul, what she conceals may be revealed. The secret would be discovered and the enigma resolved. Doubt, suspicion, and illness would disappear. Without this complement, the wife would remain, according to the husband, incomplete. Her being would remain intact. She would remain virgin.

Unravelling the Hospitality only takes on meaning when one grasps how and why these ritualised, systematised and dramatised practices fail in real life. Our theologian's long and tortuous reasoning is to be read, with all its strayings and contradictions, as an attempt to account for the impasses encountered when applying this law, and the means employed to get out of them. At the heart of the practice of Hospitality lies a crucial point of impossibility that no amount of willingness or determination

17 Klossowski, P., 'Le Souffleur', *op. cit.*, p. 187.

18 *Ibid.*

19 *Ibid.*

20 *Ibid.*

on Octave's behalf will ever reduce. He experiences the effects and consequences of a denial coming from the real. Octave's *theoretical* fictions, included in Klossowski's narrative like a dream within a dream,[21] indicate a tighter relationship between these astonishing theorisations and what is excluded from meaning: the real. Theoretical fiction and caricatured theological arguments are not an innocent addition to the staging of the Hospitality. They alone enable this real to be put into logical form. The real, as the point of impossibility, constitutes an end-stop in the voyeuristic practise.

Propounding this theory also helps Octave to target what Roberte hides. The illuminated word has a revelatory function: the spouse is put beside herself. Beyond words, the gesture as a bodily manifestation will inscribe a truth: Roberte, the wise and loyal spouse, is annulled when the Other Roberte surges up, eager for betrayal and offering herself up to pornographic rituals that, in violation, fulfil her sexually. Discussion stops, Octave becomes the gaze and Roberte is silently invaded by her bodiless demons, increate intellects and '[...] workings of the flesh the pantomime of spirits'.[22] Octave's reading of her soul begins. The voracious eye finds its feeding ground, and the gaze as fallen object stands apart from its backdrop, active and sovereign.

Communicating the Laws of Hospitality?

Like his characters Octave and Théodore Lacase, Klossowski tirelessly insists on the incomprehensible character of the principles that govern the Laws of Hospitality. This incomprehension is no way due to the quality of the interlocutor's listening or reflection. The reason for this is

21 Lacan, J., 'Kant with Sade' in *Écrits, The First Complete Edition in English, op. cit.*, p. 648.

22 Klossowski, P., *Roberte Ce Soir* and *The Revocation of the Edict of Nantes*, *op. cit.*, p. 56.

structural. The ordering principles of Hospitality are devoid of meaning. In reading these three narratives, the first risk would be to consider the Hospitality as something that is both *practicable* and *demonstrated* in the fictional depiction. The Hospitality would be practicable and practised: Octave adulterates Roberte and, faced with this spectacle, turns into a gaze. There is no shortage of terms to qualify this private practice. Octave is a sleazy old man, a pervert whose jouissance is enciphered by means of his fantasy of seeing his wife violated by a third party of his choosing. In short, Octave is a voyeur and the Hospitality is a system of perversion put on the stage. It is even sometimes for this that Klossowski is read and admired. Now, Klossowski is no dupe to this possible interpretation of his oeuvre. He himself qualifies Octave as a dirty old pervert, and he does not fail to designate himself as a maniac, a crank, a freak, and a man possessed. But this interpretation reduces Klossowski's work to an illustration of a doctrine of perversion, albeit a remarkable illustration, even an exceptional one.

The true relevance of Klossowski's work does not lie there. Octave or Théodore's system is relatively poor and lacking in original detail. These fictional scenes of stereotypical rituals are very limited compared to the perverse systems that we see in clinical practice or even in investigative journalism.

Klossowski's relevance lies elsewhere. Does it reside in the fact that the characters put words to what they perform? That would be to forget what Klossowski lays bare: the true conversation between the characters is a silent one. Should we deduce that they keep quiet in order to act? We are spared this kind of naivety. The muteness that constitutes the heart of each scene where, given over to a man, Roberte is violated, brings about the emergence, at the core of a conversation where words are exchanged, of both a painting and a spectacle. At the very instant the Other would finally be present, *hic et nunc* in the ritual that is its crucible, the image appears and is fixed in a frozen, halted scene that hangs in suspense. The final moment slips away and silence prevails. This silence is not nothing. It has chased away all speech content, and now opens onto another scene of gestures, attitudes, and bodily movements. Klossowski names them with a theological term: 'corporeal idioms'. He warns us:

> If an exchange of words is worth something exchangeable – ideas, feelings, promises, decisions – then this practise delimits the fact that people, as soon as they are responsible for what they say, cannot in fact exchange one for the other, nor replace one by the other, in the sense that they must rather use an agreed upon counterfeit in order to mutually propose some equivalent to their own unexchangeable substance.[23]

All in all, this system spells out how Roberte rushes in, 'heart and soul'.[24] In the muteness that sets in here, we are to read the reign of corporeal idioms that censor speech.[25] Since Roberte's substance is unexchangeable, idioms are exchanged. On the other hand, the '[...] exchange of words' tends to 'postpone or annul any *fait accompli*'[26] wherein substance reveals itself, but as something fragmented, fortuitous and singular.

The pertinence of this oeuvre lies neither in the lengthy, dramatised description of a voyeuristic ritual, nor in the characters' explanations of their sexual choices, practices and activities. Klossowski is not a psychological author; he does not take everyday psychology as a reference (i.e. an imaginary rationalisation caught in the narcissistic duality of *you* and *me*). The success of the three fictions in *Les lois de l'hospitalité* lies in their demonstration that Hospitality is impracticable not for contingent reasons based on any chosen means of application, but due to a structural cause that binds statement and enunciation together. No real subject can utter the statement of the Laws. No subject can say *I* in the logic of the Laws, for their wording only authorises the grammatical *I* of the subject of the statement. The subject of the enunciation meanwhile experiences subjectively the impossibility of the practice of Hospitality. Faced with this impossibility, Klossowski does not choose impotence or the silence of renunciation, but rather produces an oeuvre. He writes the three fictions of the Laws, and makes paintings that he calls, precisely, his *mutism*.

What then accounts for the impossibility of the *I* of enunciation, when it utters the statement of Hospitality and strives to carry it through into

23 Klossowski, P., *La Ressemblance*, *op. cit.*, p. 53.

24 *Ibid.*, p. 54.

25 *Ibid.*, p. 53.

26 *Ibid.*, p. 51.

practice? In his article 'On the Use of Stereotypes of Censorship Carried Out by Classical Syntax' subtitled precisely 'On the Incommunicability of the Laws of Hospitality', Klossowski gives his most concise formulae concerning these questions. Our author makes a distinction, which can be found again in his notional oeuvre, between the *code of everyday signs* and *the unique sign*. The everyday signs constitute the code by which we express ourselves, and thus this code designates spoken language. The unique sign is of an altogether different register. It is not a sign of everyday code. It is not a signifier, which, by definition, is always differential. It even serves Klossowski in designating what eludes the signifying code:

> [...] I've noticed at what point this code (the everyday signs) are limited when it comes to expressing that which does not always recur – that which recurs sometimes does not always happen again in the same way to justify this use of the same signs. So starting from the difference between a common, everyday sign and what it expresses, be it from a greater and greater inadequation, it seems to me that everything points to these variations and these rises and falls in intensity [...].[27]

These variations and the waxing and waning of intensities bring us back to Nietzsche's semiotics of impulses. Klossowski continues:

> [...] Behind the use of everyday signs we always insinuate some sort of 'unique sign'. We each coincide with the meaning of this sign, in virtue of its own intensity that assures its uniqueness.[28]

Klossowski says he is obsessed by one unique sign that exerts a force of constraint. This is the effect of the phantasm, which is silent and constraining for the subject. The unique sign founds the coherence of thought and the unity of being. It is their actualised base. The everyday signs set off the sliding movement of signifiers wherein the subject loses his coherence. On one side there is fixity and assurance, on the other, slippage and uncertainty.

This sign is the name *Roberte*. Its sonority is immediately taken up in an interplay of shattered images that belie any synthesis. It most accurately

27 *Ibid.*, p. 12.

28 *Ibid.*, p. 13.

enciphers the (impulsive) intensity of the dark forces. Klossowski oscillates between these two poles, which have become the walls he runs into: 'To remain in the coherence of a unique sign is to renounce living in a world constituted by incoherence where the code of everyday signs reigns'.[29] To choose the unique sign is to annul any possibility of a social bond; opting for the code of everyday signs means losing the coherence and intensity that encipher being as such.[30]

For Klossowski, drafting the Laws is his particular attempt at reconciling the two poles, at making them compatible, or at least tying them together and making them co-exist. He affirms this at the outset:

> In the world of everyday signs, the laws of hospitality, as described in these novels, are as much an aberration as they are a custom. As soon as the name of Roberte as a unique sign is divulged and spread in the world of the everyday code, what manifests then is both the absence of the conceptual place of this custom, as well as the presence of the traditional place where diverse customs, due to the incoherence of the world, continually defy the meaning of the impracticable, here proposed as hospitality.[31]

Klossowski drafts the *Laws* under the pressure of the unique sign: the name 'Roberte'. He says as much himself: he had to find a 'ruse to [...] find an equivalent'[32] to the unicity of the sign of Roberte. By using the signs of everyday code in writing (the narratives employ classical syntax) an equivalent is provided for that which cannot have any equivalent: intensity and its essence, together enciphered by the sign of the name 'Roberte' (which is precisely unique and without equivalent). There is no conceptual locus that can spell out the unique because what is proper to the concept is that it abolishes the unique in favour of comparison, measure, and the relation between signs. On the other hand, loci do exist where this practice is realised, but the practice is debased because

29 *Ibid.*

30 In the Afterward to *Les lois de l'hospitalité*, Klossowski elaborates on the effects the unique sign has on him; he brings up the question of folly that runs throughout the *Roberte* cycle.

31 Klossowski, P., *La Ressemblance*, *op. cit.*, p. 14.

32 *Ibid.*, p. 13.

it is shared. It becomes plural and therefore by definition annuls what is unique and un-transmittable.

Klossowski will develop the consequences of this structural incompatibility (thus in no way contingent or relative) between the unique sign and everyday signs, between intensity (jouissance) and the signifier. In the terms of the everyday code, the custom of Hospitality may be translated as: the husband adulterates the wife – 'this means that the husband brings the wife to commit adultery'.[33] Why would the husband make such a decision? What is he aiming at? The question of the husband's goal will be the object of all the demonstrations of the narrative of the Laws. Here is a simplified (descriptive) formulation:

> Octave thus wants to discover Roberte's real identity in her contact with a stranger, an unknown because he believes to know, in his conjugal ties, only an outside and thus fallacious identity of his wife [...].[34]

He adds: '[...] in essence, he discovers in Roberte a plurality of natures that are each time revealed only through the intermediary of fortuitous lovers'.[35]

Presented in this way, Hospitality would reportedly be practicable, though its dimension of a perverse (voyeuristic) system is not lost on anybody. However, the mainspring of this practice does not lie in the system that is being presented. If one becomes preoccupied with the staging, one forgets what brought it about, and it is reduced to a mere spectacle in front of witnesses. Here is the thesis: '[...] Roberte must remain Octave's unexchangeable good, or the entire enterprise makes no sense [...].'[36] If Roberte is Octave's unexchangeable good, then she is an incomparable good, one that lies beyond the full set of goods and is therefore priceless (price being an abstract assurance of relative comparison and measure). As a unique good, she can be neither given away nor presented as a gift.

33 *Ibid.*, p. 14.
34 *Ibid.*
35 *Ibid.*
36 *Ibid.*

She cannot circulate, she cannot even be the gift made to the guest that constitutes the Hospitality. This custom '[...] makes sense only because it is contradictory.'[37] In the terms of the everyday signs, the wording of the Hospitality is contradictory. When it is related to the unique sign of the name 'Roberte', it has a unique and thus un-transmittable meaning, and there is no name to designate it. Once underway, this custom enciphers Octave's jouissance, and for Klossowski, one's jouissance is precisely that incommunicable part of one's essence: 'Octave does not feel the jouissance of his inalienable good except through alienating it each time.'[38] To take stock of his wife's unexchangeability, our protagonist must necessarily go via everyday exchange. To bring about the unique sign as impossible and nameless, the interplay of signifiers must necessarily be engaged. The other's gaze increases the wife's value. When this scene is reproduced, Octave's jouissance gains in intensity. The split between coherence and incoherence, between jouissance and everyday code, remains exasperated, and is pushed to its limit.

Klossowski continues, pointing out the misunderstandings that can arise from reading the *Laws*. How is Octave's attitude to be described?

> Since it concerns the life of a couple, Octave's behaviour with Roberte and her reactions are understood by the reader only through the schema of the monogamous logic of adultery.[39]

What is practiced is referred to common conceptual tools that are supposed to give a communicable meaning. For example: whoever speaks of adultery presupposes the existence of monogamous marriage. In this way, incomprehension logically arises:

> If one tries to formulate the laws of hospitality, Octave's behaviour comes to the simplest representation one can have of his attitude: the husband orders his wife to commit adultery. It is the same with Roberte's behaviour: she betrays in order to

37 *Ibid.*
38 *Ibid.*, pp. 14–15.
39 *Ibid.*, p. 15.

> stay faithful to the husband. When you come right down to it, neither statement is comprehensible – 'to stay faithful to the husband' seems absurd.[40]

The absurdity that emerges from these statements is down to the use of the code of everyday signs which segment and analyse piece by piece in order to understand and explain:

> [...] to describe the contents of the experience according to this logic (the everyday code) [...] is to decompose it directly into intelligible experiences that never correspond with the indissoluble whole lived by Octave.[41]

This 'indissoluble whole' is the intensity of the waxing and waning, and above all in its highest degree of manifestation where coherence of thought is reached and exercises its constraint over the subject's mental life. Klossowski names this high point of intensity for Octave: jouissance.

Our theoretician argues that another possibility would be to say: 'Octave is a voyeur.'[42] Such an explanation continues to ignore the whole that Octave experiences since, in this case, it contents itself with designating Hospitality by another reference from the everyday code: libertinage. Now, libertinage is simply the term-for-term inverse of the fidelity of monogamous marriage. The question lies elsewhere. It comes down to the very code of everyday signs.

> No content of experience can ever be communicated except by virtue of conceptual ruts that are dug into minds by the code of everyday signs; and, conversely, the code of everyday signs censures all content of experience.[43]

Going via the everyday code always ends up at the same result: the content of the intensity leaks away.

40 *Ibid.*, p. 16.
41 *Ibid.*
42 *Ibid.*
43 *Ibid.*, p. 17.

At this stage in his demonstration, Klossowski's step forward envisages the consequences of the logic of everyday signs. '[...] all that is communicable must be able to be enounced according to the very principle of this logic: i.e. the principle of contradiction that excludes all possible ambiguity.'[44] Monogamous marriage must be restored within the framework of this founding principle:

> The monogamous logic of adultery disposes of a general and precise communication, implicit in the transgression of the forbidden: you must not covet the other's good. The forbidden affirms ownership of a person, here an inalienable object [...].[45]

This logic is based on a presupposition: the ownership and identity of the 'responsible ego'.[46] Non-contradiction, identity, ego and ownership are inseparable.

Libertine logic has the same presuppositions:

> We remain here in the same conceptual place: in the name of the principle of identity, be it of propriety, both adultery and (libertine) prostitution are forbidden. [...] And because both are enounced together as forbidden, it is precisely this interdiction that guarantees the intelligible expression of the contents of the experience named adultery or prostitution.[47]

These remarks, which allow us to grasp what is at stake in drafting the Laws, cannot be dissociated from the lessons learnt from Sade and Nietzsche. The text of the Laws takes up the same advances in the numerous texts written by Klossowski on the Marquis and the Sils-Maria philosopher. But because the concepts employed and the problematic chosen redeploy these theological examinations in fiction this time, our author will say that the custom promoted by Octave has no historical or conceptual reference points.

How is one to move forward? How is one to get out of this impasse? In what way will the Laws

44 *Ibid.*
45 *Ibid.*
46 *Ibid.*, p. 18.
47 *Ibid.*, p. 19.

> [...] get around the unilateral interpretation of adultery, how will the couple avoid the interdiction placed on adultery and libertine prostitution if these things are the conditions of the hospitality they offer?[48]

The response is a remarkable one: the practice of the Laws 'would logically [...] respond to the content of the experience, at its origin.'[49] What does this mean? How could such a thing be possible? Hospitality brings about, in the *hic et nunc* of what it stages,

> [...] the apprehension of many women inside the one and only wife (interiorised polygamy), and this at the dictates of de facto polyandry, the wife's commerce with several men, that each time reveals a different woman inside the same woman.[50]

The ego is abolished along with the unity that ensures it. The person is shattered, despite its unique agent and self-same physiognomy. The person metamorphoses and becomes multiple, which is incomprehensible for a logic of non-contradiction, the guarantor of egoic unity.

> [...] misunderstanding Octave's experience, according to the directives of this logic, [the reader] will 'conclude' only jealousy and infidelity, both of which only express the states of jouissance and suffering that result from despoliation – while for Octave, these two pathetic instances reunite in a supreme possession.[51]

To speak of jealousy or infidelity is to presuppose a unity: the person. If the person falls apart, if the person becomes plural, speaking in terms of jealousy or infidelity no longer has any meaning.

In the conclusion of this oeuvre we meet an unusual formulation that unpicks the currently accepted schemes of thinking and interpreting:

> The logic of the adulterer, based on propriety and that consecrates the inalienable, must ignore the unexchangeable emotion of this supreme possession and remove its internal contradiction: nothing makes one prostitute his goods, or his wife. [...]

48 *Ibid.*

49 *Ibid.*

50 *Ibid.*, p. 20.

51 *Ibid.*

> There is nothing to impose this on the other. Common sense ensures a silence on this type of communication, because the principle of non-contradiction is the basis of intelligible, monogamous propriety [...].[52]

This is why, in affirming the ego's abolition in favour of several women in one, and several men for one woman, Klossowski posits (and herein lies his key contribution) the '[...] *a contrario* demonstration: I do not think of taking back that which I give to another.'[53] This is the lack of jealousy and infidelity. 'Here, any comprehension of the formulation of the laws of hospitality is excluded: only through the alienation of my goods do they remain inalienable'.[54]

Hospitality is not communicable and therefore non-practicable using the criteria of the signs of current comprehension. No man or woman may perform this custom, or rather, it might happen that by performing it they become other, multiple and plural. Only to implement it, the agents would each have to bring together several persons, the multiple and the plural would thus have to be actualised. Utopia is rearing its head! The same gnawing question is back: 'How to extract the emotion from its stereotypical communication?'[55]

The Practice of Hospitality

Antoine's Troubles

Roberte Ce Soir occupies a pivotal place in Klossowski's oeuvre (as much his art oeuvre as his literary oeuvre). On the first pages of this narrative, Octave's declaration of the Laws is minutely relayed by Antoine, Octave's

52 *Ibid.*
53 *Ibid.*
54 *Ibid.*
55 *Ibid.*, p. 11.

nephew, adopted by the childless couple at the age of thirteen. Today, around seventeen years of age, he is studying for his Baccalaureate with private tutors chosen by his new parents. The fiction hints that these various tutors have been recruited for odd reasons, bearing little relation to schooling. They seem to have been Octave's 'guests', and therefore Roberte's lovers. This is explicit in the case of Victor, whose real name is Vittorio comte delle Santa-Sede (i.e. the Holy-See)!

> My uncle thought it necessary I be given a tutor, and I had a series of three, all chosen from among his and my aunt's acquaintances. They used to have a good many visitors at their summer home. This or that guest would suddenly be declared responsible for my education; a few months later, sometimes a few weeks later, he would disappear.[56]

Antoine's home education is caught up in the implementation of the laws of Hospitality. Indirectly, his education is a veritable sexual education that for Octave ties together the carnal and spiritual.[57] Antoine is the narrator of the introduction to *Roberte Ce Soir*, and of what follows in as much as he 'thought it worthwhile to note certain of [Octave's] digressions and to reproduce them in the context of this extraordinary experience of my student years'.[58]

Antoine's adolescence has been 'trying'.[59] What was going on? 'My aunt treated me like a brother [...].'[60] As for the professor, he made his nephew 'his favourite disciple'.[61] He teaches him theology and instructs him in scholastic argument. Octave goes further by setting Antoine practical work projects on this teaching. What is debated in theological and scholastic theory must become for the teenager an involving practical experience. This experience will be the staging of the laws of Hospitality: 'I served as a pretext for the practise of that hospitality which was practised at my aunt's

56 Klossowski, P., *Roberte Ce Soir* and *The Revocation of the Edict of Nantes*, *op. cit.*, p. 10.

57 *Ibid.*

58 *Ibid.*

59 *Ibid.*, p. 9.

60 *Ibid.*

61 *Ibid.*

expense.'[62] Such an 'atmosphere in the house'[63] is only possible due to the disturbance Roberte provokes in her nephew:

> It is true enough that Aunt Roberte had aroused a storm of emotions in me. But my uncle, having correctly guessed what the matter was, took perfidious advantage of it in order to contemplate his own perversity at work in me.[64]

Octave needed a locus in which to experience his theological-doctrinal flights of fancy, and Antoine's sexual disturbance faced with his aunt Roberte's youth and beauty was his pretext. Octave will provoke Antoine's troubles, sustaining them and giving them greater density:

> As with most boys at that age, my passion strove along thoroughly platonic lines. My uncle managed to transform it into a perfect nest of vipers, I don't know how else to describe the awful tangle of carnal and spiritual desires which the mental torture he inflicted upon me shortly had seething inside my breast.[65]

Such a scene is reminiscent of Sade's *Philosophy in the Bedroom*. Octave is a new immoral instructor, a new Dolmancé. Antoine will be witness to a hospitality, 'which our traditions condemn as shameful';[66] it will reveal to him his carnal desire for his aunt, and it will disturb him.

How does Octave go about perverting his young nephew (the actualised form of his authentic education)?

> OCTAVE: [...] I should have to ask you some rather pointed questions.
> ANTOINE: Uncle Octave, I should be only too happy ...
> OCTAVE: You must realise from the start that once they are asked you are going to be less free, even if you refuse to answer.
> ANTOINE: What good is my freedom? I don't know what to use it for. Hearing you say what I don't dare admit to myself will be a relief for me. Your words will give me a clearer image of myself.[67]

62 *Ibid.*
63 *Ibid.*
64 *Ibid.*, p. 10.
65 *Ibid.*
66 *Ibid.*, p. 9.
67 *Ibid.*, p. 21.

The dialogue continues.

> ANTOINE (puzzled): Whatever are you aiming at?
> OCTAVE: Simply at fulfilling your dreams.
> ANTOINE (startled): You ... my ... with my aunt?
> OCTAVE (reassuring him): Don't rush to any conclusions. Nothing is more ... impalpable in spite of appearances ... [...].[68]

The teaching begins: Octave makes his nephew recite the theological principles he has learnt and immediately gets him to apply them to the person of Roberte, constantly titillating and exasperating his troubled desire. Antoine confesses that for him Roberte is both an unbeliever *and* austere. Octave pounces on these words, twists them around and fires them back at the dumbfounded Antoine who exclaims: 'Uncle Octave, I'm afraid I don't know.'[69] The professor's demonstration is to shed light on Antoine's hesitant carnal desires:

> OCTAVE: As for her unbelief, I know all about that. But what am I to make of this austerity you ascribe to her?
> ANTOINE: That's an unfortunate term.
> OCTAVE: Could it be your way of indirectly referring to your pique?
> (Antoine is silent.)
> OCTAVE: She looks austere to you because her unbelief does not lead her to loose behaviour?
> ANTOINE: Maybe.
> OCTAVE: But you none the less hold out hope of some loose behaviour from her?
> (Antoine is silent again.)
> OCTAVE: Still, everything about her encourages you to anticipate such behaviour?
> ANTOINE: It's simply a mental picture I have of her.
> OCTAVE: [...] For the only inactuality that is familiar to you is that she is unbelieving and that your desires cannot exploit this quality as you would like it. From this you conclude she is austere [...].[70]

68 *Ibid.*, p. 23.
69 *Ibid.*, p. 34.
70 *Ibid.*, pp. 30–1.

Even if he only knows it in a very confused way, Roberte's austerity designates for Antoine her sexual reserve towards him. Her unbelief should lead to loose behaviour that is not forthcoming. Or, more specifically, not yet forthcoming.

Indeed, and this is why the initiatory education exists, the end of *Roberte Ce Soir* presents a scene that has been set up for Antoine: Victor comes in and starts to attend to Roberte sexually while she is giving the teenager a lesson on fraternity in work:

> Free yourself from the obsession of a dogmatic transcendence and discover a real transcendence in the brotherhood of practical effort; that is the only effort which can possibly give meaning to this life.[71]

Antoine is elsewhere; he listens to these conventional statements with a distracted ear. His attraction for his aunt sweeps over him with particular intensity:

> She still has to come to the end of her sentence when Antoine sees Victor enter the room. And as the call comes from Antoine, 'Don't talk, I want to see some more ...', Roberte turns around, stands rooted to the spot at the sight of Victor [...].[72]

There follows a description in which Roberte is violated by Victor. For both of them, Antoine is the spectator to whom they show what he must now learn and know. The mental fiction that preoccupies the teenager emerges in reality, taking on form. His own fiction, stirred up by Octave, erupts.

> Then, having twirled Roberte around only so fast as to give Antoine a view of his young aunt's buttocks, her thighs, the back of her knees and her long legs sheathed in black, Victor settles her upon his sedcontra,[73] holding her by both wrists from the rear while she receives the major probation, perched on the tip of her toes. And as Antoine has fled into hiding behind a curtain, too moved to bear the sight, he is startled by a hoarse howl and made to look again [...].[74]

71 *Ibid.*, p. 90.

72 *Ibid.*

73 His penis.

74 Klossowski, P., *Roberte Ce Soir* and *The Revocation of the Edict of Nantes*, *op. cit.*, pp. 91–2.

The fact that Antoine is a spectator of this scene orchestrated by the elderly Octave is essential, and is a reference found several times in the novels. Antoine is *the one who is shown*, with an aim that is pedagogical, educative and initiatory. This is how the logic behind Octave's drafting of the Laws, and Roberte's submission, will be understood. In his 1994 interviews with Alain Jouffroy, Klossowski makes reference to the presence of the adolescent, at a time when for several years he had been painting only young, somewhat androgynous boys.

> KLOSSOWSKI: In general [...], the adolescent was a theme I never talked about, even though it was often present in the *Roberte* books, the adolescent being Roberte's nephew Antoine, behind whom Uncle Octave was hiding, the one who made sure Antoine got aroused by Roberte. In a way, the subject was the emotion produced by Roberte, a mature woman, on young boys of thirteen, fourteen or fifteen.
> JOUFFROY: In your written works, the theme of the adolescent constitutes, [...] in perspectival terms, the vanishing point.
> KLOSSOWSKI: Yes. In fact the theme of the adolescent was declared right back on the opening pages of *Roberte Ce Soir*. Psychologically speaking, the adolescent has the role of a screen in relation to the mature woman, in as much as she can overwhelm such young people. [...] Her image is very important to an adolescent who has not yet had a fling. [...] His fling is these representations. The adolescent is the emotional screen onto which the figure of Roberte is projected, all of which is penned as it would be pictured by a young boy, who is in some sense traumatised, – and not by a lover.[75]

Klossowski specifies that there are

> [...] accomplished women, therefore authoritative and all the more so since they appear to be frivolous, though they know perfectly well how to master their temperament, and who seem austere and severe in relation to the emotions they might give rise to. These are the situations I tried to describe. They make for [...] interesting scenes: the young boy's contemplation of a woman's radiant body.[76]

Jean-Noël Vuarnet points out the age gaps between the three characters: Octave, Roberte and Antoine.

75 Translated from Jouffroy, A., and Klossowski, P., *Le secret pouvoir du sens, Entretiens*, Editions Écriture, Paris, 1994, pp. 28–30.

76 *Ibid.*, p. 31.

> Roberte's representation (for an old man of whom she could be the daughter, and by virtue of the intercession of a young man of whom she is not the mother) of [...] an educating aunt [...] works only because the stereotypical old man still exists, and because the young man is the 'virgin' witness. In this way, the gaze of an aged man, as well as the gaze of one too young, bring the marionette to life and animate it [...].[77]

Octave tires himself out trying to ascertain a young boy's first sexual turmoil. Far from simply lying in wait for it in passive contemplation, he must be active: if he is to organise the boy's education, then he must experientially isolate the very moment Roberte becomes explicitly insinuated in the teenager's dreams for the first time. Octave has to come back to this point of origin where the disturbance is first embodied as an image on the unblemished screen of the teenager's mind. Klossowski's narrative makes a picture from this image, the same picture that is described (and shown) to the reader. Klossowski will unhesitatingly confirm that this teenager is himself, the adolescent he once was:

> JOUFFROY: But isn't this adolescent you, when you were younger?
> KLOSSOWSKI: Yes, it's me, in the sense that I was moved, like others, back when I was twelve or thirteen, by the seduction of women who were no longer young girls [...].[78]

Octave (and Klossowski with him) wants to get back to this first turmoil, to his first visions where a married woman is implied in his desire, to those ancient images that encipher the disturbance from back when.

In the fiction *Roberte Ce Soir*, one has to reckon with the perfidy and 'perversity'[79] of the theologian Octave. Antoine becomes the screen on which the terrible pornographic scenes of Hospitality will be played out. Octave produces a spectacle for his nephew, to excite and torture him, of his aunt's irrupting sexual pleasure when her violator takes her:

77 Translated from Vuarnet, J.-N., 'Trios fragments pour Pierre Klossowski', *Roberte au cinema*, Obliques, Editions Borderie, Paris, 1978, p. 100.

78 Jouffroy, A., and Klossowski, P., *Le secret pouvoir du sens, Entretiens, op. cit.*, p. 31.

79 Klossowski, P., *Roberte Ce Soir* and *The Revocation of the Edict of Nantes, op. cit.*, p. 10.

> But while [Victor] fondles her buttocks, Roberte [...] gradually lowers her hand, straightens out her fingers, finds Victor's sedcontra, would thrust it aside and, without letting loose, leans slowly back. [...] Roberte, her skirt still raised, with one hand seems to be adjusting her girdle or her stockings while with the other, holding them between the tips of her fingers, she tenders Victor a pair of keys which he touches without ever taking: for the two of them seem hanging in suspense in their respective positions.[80]

After the violation, where Roberte had in fact consented to her degradation and debasement, the scene becomes immobilised. It is jammed onto the image of Antoine's fascination; without the screen of his mind, the Laws could not have been practised. The image comes to a halt with Antoine's fascination as he is forced to watch, immobilised and paralysed, from the point at which he has become a blind gaze. At the end of the line, is he not identical to the gaze of the sleazy Octave? Unless Octave himself has not been reduced to the de-subjectified gaze of the adolescent he has initiated?

The Instant of the Opened Door

We are now aware of Octave's illness. Antoine reports that Octave believes himself to be 'the foremost victim of this equivocal situation',[81] in other words, of this impossible overlay of Roberte's (hidden) soul onto her (apparent) body. The law of hospitality has no other goal than to bring Octave out of his 'perplexity'[82] in the face of this equivocation: her austere physiognomy is mere appearance – but the invisible essence that makes up her very being is restless with frivolity. This is Roberte the whore. The necessity of this being put into practice, in calling upon a guest, emerged at the instant their bodies met. In Octave's mind, the encounter would take place as follows: 'When my Uncle Octave took my Aunt Roberte in his

80 *Ibid.*, pp. 90 & 92.
81 *Ibid.*, p. 9.
82 *Ibid.*

arms, one must not suppose that in taking her he was alone.'[83] Before he even takes her, a third party – the guest – has appeared.

In this system he has organised, Octave lowers himself to the role of he who walks in on Roberte and the guest 'just in time'.[84] He makes himself the witness of his wife's sexual encounter with the lover he intended for her. This instant '[...] was all over and done with in the twinkling on an eye, and once again [Octave] would be on the point of taking [Roberte] in his arms.'[85] It was the instant of the 'opened door':[86]

> [...] Octave would have been asking too much had he wished to prolong the instant of the opened door, he was already doing exceedingly well in getting the guest to appear in the doorway at the precise moment he did, getting the guest to loom up behind Roberte so that he, Octave, might be able to sense that he himself was the guest as, borrowing from the guest his door-opening gesture, he could behold them from the threshold and have the impression that it was he, Octave, who was taking [Roberte] by surprise.[87]

This moment of 'fulguration'[88] where, in the crack of the door that opens onto the eagerly awaited scene, the gaze that Octave has reduced himself to is released; the husband makes himself the voyeur of his wife in the arms of the guest.

From this point on, the husband has become the guest: he has come from without, he has taken on his gestures, he becomes his gaze settled on Roberte. But Octave has not, for all that, left his own place behind: he sees the guest he has become approaching the wife and surprise her with his unforeseen, fortuitous presence. He is at once the guest and the spectator of the scene. He sees himself as the guest about to take Roberte; he becomes his step, his arm, his mouth. He is both a spectator and an actor of this

83 *Ibid.*, p. 11.
84 *Ibid.*
85 *Ibid.*
86 *Ibid.*
87 *Ibid.*
88 Lacan, J., 'Logical Time and the Assertion of Anticipated Certainty' in *Écrits, The First Complete Edition in English*, *op. cit.*, p. 167.

scene. He sees himself as he might observe himself in a film rolling under his control. The goal Octave is seeking – he insists on this by employing expressions from Thomist theology, amongst others – is for there to be an 'essential' relationship established between his wife and the guest – i.e. a relationship in which both their essences encounter each other, join, and become one, as opposed to an accidental relationship that is only a partial, limited, and fragmentary encounter. It is a question of bringing about, between the husband and his guest,

> not [...] a relative relationship but an absolute one, as though, the master becoming one with the stranger, his relationship with you who have just set foot here were now but a relationship with yourself.[89]

By identifying himself with the gaze of the third party, the latter becomes for Octave a kind of double. It is no longer another party who would be part of him, it is utterly him, with no leftover, no loss. In this mirroring, the guest stands as the reflection of the husband who, in return, is laid bare as a pure reflection of this third party he has merged with. The guest is Octave and Octave is the guest, but Octave is also Octave, he remains Octave, who sees himself become the guest outside him. Our theologian insists on this total reciprocity, where, by means of imaginary identification, two people (one and his reflected double) become one essence. We obtain through the image what the image cannot provide: fusion between the guest's and the husband's very being.

> For with the stranger he welcomes, the master of the house seeks a no longer accidental, but an essential relationship. At the start the two are but isolated substances, between there is none but accidental communication: you who believe yourself far from home in the home of someone you believe to be at home, you bring merely the accidents of your substance, such accidents as conspire to make a stranger of you, to him who bids you avail yourself of all that makes a merely accidental host of him. But because the master of this house herewith invites the stranger to penetrate to the source of all substances beyond the realm of all accident, this is how he inaugurates a substantial relationship between himself and the stranger [...].[90]

89 Klossowski, P., *Roberte Ce Soir* and *The Revocation of the Edict of Nantes*, *op. cit.*, p. 13.
90 *Ibid.*, p. 12.

Such insistence brings out the subject's furious determination, within the logic of the imaginary process, to rid identification of anything left out: the switchover to the other party must be total. Nothing can, nothing must remain outside its realisation.

For Klossowski, his character's reasoning demonstrates this. He who watches on is beside himself, becoming another party entirely, and this other party is him. Théodore, the narrator of *Le Souffleur* and Octave's alter ego (as well as Klossowki's), will most accurately describe the subjective effects of this switchover to the other party, this massive imaginary identification:

> I have been trying for years to slip behind our life, in order to see it. I have thus been endeavouring to grasp life by staying outside it, where it has a completely different aspect. If we see it from there, we approach an unsustainable bliss [...].[91]

Without all this he would have the 'the strong sensation of being blown out like a humble candle.'[92] Becoming the gaze gives him a consistency of being that, in practical terms, his everyday existence absolutely cannot give him, riddled as it is with doubts, ambiguity, and suspicions. We can see here the pertinent contrast between becoming an object and experiencing oneself as a subject. By making himself an object in his fantasy, the subject Théodore receives assurance. Théodore insists a great deal on this loss of consistency that disconnects him – where the reality of his life and his world splits in two.

> I've been looking in vain for the facts of this last period of my life, but I find only reflections, resonances, and I don't manage to get back to their source. Some events lead to others, and we attach ourselves to them, working things out so as to live with the least amount of pain possible. But these reflections blind me, the resonances deafen me. [...] Faces, gestures, light and shadow and an incessant murmur take over my thoughts, and I am surprised that these perpetual undulations can reflect so much in the uncertainty of having lived them.[93]

91 Klossowski, P., 'Le Souffleur', *Les lois de l'hospitalité*, *op. cit.*, p. 187.

92 *Ibid.*, p. 245.

93 *Ibid.*, pp. 191–2.

He describes 'the inconsistency of thought'.[94]

In an attempt to halt the flight of being, where any grasp that might provide a stopping point and mark out a boundary simply slips away, Théodore (like Octave) makes himself the object gaze. He wants to pass over to the other side where, he supposes, he would be able to observe, from a calm and concrete place, the whirlwind of the lives of others, and his own, with the changing and enigmatic Roberte. '[...] I force myself to look [...].'[95] We can see here his ultimate attempt to get back to the 'source'[96] of these multiple mirrorings and dual reflections devoid of substance. It is a question of being able to see from this invisible, unlocatable vantage point – to see life from outside life.

Théodore must pay the highest price in order to slip behind the scene of his life: exchanging his own 'time to live for the time lived by another.'[97] This other party is a dead man whom he will call his 'Guide'.[98] Having become this old man now deceased, he can see life from the beyond, from death. Théodore signs a contract with the old man.

> Does this mean that I've swapped my own gaze for that of an old man in decline? Could my eyes not bear what would be seen as our own life, once and for all? Did I have the confused feeling that Roberte's face would deteriorate and withdraw as soon as it stopped offering itself to the greed that forms the warp and weft of life?[99]

Théodore knows he must reply in the affirmative to these terrible questions, where a subject relinquishes his own life for that of a dead other. It was the price to pay to discover his wife's hidden soul. 'Rather than grow old tranquilly near [Roberte], I conjured an old age that did not belong to me, so I could [see] from the shadow of a senile figure's past perversity [...]'.[100]

94 *Ibid.*, p. 192.
95 *Ibid.*, p. 191.
96 *Ibid.*
97 *Ibid.*, p. 187.
98 *Ibid.*, p. 181.
99 *Ibid.*, p. 187.
100 *Ibid.*

Our protagonist relays a very odd scene: just as he is passing away, the old man 'removed his face',[101] and said to Théodore: 'I've constituted myself only by making you out of all that I've hidden from view. [...] I leave you my hollow face so that you can fill it as you will [...].[102] Since then, Théodore has been no more than 'his gaze – a gaze that someone with marital status could never cast.'[103] Théodore can become Roberte's voyeur by identifying himself with this absolute Other. On one encounter with the already deceased old man, he slips away from himself:

> [...] I had a blind spell [...] I stopped seeing. Was I moving like a drowning man? Almost immediately I heard steps approach, and then I felt support. (The old man appears). Things aren't going well with you? Now, now, don't hit yourself [...] here, I'll guide you! [...] He made me sit down in his invalid's chair, I, who had been agile just minutes before, and massaged my temples with his skeletal fingers. I was taken over by an unspeakable relief, even though the chair had started sliding, pushed as I was by the core of his own thoughts.[104]

Now that he has become the Guide's thought, Théodore sees associated visions. Where a moment ago he was blind, he now sees the Other Roberte:

> In the greenish shadows, a young woman in a flat, straw hat, a white veil covering her face and wearing a turquoise suit, leaned against one of the trunks, looking furtively around her from the shrubs.[105]

The Other Roberte is in her stage clothes, and the show is about to begin. This is what permits an identification with the old man's gaze.

What does this show present us?

> She slowly took off her gloves, removed her jacket and, suddenly nude, stretched herself out in the ivy, arms folded under her veiled head revealing her underarms, and then, with a finger raising the veil over her lips, started to kiss the curve of her shoulders. Still keeping one arm under her head, she brought the other to her chest,

101 *Ibid.*, p. 188.
102 *Ibid.*
103 *Ibid.*
104 *Ibid.*, pp. 188–90.
105 *Ibid.*, p. 190.

> moved her fingers around her breasts, and sliding the palm of her open hand over the fullness of her belly, slipped her long fingers into her fleece while raising a superb thigh, her head falling into the ivy.[106]

Théodore, who watches this scene immobilised in the old man's invalid seat, speaks of 'revelation'.[107]

However – and this is an important point – our protagonist is also on stage, going about his everyday life with his spouse. But this life loses all relevance, is undermined and emptied from within: it unfolds under the dead man's all seeing, tirelessly active eye. Théodore insists on his own position in the scheme: he has become invisible, now no one can suspect his presence. '[...] vision had become my last chance for salvation. [...] The only certitude of my existence consisted in the fact of my seeing what happened, when one believed I wasn't there'.[108]

According to Klossowski, only by making himself an object, equivalent to another's de-subjectified gaze (the paradigm being the gaze of the dead man who steals his life) can the voyeur become certain of his existence. Turning into the gaze is an eloquent process of the lowest de-subjectification, and once it is accomplished, the voyeur, as a subject, is an 'entirely hidden gaze',[109] to use Lacan's expression. For this gaze can only operate when, as Théodore affirms, 'they believe I'm not there!'[110] This hidden gaze is the last residue of any kind of subjectivity. This set-up reveals itself to be a progressive and logical process of symbolic reduction: a minimal, implied subjective structure is the counterpart to a maximum of libidinal investment – as Théodore says, 'unsustainable bliss'.[111]

The Klossowskian voyeur is, in the strict sense of the term, Living dead. This is what *Le Souffleur* shows us: a living being that can approach life only through the gaze of someone deceased and who, in this capacity, sees

106 *Ibid.*

107 *Ibid.*, p. 191.

108 *Ibid.*, p. 192.

109 Lacan, J., *The Seminar Book XI, The Four Fundamental Concepts of Psychoanalysis*, trans. A. Sheridan, Penguin, London, 1994, p. 182.

110 Klossowski, P., 'Le Souffleur', *Les lois de l'hospitalité*, *op. cit.*, p. 192.

111 *Ibid.*, p. 187.

his life stolen from him. A dead man who, on becoming eternal, maintains the comic spectacle of life but only by immobilising and suspending it. The Klossowskian voyeur is a dead man in the imaginary sense: though dead, he remains eternally present like a statue – he cannot die. Such is the subjective result of imaginarisation, which multiplies the symmetrical reciprocities of narcissistic duality. Here, the prevalent imaginary dialectic turns round and round with no way out. Indeed, Hospitality such as it is written down by Octave (and Théodore) implies a practically endless stream of guests to whom our protagonist offers Roberte, one after the next. It is the compelling renewal of viewpoint: what if this next guest were finally to enable him to know whether Roberte is pure or defiled, loyal or a whore? By multiplying these others who repeatedly divest him of his life, the Klossowskian voyeur is thus broken into a multitude of massive identifications, diffracted into an anonymous 'thousand-fold gaze'.[112] These split and redoubled gazes cannot form a closed set in which Roberte might deliver up her hidden soul, her closely guarded secret. One guest is always missing, a new vantage point on Roberte is always possible. *Walking in on the wife with the guest* becomes an endless task whose completion is all the more elusive at each attempt: the instant of the opened door strains to be interminably reproduced. The practice of Hospitality cannot bring it about: it fails through the very means of its performance. The imaginarisation of this system runs idle, stuck in an infinite, fragmented logic – the prerogative of metonymy where only the arbitrary and relative govern.

This is what Théodore, disillusioned and in particularly bad shape, acknowledges:

> Nothing other than this grievous need to have what is most intimate to me verified by the strangest, most foreign minds, the antipodes of my soul, this tragic weakness to solicit others' arbitration, which itself reposes on the arbitrary, was in order to obtain the ratification of everything in my life that should have remained forever unutterable.[113]

112 *Ibid.*, p. 213.
113 *Ibid.*, p. 279.

Our voyeur suffers from his conjugal happiness. This is the illness he thinks he can rid himself of by communicating it to others. But each gaze that bears down on the enigma of Roberte poses anew the question of the last word: the enigma echoes on. No certainty whatsoever can be obtained. By becoming the gaze the subject does indeed obtain a point of assurance and certitude: the enciphering of the jouissance localised in the phantasmatic scenario leads to the creation of the ritual, but what is being aimed at, namely Roberte's soul, slips further away with each repetition. Octave/Théodore is ill forever.

Roberte in her Entirety?

There is no 'whole' Roberte for Théodore in *Le Souffleur*. But in the fiction of the first two narratives of the trilogy, *Roberte Ce Soir* and *The Revocation of the Edict of Nantes*, Octave tires himself out willing her into being. To manage this, he will call upon the knowledge of his profession: theology. Of course, Octave will inevitably run aground on this same impossibility: Roberte's essence cannot be isolated and hoarded, but his reasoning, with its exemplary verve emptied of all psychologising, teaches us a valuable lesson about what such a subject aims at, and the logic behind his fantasy. This lesson is presented in three phases which we shall examine below.

The Essence of the Wife

What Octave/Théodore can now see thanks to the gaze of the guest (the dead Guide) is this: Roberte is prey to a sexual turmoil that she provokes in herself by touching herself and masturbating – 'More stunning than ever, Roberte smiled, embarrassed by the pleasure she gave herself.'[114] But what

114 *Ibid.*, p. 190.

our voyeur aims at is something else. In other words, what does he try to grasp through this gaze that settles on Roberte?

According to the principles of Hospitality drawn up by our theologian, parodying the terminology of Saint Thomas Aquinas, it is Roberte's 'inactual essence'[115] that must be revealed. One must 'judge and discover the underlying Roberte'[116] behind the appearances of the physiognomy of her body, and invoke the guest to 'reveal the inactuality of Roberte which escapes us and which is nothing other than her essence.'[117] Her essence then merges with inactuality, but actuality or inactuality only exists when a third party seeks it out. For Octave, the essence of his spouse is that part of her that is hidden to him – and everything that eludes him constitutes her essence. In other words, Octave's definition of essence is an oriented one: for him there is an absolute, necessarily present secret from which he is excluded; uncovering this secret would allow him to know the essence of his spouse. Roberte's secret is her essence. Her essence is what is unknown for the husband, and therefore, what is stolen from him. In Octave's reasoning, secret and essence become strictly synonymous. Hence the following example, which presents itself as a degraded form of the secret and therefore of Roberte's inactual essence:

> OCTAVE: [...] didn't you say that for you your aunt is like an elder sister, attentive and severe at the same time?
> ANTOINE: I did.
> OCTAVE: Attentiveness and severity are things you grasp in her whereas I do not; they are inactual for me, actual for you.
> ANTOINE: Granted.
> OCTAVE: And didn't you go on to say that she is somewhat contemptuous of my most serious studies?
> ANTOINE: I said that too.
> OCTAVE: And just a moment ago didn't you sum up your impressions in calling her unbelieving and austere?

115 Klossowski, P., *Roberte Ce Soir* and *The Revocation of the Edict of Nantes*, *op. cit.*, p. 13.
116 *Ibid.*, p. 30.
117 *Ibid.*, p. 31.

ANTOINE: I did indeed.
OCTAVE: All this – tell me, is it actual for me or for you?
ANTOINE: It is exactly how it appears in my mind.
OCTAVE: In your mind. So here is a part of my wife's inactuality revealed to me: the 'attentive and severe elder sister' posture she adopts as regards my nephew.[118]

What Antoine knows about Roberte, his would-be older sister, attentive and severe, constitutes an inactuality for Octave, and is therefore part of her inactual essence. If he is to gain access to this essence by making the actual inactual, it is then indispensable to go via another, in this case the nephew Antoine.

As for the *apparent* Roberte: the 'mistress of the house', the 'pampering spouse', she is without interest. She even constitutes an obstacle to Octave's research. 'The notion of mistress of the house reposes upon an essential basis: this essence is therefore subjected to restraint by her actual existence as mistress of the house.'[119] It is in defiance of the everyday spouse (the mistress of the house) that Octave will pursue his search for the 'absolute Roberte',[120] for the 'whole of Roberte',[121] the only one able to 'yield us her secret'[122] and who actualises herself only in the system of Hospitality: as the hostess. Only here can her essence be actualised, where she metamorphoses into the hostess that offers herself, at the beck of the host, to the guest who has come from the outside. In this capacity, the guest is very much a 'liberator'[123] of the inactualised essence in the banal mistress of the house.

This 'actualisation'[124] of the hostess's essence only has any value if the host can take part in it, if it is accessible to him. In other words, how will he be able to participate in the revealed essence of Roberte? This question leads to another: what about the essence of the host himself?

118 *Ibid.*, pp. 28–9.
119 *Ibid.*, p. 13.
120 *Ibid.*, p. 39.
121 *Ibid.*, p. 27.
122 *Ibid.*, p. 39.
123 *Ibid.*, p. 12.
124 *Ibid.*, p. 13.

He replies with a reference to the cause that he spells out at length: 'The host's essence – hospitality – […] aspires to convert into a presence the absence of cause […], and to actualise itself in that cause.'[125] Octave will insist that the host is 'not even anyone',[126] not even a subject. He stands, curious, in the place of the cause, at the instant of the opened door: the essence of the host 'is proposed as a homage of the host's curiosity to the essence of the hostess'.[127] This curiosity is the cause become present and actual. It is what gives body and shape to absence by (imaginarily) making positive that which initially inscribes itself as pure negativity. Here, the host must be distinguished from the master of the house. 'The host however is neither suspicious nor jealous, because he is essentially curious about that very thing which, in everyday life, would make a master of the house suspicious, jealous, unbearable.'[128] Jealousy and suspicion are typical of a master of the house, a subject caught up in the stereotyped affects of the logic of monogamous marriage. Curiosity is something quite different: it is what drives Octave to want to find out the enigma of Roberte's essence. It does not qualify a subjective position, but rather names the cause of what becomes an object set in motion: the gaze. The guest's responsibility lies here:

> […] it is for you, the guest, to discern the hostess's essence in the mistress of the house, for you to cast her forth from potentiality into existence: […] the hostess remains sheer phantasm and you a stranger in this house if you leave to the host the inactualised essence of the hostess […].[129]

According to the professor's reasoning, the guest is not the cause of anything at the start of the set-up. He is merely a means, an auxiliary, to 'make proof of the host's curiosity':[130] an absolute, pre-existent curiosity, the very essence of the host. Octave wants to establish his curiosity

125 *Ibid.*, p. 15.
126 *Ibid.*, p. 14.
127 *Ibid.*
128 *Ibid.*
129 *Ibid.*, p. 16.
130 *Ibid.*, p. 15.

(Théodore will later speak of his 'undisclosable dread'[131]) as the cause of the voyeuristic arrangement, as the veritable motor of the scene that gives the law of Hospitality its concrete form. This alone can bring forth Roberte's 'quiddity'. Curiosity is the essence of the host. However, by making himself gaze-object, by making himself sheer curiosity, what Octave cannot grasp is that he is not the cause of what is happening, but its effect. This subjective process is what our voyeur tries to evade. By refusing jealousy and suspicion – making them the sole privilege of the master of the house – he is no longer a divided subject with all his doubts, but sheer curiosity freed of all doubt. What he utterly cannot fathom is how he entered this system as a subject. For it is only at the end that he is reduced to the object-gaze, to this curiosity emptied of any signifier that would give him consistency of Being.

As Klossowski indicates, not without malice, '[...] realising that to attain his ends he needs means which concrete life does not afford, [...] Octave goes off to hunt for them in the obscurest mysticism.'[132] Indeed, converting the absence of cause into presence necessitates the 'visitation of an angel'[133] and not the simple presence of a human existence with its accidents and limitations. The guest would no longer be anything other than the mask of an angel: '[...] the angel is capable of concealing himself in the guise of the guest – is it you? – whom the host believes fortuitous.'[134] Only an angel, an 'increate intelligence',[135] because he is a bodiless, simple substance produced without the flesh,[136] would be able to actualise, in the mistress of the house, the essence of the hostess that 'is known to none but him who beyond all being knows.'[137] In this last remark the professor's secret wish is laid bare: to know Roberte's essence just as God knows it.

131 Klossowski, P., 'Le Souffleur', *Les lois de l'hospitalité*, *op. cit.*, p. 213.

132 Klossowski, P., *Roberte Ce Soir* and *The Revocation of the Edict of Nantes*, *op. cit.*, p. 15.

133 *Ibid.*

134 *Ibid.*

135 *Ibid.*, p. 40.

136 *Ibid.*, p. 70.

137 *Ibid.*, p. 16.

This is what is at stake in his curiosity: to be equal to divine knowledge. Roberte's equivocation would be dispelled. Through the visitation of this angel, God's direct messenger, 'solicited by the host's piety',[138] Octave's curiosity is led 'to the point where the mistress of the house [...] will be completely actualised in an existence which shall be determined by you alone, by you, the guest, and not by the host's curiosity'.[139]

A logic is deployed. First there is Octave's curiosity. He makes himself the voyeur of a scene that must actualise Roberte's essence, her un-dented being. But this essence slips away because his wife has a body. Only an angel can carry out such a task. Next, there is the point of subjective detonation where the actualisation of his wife's essence – this is Octave's supposition – would dislodge him from the place of mastery, the place of the absolute and explicit cause of the system. He immediately becomes an instrument: '[...] you are indeed that angel, and by your presence you give an actuality to the hostess: you shall have full power over her as well as over the host.'[140] In fact, '[...] the host shall be master in his house no more: he shall have carried out his mission.'[141] This turnaround whereby Octave reveals the place he occupies needs to be explained: whereas before he was the accidental master, now he becomes the 'black fetish'[142] essential to the service of God. *In fine*, Octave will have become God's angel – and Roberte's guest! The system freezes: by means of the angel with which he has now merged, our protagonist would be *the* gaze of God – his eternal voyeur.

The gaze of the stranger, the unknown party, the guest, the lover – a gaze that is almost infinitely multiplied in the practice of Hospitality – as well as the gaze of the deceased man (Théodore's Guide) are seen to be mere ersatz of the eternal, absolute gaze which nothing can escape: the gaze of God. The gaze of the third party with whom he identifies at the instant the door opens on the scene will forever bear the imprint of the gaze of the divine other. Only this panoptical gaze can reveal Roberte's

138 *Ibid.*

139 *Ibid.*

140 *Ibid.*

141 *Ibid.*

142 Lacan, J., 'Kant with Sade', *op. cit.*, p. 652.

entire essence. In this respect, God's gaze would be able to bring to a close the limitless series of the anonymous 'thousand-fold gaze'. The stream of endless identifications with the third party stops here: Hospitality can be realised. For the theologian Octave, God's gaze is the form taken by the *push-to-the-woman* that his fantasy subjects him to. We might recall Jacques Lacan's sentence in his unpublished Seminar *R.S.I.*: God is The Woman in her Entirety – wholly liberated from castration.

This reference to the angel, and then to God, explicitly opens Octave's reasoning to theological demonstration. To know Roberte as God knows her introduces the questions of hypostatic union and the Holy Trinity. What does this maze of thought amount to for our theologian? What does this appeal to theology and the mediaeval bring him?

The Pure Spirit

Realist naivety would equate the guest, Roberte's lover, with an embodied character: some man or other. Admittedly, Klossowski's narrative gives body to the guest. Precise physiognomies and agents actualise him in the practice of Hospitality. But even when the lover is a specified man, something else is involved. What Octave aims at above all else is the spirit.

What does the theologian mean by *spirit*, since this is the vocabulary our author employs, examines, and makes light of? The spirit is a being that is characterised by a double opening: on the one hand, onto absolute Being, God the Being par excellence, and on the other, onto what it is and what it is not in itself. This double opening onto universal Being and onto itself defines the two fundamental features of the spirit: transcendence and reflection. The human spirit has above all a finite, limited character. The finite character of the human spirit appears in the fact that it is bound by the necessity of a partial and unpredictable encounter with the 'stranger', and also, as a consequence of this, by his own body which is a mediator. The human spirit is not a 'pure spirit'; it is essentially a 'spirit-cum-soul', which is a specifically human spirit by virtue of being linked to a body, and therefore to space and time. Owing to its opening onto absolute being, the human spirit's ever finite reflections allow this immensity to subsist, although they can never respond in an adequate way to the infinite expectation of the spirit. Here then is the basic definition of the spirit for the human creature. On the other hand, God, as existing-absolutely-in-and-of-himself, cannot be said to be 'existing' in the same way as created beings. Being belongs to him absolutely and totally (*esse ipsum subsistens*). Being absolute and in eternal possession of himself, nothing can limit and nothing can be added to God. He is pure Act. It is this possession of the absolute, original and limitless self that makes God absolutely spiritual. He is pure Spirit.

What possible relationships are there between the human spirit, which is always *contaminated*, never pure, and the pure Spirit that is God? In his infinite Being, God remains absolute and absolutely Other, incomprehensible for this human and finite thought. God's infinitude can be neither circumscribed nor comprehended by any other party. On the contrary, it remains Unfathomable. It is the foundation of all cognition but can never become an 'object' within human cognition. God remains the absolute and impenetrable mystery. It is only by acknowledging him as such that God can be grasped as a 'he'.

It is in this context that Octave endeavours to track Roberte's essence. How does he go about it? His demonstration addressed to Antoine has the goal of instructing him and above all of initiating him into the mysteries of femininity.

> OCTAVE: At this very moment someone is standing between you, my nephew, and me, your uncle. [...] someone there all the same [...].
> ANTOINE: But between you and me? Who else is there, Uncle Octave?
> OCTAVE: He who even now is preventing us from understanding each other. [...] And yet without him we'd not be able to bring this off.
> ANTOINE: Some fourth person is involved?
> OCTAVE: No, a third, he who intrudes between you and me, between me and Aunt Roberte, between your Aunt and yourself.[143]

143 Klossowski, P., *Roberte Ce Soir* and *The Revocation of the Edict of Nantes*, *op. cit.*, pp. 21–2.

Antoine's retort is understandable: who on earth can this inhibiting third party be who puts up a screen between Octave, Roberte, and Antoine? Without him, an authentic communication would be possible between these three persons – Roberte's essence could be grasped, the mystery that makes her a woman would be dispelled.

> OCTAVE: And this third person is a pure spirit.
> ANTOINE: You're joking!
> OCTAVE: I have never been more serious. I have *named Roberte* to him.[144]

Here we see Octave's operation set in motion. This is where he starts to do his true practical work of theology! In what does appointing Roberte to the 'pure spirit' consist? What consequences does he expect? Recall the theological definition: the pure spirit is God, or the angels who are his messengers. Octave has appointed Roberte to God.

> OCTAVE: I named Roberte to the pure spirit. [...] Don't bother yourself with doubts of the possibility of doing something that has been done. And there is no undoing it now. You have got to accept things as they are, Antoine, otherwise it will be useless for us to continue.[145]

Octave insists on the extreme gravity of what he has just accomplished.

> OCTAVE: [...] instead of naming the spirit to Roberte, as my relations with her would ordinarily have led us to expect, the reverse took place. Unbeknown to your Aunt Roberte, I, your Uncle Octave, denounce my wife to a pure spirit.[146]

What would permit, according to the husband, such a denunciation – to be taken in the strongest sense of the word? 'Whereupon Roberte is made the *object* of a pure spirit, the latter thereupon becoming my accomplice.'[147] The Roberte who has become an object of pure spirit is no longer Living Roberte, present and palpable in her body. She is rather the object of a

144 *Ibid.*, p. 23.
145 *Ibid.*, p. 24.
146 *Ibid.*
147 *Ibid.*

pure symbolic entity, 'impalpable in spite of appearances.'[148] From now on, 'everything depends on the spirit.'[149] Octave is not saying that Roberte becomes an object for the thought of the one who thinks or speaks about her – such as himself or Antoine. Rather, the spouse becomes 'the object of that spirit's preoccupations',[150] the pure divine spirit. The mainspring of the professor's demonstration lies here: Octave does not know Roberte, he is not acquainted with the 'whole' Roberte beyond the pampering spouse. He does not know her essence. By naming her pure spirit, a way out of this impossibility seems to come into focus: 'Roberte eludes me to the point where I am obliged to invoke the pure spirit. [...] she becomes the object of his attention, in his attention to her there is revealed to me what she hides from me'.[151] Octave does not let go: Roberte, albeit unbeknown to her, hides something from him. By denouncing her to the pure spirit, she becomes one of his objects: an object that has consistency only as pure divine breath, her spirit freed of the contamination of language and of the body as a symbolic Other.

Should Octave manage to communicate with the pure spirit, Roberte, as an object of this spirit, would then become knowable, since the purity of this spirit indicates that it can be entirely communicated without any loss: like God unto himself, the spirit is pure transparency, pure communication. Being, as theology stipulates, belongs to God absolutely and totally. He is in eternal possession of himself. To denounce Roberte is to appoint to the pure spirit what constitutes an enigma for Octave – i.e. what he does not know of God, so that this secret, having become an object of the divine spirit, immediately opens up because God cannot, by definition, have any secret for himself. 'In Roberte', says the professor,

> it is not the dutiful helpmate I would denounce, it's that in her which, lurking behind all the little helpfulnesses performed and duties fulfilled, perpetrates great wrongs, steals in the act of giving and can't be found out because the helpmate activities cover

148 *Ibid.*, p. 23.

149 *Ibid.*

150 *Ibid.*, p. 25.

151 *Ibid.*, p. 26.

> up the evidence. [...] What I denounce to the pure spirit is not the everyday actuality of our conjugal life but that very inactuality the pure spirit shares with Roberte.[152]

Saying that the pure spirit shares Roberte's inactuality amounts to saying that, for this spirit, Roberte is not an enigma. What is actuality for Octave is inactuality for the spirit. Now, this inactuality of Roberte bears a name: it is her essence. For Octave, a relationship of equality is established between what is hidden from him and Roberte's essence. Roberte's essence is her secret, which for him, the husband, is a secret in his wife. The definition, de facto, that the professor gives of Roberte's essence is notably different from its common definition, in its philosophical and its theological uses alike. For Octave, essence is less the permanent and lasting fundamental structure of the created being Roberte, than the secret (of her femininity and the jouissance he posits as being there when she is taken by the guest) that this same Roberte would conceal from him if need be. Roberte's essence is what Octave is unaware of and what he tenaciously holds onto as regards her presence: the secret is there, absolutely.

A question remains: while appointing Roberte to the pure spirit and denouncing what in her is enigmatic, the only way of dispelling her secret in the end is with the following condition: can there be any '[...] communication possible between Roberte and the spirit'?[153] Between Roberte as an embodied creature and the pure divine spirit transparent to itself? The question is voiced by Antoine, caught as he is in the heat of the dispute. By way of reply, Octave calls upon the theological concept of hypostatic union. For the spirit to know Roberte, Roberte must no longer be Roberte, as a reasonable substance; she needs to have been transformed. But what is hypostatic union? Theology defines it as the realisation and permanent result of a union in one sole hypostasis or person. It is a technical term used with regard to Christ: by the union which in Jesus Christ is realised and endures between a human nature and the divine person (hypostasis) of *Logos*, a human reality itself becomes the created expression of the Word of God. The 451 Council of Chalcedon defined this Christological dogma:

152 *Ibid.*, p. 28.
153 *Ibid.*, p. 28.

Jesus Christ, the word of God made man, is a person of two natures, present in this unique person without confusion, unchanged, undivided and inseparable. Therefore there is no mixture whatsoever of the two natures, but coexistence in one person who is neither divided nor split.

Octave's reasoning continues. What is the necessary condition for the realisation of hypostatic union? Antoine takes pleasure in replying. He recites his obediently learnt lesson: 'The loss of the incommunicability proper to human nature' –incommunicability being 'the principle according to which the Being of an individual cannot be attributed to several individuals, and which properly constitutes the person identical unto himself.'[154] In other words, the privative function of the person is that of '[…] rendering our substance incapable of being assumed by a nature either lower or higher than ours.'[155] Hence the following crucial question: 'Is there a situation in which the reasoning substance loses personal incommunicability?'[156] Depending on the reply, knowledge of Roberte, in her Entirety, shall or shall not be possible. With the death of the person, substance, composed of both a soul and a body, is dissociated, and ultimately separated. The soul, set free, can associate itself with another body. 'As a consequence', our theologian adds, 'the separated but subsisting soul loses personal incommunicability, as shown by the fact it recovers its capacity to unite itself to a body.'[157] For Octave, such a possibility allows for the possibility of his intervention: how might one manage to separate the soul from the body (as occurs when a person dies) so as to allow this soul, henceforth open, to be grasped in and of itself?

> Now, may we imagine an operation occurring in the actual person whereby, dissociating the soul from the body and the spirit from the soul, the actual person is placed in suspense?[158]

154 *Ibid.*, p. 32.
155 *Ibid.*, p. 33.
156 *Ibid.*
157 *Ibid.*
158 *Ibid.*

If the actual person is suspended, losing the incommunicability of the soul, hypostatic union is realisable. God's intervention is necessary. He is the one that can suspend the actual person. Octave observes very well the danger of such a step forward in his argumentation: what he is aiming at (namely, making Roberte's essence, through the hypostatic union, associate with the pure spirit without melting away) implies a decision he has no hold over. It is a decision submitted to the good will of God, which is clearly about as hypothetical as you can get: '[…] if God permits it to be so'.[159]

Octave is not naïve: he knows very well that hypostatic union is a mystery, and in no way a phenomenological entity accessible to reason. He acknowledges that this union, in this capacity, '[…] cannot of course serve us as an example […].'[160] Nevertheless, it will have taught us something about both personal incommunicability and its possible loss, but only if God allows it. Supposing that this union might ultimately be possible, Octave qualifies it as 'dreadful'.[161] Dreadful indeed is the union that would actualise two essences in one same person: feminine jouissance and the pure spirit, Roberte's secret and the absolute Being.

This reference to hypostatic union – realisable should God allow it – has one of the most important consequences in theology, and Klossowski will make excessive and specific use of it: the *communication of idioms*. The idiom, in its accepted use in theology, is a property of nature attributable to a person who possesses a nature. Christ possessed two natures, and the idioms of both may be attributed to him. There is communication of idioms in the logical sense when the person of Christ is designated by a name that characterises him as bearer of one of the two natures and when, at the same time, the subject thus designated is attributed with the properties of the other nature. In a sense, the rules of the communication of idioms constitute a grammatical transcription of the reality of hypostatic union. For example: the Word of God was sacrificed. The natures do not by definition communicate, but their idiomatic properties are exchanged. Divine idioms

159 *Ibid.*, p. 34.
160 *Ibid.*
161 *Ibid.*, p. 35.

may be attributed to Christ-the-man: power, glory, eternity, absolute being, and so on; and human properties may be attributed to Christ-the-God: terrestrial birth, suffering, death, and so forth. The scholastics established very precise rules for the employment of the communication of idioms. For instance, abstract, divine and human attributions are not interchangeable, and the abstract cannot be attributed to the concrete: thus it would be false to say, 'Christ's humanity is the Word made flesh.'

According to the communication of idioms, Roberte shall be austere and abandon herself to the carnal desires of her husband; there are in Roberte essential relations and accidental relations, and so on and so forth. In other words, 'Roberte belongs to two universes: one of immediacy, where someone possesses her; and her particular universe, where she escapes from it all.'[162] Alain Arnaud recalls quite rightly that three of the twelve rules for the communication of idioms set out by Denis Pétau are particularly at work in Klossowski:

- there is only one agent, considered either in regard to his two natures, or in regard to just one;
- one can simultaneously affirm contrary properties belonging to each of the two natures;
- communication is accomplished according to the agent and not the natures; one must therefore respect both the unity of the agent and the duality of the natures.[163]

One example of this communication of idioms in Klossowski's narrative is to be found in the following reasoning of Octave to Antoine:

> The pure spirit is inactual in relation to me just as in relation to Roberte: inactual in relation to himself, so he remains up until the instant I invoke him for the purpose

162 Arnaud, A., Pierre Klossowski, *op. cit.*, p. 101. 'We return to the paradox of the communication of idioms of whom Roberte is the perfect illustration in the Klossowkian universe. The more she reveals in the scenes, through postures, gestures, etc., the more her nature is hidden. The more she shares, the more she affirms the incommunicable ... We see Roberte stripped, spanked, assaulted ... but her smile, her look, her hands deny these outrages. These aggressions only touch the person's simulacra, she seems to be saying; in the strict sense, she has nothing to do with it.'

163 *Ibid.*, p. 95.

> of designating the actual Roberte to him, then and only then does he become actual. Previous to this the inactual Roberte could not be known to the pure spirit: but while we continue in ignorance of Roberte, once she is designated to him not only does he know what escapes me but he will himself be the actualisation of inactual Roberte. [...] Roberte does not at all know in relation to me or in relation to you what she very well knows in relation to the pure spirit. So long as the pure spirit did not know her she did not know what she knows with him, just as he did not know what at present he knows with her.[164]

In this long demonstration, both Roberte's openness and her absolute closure are affirmed at the same time: she is actual and inactual, actualised and inactualised by the pure spirit. A *coincidentia oppositorum* is affirmed. We understand that Antoine is losing the argument and Octave is no more than 'an apologist for international fraud'[165] as Roberte reminds him, sickened!

For Klossowski, the communication of idioms will forever bear the stamp of the simulacrum: the nature, the essence, and the being of Roberte as the paradigm of womanliness, of the Other sex, will always be closed off and unexchangeable. The fiction of 'grammatical transcription', as stipulated by the theology of idiomatic communication, alone endures as a concrete consequence of the mystery of hypostatic union.

The Impossible Trinity

In this initiatory dialogue, Octave (Antoine specifies this) carried away by his reasoning, starts rambling. His nephew shows great perspicacity when he refers his uncle's ramblings and flights of fancy to the power of language: the trap lies not in the logic of the exposition but in the words. '[...] the professor's behaviour demonstrates into what kind of pitfall language can

164 Klossowski, P., *Roberte Ce Soir* and *The Revocation of the Edict of Nantes*, *op. cit.*, pp. 35–6.

165 *Ibid.*, p. 69.

lure even the most lucid intelligence [...].'[166] Plunging into the maze of theological quibbles, Octave gets lost, gets into a tangle, and becomes desperate. However, and this is the decisive point, he produces the same kind of effect in his interlocutor. Roberte herself, being used to the interminable scholastic disputes with her elderly husband, speaks of the tortures[167] she has to bear the brunt of.

One of these flights of fancy concerns the Trinity. The professor's question is clear from the start: does the strict reference to the mystery of the Trinity permit discovering who Roberte is? In other words, does this theological concept have any pertinence whatsoever when it comes to examining and resolving what lies behind his illness?

In theology, the dogma of the Trinity designates the mystery of the unique nature of the three Persons in the Godhead (Father, Son, and Holy Ghost), which is the fundamental mystery of Christianity. Starting off from this, Octave will consider his relationship with his wife, adding his own ha'penny's worth, to wit, a practice that hijacks the mystery and then debases it into 'mystification'.[168] The theology of the Trinity specifies that the unique divine reality exists in a *trine* manner of being which is relational and 'hypostatic' because, as relation, it is always interchangeable: by being communicated in a generative expression of self (itself being without origin); by being communicated as expressed and begotten; by being communicated as if breathed, 'spirited', in the loving inclination or adhesion of those who love.

In what way are these founding theological remarks useful to Octave's reasoning? What is he striving to produce, to bring about? Our professor effectively starts off from the dogmatic principles of the Trinity:

> [...] divine essence expresses itself in three persons who are not three essences but a single essence, since there is only one divine essence. And each of them is at all times that essence in which each person is established as an essential relationship.[169]

166 *Ibid.*, p. 10.
167 *Ibid.*, p. 82.
168 *Ibid.*, p. 38.
169 *Ibid.*

The notions of a hidden face, of an unknown essence, of an authentic nature that is incommunicable, each fall by the wayside in such a context. Between the three Persons of the Father, the Son and the Holy Ghost, there is an essential relationship, i.e. nothing can escape each Person of the essence of the two others. This is the starting dogma: God is one, the divine essence is unique. The relationship between these three Persons leaves nothing left over, there is no obscurity, no inactuality. Everything is inevitably and immediately actual for each of the three Persons. There is no third party among them, no distance, and each Person is entirely present for the two others.

What happens when there is a relationship between created beings?

> With created beings, on the other hand, this relationship is merely accidental, and from one created nature to another, [...] there is no communication of essence like the intercommunication of the three persons within divine nature.[170]

The essence of the created being is limited by his existence. As Octave observes: 'Roberte, it must be recognised, limits Roberte [...].'[171] Our professor is aiming at the moment when 'the human soul's essence, withdrawing from personal existence, recovers the power to multiply itself in several persons or to express itself in as many persons as there were various subjects to perceive [...].'[172] This possibility comes up against a difficulty: 'Would not this essence then have to be able to maintain itself, or be able to be maintained, as form?'[173] This form can be realised by the image of the representation: this is the viewpoint that each person can have of Roberte in his spirit, the viewpoint of each lover who practices Hospitality with her. As the uncle says to Antoine:

> Suppose that between you, me, and a third person, Roberte reproduces within herself her relationship to all three of us; these inwardly produced relationships reflect

170 *Ibid.*
171 *Ibid.*, p. 61.
172 *Ibid.*, p. 38.
173 *Ibid.*

> not our own images of her but, instead, the three different images of her we each respectively form of her.[174]

According to this reasoning, if the system is carried through, Roberte falls apart as One: she is no longer one person in whom three different images are actualised (i.e. the successive viewpoints of the husband, the nephew and the third party – the guest). On the contrary, she becomes plural: '[...] a triple relationship to Roberte is constituted in her own spirit: and now she is three persons.'[175] Why has the unity broken into pieces like this? Because each vantage point, each image, is proper to each of the three persons summoned: the husband, the nephew and the third party. These three images that have come from the outside, each one of them dispossessing Roberte of herself by diffracting and multiplying her, are heterogeneous. They cannot be synthesised. There is no longer one Roberte, but three Robertes in one sole 'apparent' physiognomy objectified as a bodily image. Would the Trinity thereby be manifested? Not in the slightest, replies Octave: '[...] for this trinity is wholly exterior to her, it comes to her only from our outside presence.'[176] It takes the presence of each viewpoint to obtain these diverse images of Roberte, images she encounters in the gaze of each person placed upon her. 'This triple representation of herself to herself' continues the theologian

> is hence not essential; the three Robertes are only accidental in their relationship to Roberte, because this triple representation of herself originates with us, and because it is we alone who modify it [...].[177]

In other words, there is no unity of measure here, as there is in the dogma of the Catholic Trinity. What is missing? In order for

> [...] these three Robertes [to] be of a single substance the minimum requirement would be that the absolute Roberte know a Roberte-to-Roberte relationship based upon her essence, that the three Robertes consummate a single secret.[178]

174 *Ibid.*, pp. 38–9.
175 *Ibid.*, p. 39.
176 *Ibid.*
177 *Ibid.*
178 *Ibid.*

Of course, the sophistication of Octave's sentences bears not on the reasoning but on the syntactical play; he loses his reasoning in his own developments. The (theological) snake bites its own tail! Indeed, Octave wants to grasp Roberte's essence, he wants all of her (unknown) essence to be knowable just as divine essence is common to the three Persons of the Trinity. But for this to be possible, the absolute Roberte would have to be present from the start and be able to communicate her essence completely and totally, without any unknown remaining. However, this essence is, at first, precisely what one cannot find. In the end, it is a matter of obtaining it by virtue of the images that are reflected back.

Does Octave finally bring this demonstration to a close? Not at all. This is particular to Klossowski's style of writing, where he pushes the irony to the limit, parodying theological language. Far from stopping the demonstration, the aporia gives it a kick-start and new concepts are introduced. The sentences at this point in the narrative verge on the incomprehensible, yet Klossowski's artful writing pushes us, despite everything, to read and decrypt them. What does Octave say? He makes a distinction, taken from William of Ockham (called Hocheim in the text) between the created being and the intelligence, the latter stemming from the increate. Let us suppose that Roberte's awareness of the representation she is the object of (in the mind of another) stems from the intellect. So, 'we at once find Roberte disposed to yield us her secret.'[179] Why? Because these intelligences, in so far as they are increate, are able to communicate with one another. Living and visible Roberte switches over to the idea of Roberte that results from each participant's relation to her; it is the passing from '*that* Roberte', who is alive, 'to become momentarily *this* Roberte, the object of the judgement, the intention, of the desire of others.'[180] If this operation is realisable, Roberte will 'begin to lose her incommunicable character and take on the capacity to enter into composition with another nature, reverting into the state of uninformed substance or the state of nonactualised but simply actualisable

179 *Ibid.*

180 *Ibid.*, p. 40.

form [...].'[181] In spite of Octave's every effort, precisely what is not possible proves to be futile. The passage from created being to increate intellect will never be perfect, will always leave a remainder. Roberte is alive – she has a body! Rendering Roberte, who has become a pure signifier, an abstraction who 'would still come into conflict with her own body as with the equivocal witness of her presence among us, of her identity about to become false [...].'[182] Using words of theology and a parody of reasoning, Klossowski quite rigorously runs up against the structural incompatibility between the real of the body and the signifier, between the jouissance that specifies the body as living and the symbolic that mortifies what it designates (*corpsification*, to use Lacan's word[183]).

Ought one to conclude that nothing is possible, that Roberte will be forever inaccessible? Klossowski, through the voice of Octave, replies both yes and no. There is always an association of irreconcilables in this peculiar oeuvre, an assembly of unexchangeables. This tension can be seen very clearly in the sentences quoted from *Roberte Ce Soir* that sometimes project Roberte onto the side of the essential relationship where her essence can never be attained, and at other times onto the side of contingent relations where only her created being, in its concrete materiality, can be discovered and possessed.

Is nothing of essence possible and attainable? At the start of the chapter 'The Denunciation', Octave shows Antoine some photos taken during a stay in Ascona. The uncle shows a picture that is 'quite a success'.[184] What does it show? Roberte is delivering a lecture in the villa of Madame de Watteville. She leans carelessly up against the mantelpiece, and all of a sudden her skirt catches fire as she is speaking. She leaps away and 'into the arms of this gentleman who has rushed up to her rescue and is snatching off her burning clothes.'[185] This is apparently what is to be seen in the snapshot taken by Octave. The photograph fascinates him and his fasci-

181 *Ibid.*

182 *Ibid.*

183 Lacan, J., 'Allocution sur l'enseignement', in *Autres écrits*, Seuil, Paris, p. 304.

184 Klossowski, P., *Roberte Ce Soir* and *The Revocation of the Edict of Nantes*, *op. cit.*, p. 19.

185 *Ibid.*

nation rubs off on Antoine. The whole dialogue between the uncle and the nephew is a sharp commentary on this image: what does it convey? What does it betray of Roberte's increate intelligence as her clothes burn while her body remains safe? This incident is fortuitous and unforeseen. It breaks through the spatial and temporal continuity. For Octave, this incident can be read and decrypted on the basis of Ockham's distinction between *created being* and *increate intelligence*, between body and mind, between living being and God's breath. In one sentence, Octave offers an interpretation of the incident:

> What then is happening here, if not that, in disactualising herself as Roberte, whose skirt is accidentally on fire, Roberte's spirit is actualising itself in as much as it provokes the gesture of another, who unveils her, by means of this disactualisation! Into creatable existence the increate intelligence rejects the subject in whom this same action is taking place [...].[186]

Roberte is giving a lecture. She is absorbed in an urbane, serious and careful presentation. Octave is one of the attendees. An incident breaks out: her skirt starts to burn and a man saves her. Roberte, the austere lecturer, at the instant the incident occurs, is disactualised: something else comes to be. Roberte's spirit is made manifest. The said 'spirit' has to be understood not as Roberte's 'mind' in so far as that would designate her intelligent and rational thought, but as Roberte's spirit in as much as a spirit, to be understood as a demon, takes possession of and invades the mind. Initially silent, it awakens and provokes this incident without her awareness. The spirit that animates Roberte is actualised. In order to come into being, the spirit needs a locus or a screen: this will be the young man's action. Thus, the gesture of another shows Roberte what will from now on disturb her in her own unique and peculiar way, all the while serving as a locus of reception or a screen for the manifestation of this (cunning) spirit. As Octave says, in a highly convoluted sentence:

> And if it is through an act of increate intellect that Roberte disactualises herself *qua* Roberte to attain consciousness of another actuality which eludes us, this intellectual

186 *Ibid.*, p. 40.

> act coincides with one of her consciousnesses whose removal from existence, broadening, lessens their distance from the increate.[187]

The complexity of this passage parodies the classical treatises of theology. But the logic that underlies the reasoning indicates a desperate attempt on the part of the professor for Roberte's essence finally to be delivered. The fortuitous accident actualises this essence in a partial, limited, and reduced way, but also in spite of everything through a disactualisation of the created being Roberte. The Ascona incident lays her bare: 'You see,' says the uncle to his nephew,

> That through this very operation Roberte lays herself bare and the lock to her identity is forced: displaced out of Roberte's subjective being, her consciousness immediately proposes itself as object to any other suppositum in whom increate intellect can be defined.[188]

The incident conveys Roberte's essence, but what it delivers of this essence remains opaque, incomprehensible and enigmatic. This is what is unbearable in this long demonstration: what the accident reveals is immediately retracted, and slips away from view and comprehension. This is the ransom demanded by the particularity of essence, the price to pay for catching a glimpse of it. In other words, what is fortuitous, 'by its own nature [...] cannot be frozen in a representation. As soon as it is exposed it is depleted.'[189] No sooner is the essence touched upon by a fragment than it dissolves into the very things that have been able to immobilise it. The photo shows and hides at the same time. What is to be concluded from the Ascona incident? That it is but a 'mere counterfeit'[190] of the Trinitarian mystery. The snapshot is only a 'simulacrum'[191] of the operation of Trinitarian union.

187 *Ibid.*, p. 41.
188 *Ibid.*
189 Arnaud, A., *Pierre Klossowski, op. cit.*, p. 88.
190 Klossowski, P., *Roberte Ce Soir* and *The Revocation of the Edict of Nantes, op. cit.*, p. 41.
191 *Ibid.*, p. 42.

> An image in itself has no Being; reciprocally, it is intellection through and through: the skirt burns, the body appears to be safe, but it is in fact the spirit that is burning in this body which Victor, ostensibly in order to save it, is exhibiting …[192]

This is why Octave's photographic snapshot has a fascinating power (for Antoine too, whose carnal and spiritual desire for his aunt is gnawing away at him): it shows another actualised Roberte, a Roberte stirred by her spirit. The Trinity has not for all that come into being: only the counterfeit, the deceptive photo, and the simulacrum remain. The exposition is a lure, a simple epiphany that covers up the wife's essence at the very instant it reveals it as real, remaining impossible to grasp in any way. Antoine notes this: '[…] I'm sure you make your prints according to your whims …'[193] Octave himself does not fail to acknowledge this: 'I might add that in other prints from the same negative there is no sign of any fire: all that remains, but in a much more striking manner, is this extraordinary tangle of arms and legs.'[194] Octave manipulates the images, modifies them for each circumstance under pressure from the questions he asks himself, and through the interpretations he gives of them. The images can be manipulated because they have been taken up in a discourse. They do not illustrate it, but rather realise it in the hesitations and aporias of the discourse, and in what it leaves unsaid.

Roberte, This Evening

The chapter 'Roberte Ce Soir', which provides the title to the entirety of the narrative that was published in 1954, holds a central place in the trilogy. 'Central' also has to be taken here in its topographical sense because this chapter (a very short one numbering only a dozen pages) constitutes the heart of the overall narrative that bears this title. For the 1965 publication

192 *Ibid.*
193 *Ibid.*
194 *Ibid.*, p. 43.

of the trilogy, Klossowski placed the narrative between *The Revocation of the Edict of Nantes* and *Le Souffleur*, disregarding the dates of their prior publication.

What does this central, pivotal scene of the three fictions give us? What does the voyeur of this spectacle (the one who uses the gaze to violate at a distance) discover? It is evening, Roberte is going home after her work at the Censorship Council, satisfied at having banned that day, 'Octave's ignoble work'.[195] This work, of course, is none other than *Roberte Ce Soir*. The operation that is set up in her dressing room (which also serves as her office) runs as follows: first of all, she is bothered by an absence – she must have left Octave's book behind; next, she catches the radiant beauty of her image in the mirror, where her face 'dissolves into a blur'.[196] Her faithful reflection is relinquished, and it is with Octave's eyes that she sees herself seeing herself. She becomes an other, and lapses into the spectacle around her: the daydreams of the elderly professor play out before her once again, seen as if they were happening on the outside. There is a tipping point:

> [...] her mind elsewhere, [she] applies some lipstick to her lips. One might think her on the point of going out again, to see her tall slender form bent that way toward the mirror, her face aglow [...], the lipstick held between her tapered fingers, her clear nails straying along the edge of her arched lips, now and then putting a fingertip to her long lashes [...].[197]

The image in the mirror becomes autonomous and detaches itself. Two Robertes co-exist and autoerotic practices ensue between the two wives: 'unbuttoning her black blouse with the white cuffs, she glided a hand under her armpit [...] she slides her fingers down her flanks to lift her long black skirt.[198] This autoerotic scene, admittedly fleeting, is cut from exactly the same cloth as the scene relayed in one of the chapters from *Le Souffleur*: Théodore, seated by the Old Man in his paralytic seat, becoming his living

195 *Ibid.*, p. 47.
196 *Ibid.*, p. 48.
197 *Ibid.*, p. 47.
198 *Ibid.*, p. 48.

dead gaze, sees Roberte undress under her furs and slip her fingers into her vulva. She caresses and rubs herself, or rather, she caresses, rubs and masturbates her reflection that has practically become her double incarnate. The scene described by Théodore is shown and seen from the outside by a third party. But the scene in 'Roberte Ce Soir' will spell out more: it will show Roberte's visions and hidden thoughts from the inside. What are these visions? What do they represent in the picture they make?

Roberte finds in the toilet paper dispenser

> [...] some of Octave's censored work, leaves from the chapter entitled 'Tacita, the Giant Guardsman and the Hunchback'. [...] for the hundredth time she rereads these lucubrations which vex her [...].[199]

The door opens precisely on the scene she is reading, horrified by the 'perversity' of her husband who has written it: Roberte has entered the scene, merged with Tacita (the Silent One), and what Octave has described happens to her: the giant Guardsman (who bears the features of Vittorio) and the Hunchback (who is the figure of one of her 'spies' at the Board or Censors) slowly start to abuse her sexually. In this censored chapter, Octave's writing reveals the truth of Roberte's desire. His descriptions make it present for her. He writes what she was waiting for without knowing it. What she had been wanting for all eternity, as Klossowski insists: the Guardsman, presenting a 'tremendous member whose smooth and admirably rounded knob is trained at Roberte', that has been there 'for all eternity' – its 'triumphant and insolent immobility'.[200] Eternity and immobility do not surprise us: indeed, the window of the fantasy opens all the more given that a silence falls; the wife becomes mute. Faced with this unbearable vision of the Guardsman and the Hunchback, Roberte attempts to expel them with a gesture of authority, but:

> [...] her face flushes and it is only barely if she succeeds in pointing imperatively with the index finger of that faltering hand: 'Get out!' she believes she hears herself say

199 *Ibid.*
200 *Ibid.*

in a pale voice, whereas all she does is urinate the harder. 'Only what is out is visible', is the reply she gets from no perceptible voice.[201]

Octave actualises the essence of the spouse through his writing, making her aware of it. The husband's words have a revelatory function: an illuminated letter is fired at Roberte like a pure missile targeting the inviolate essence that lies still unknown at the heart of her:

> [...] so strong has been the intruding image that a curious disappointment suspends her agitation when she verifies that the door has remained bolted while emotion has raised the tingling warmth in her limbs to an almost fever pitch, and as she is at loss to know what to do with it, and despite herself has felt it delicious, Roberte is more than irked [...].[202]

There follows a long description where our author sets out a thorough theological argument. While the Guardsman addresses Roberte in the manner of the Doctors of the Church, his actions become more precise with the aid of the Hunchback:

> [...] taking her from behind, the Guardsman's gauntlet sweeps slantwise, rips through her black blóuse, moves downward grazing Roberte's chest, splits her brassiere and lands squarely upon her breast, leaving her shoulder bare. At the very first bite Roberte lets go of the whip while her other breast tumbles through the tear in her blouse, beginning with a pink nipple popping through a curtain of black silk.[203]

The narrative becomes more precise:

> While he fixes her hand [...] the Inspectress thinks to move the other to the gauntlet fondling her breasts; thus to see them become the object of a separate intelligence, it seems to Roberte she is feeling them for the first time, never has she seen them so docile nor their nipples swell and harden so readily as in the hollow of the broad gauntlet which is massaging them.[204]

201 *Ibid.*, pp. 48–9.
202 *Ibid.*, p. 49.
203 *Ibid.*, p. 51.
204 *Ibid.*, pp. 51–2.

Previously, Octave's flight of fancy that so surprised Antoine was examined: the husband had denounced Roberte to the pure spirit in order to know, by means of vision, her hidden soul. In this quotation, Klossowski shows the effect of the pure spirit on the wife, the Guardsman and the Hunchback being mere separate intelligences, 'dead thoughts'[205] – a type of demon or angel freed of a bodily envelope. They are divine breaths, i.e. 'simple substances produced without the flesh.'[206] Roberte on the other hand is a double substance: body and spirit. Through their presence, the different parts of Roberte's body become autonomous, they take on consistency, and in this case they bear the turmoil she feels. Through the pure spirit, the parts of her body become 'objects' of thought, and little by little her body becomes sexualised, bringing on sexual turmoil. The pure spirit corrupts, animates the flesh, provokes what the wife, otherwise passive and occupied, was hoping for without even knowing: sexual desire.

We must understand this moment when, bit by bit, Roberte's body escapes her and becomes autonomous as it is exteriorised on the outside in the thought of the pure spirit ('separated intelligence'), with regard to what she still wants to censor in the name of the ego's mastery and the unity of self-identity. This mastery turns out to be futile, its unity comes undone: the parts of her body (breasts, legs, thighs, hands, etc.) become separate. What happens to her sexually, by multiplying her (how many Robertes are now present?), is effectively discovered as if for the 'first time': '[...] never had Roberte found herself so overwhelmed by this body of hers',[207] writes Klossowski. To be overwhelmed is to see the limits of unity splitting at the seams, if not to see homogeneity being annulled in favour of the multiple.

There is another characteristic of this scene:

> [...] the gauntlet, parting the fleece [...] entirely liberates the Inspectress' quidest;[208] and as she would yet put a covering hand to this attribute of her taciturn arrogance,

205 *Ibid.*, p. 51.
206 *Ibid.*, p. 50.
207 *Ibid.*, p. 50.
208 *Quidest* is Latin for 'clitoris'.

> of unsuspected size, the Guardsman deftly nips the quidest which erects prodigiously between the aggressor's leather thumb and forefinger.[209]

The reading is developed:

> Roberte has been unable to anticipate the gesture of the gauntlet which upon the Inspectress' quidest, in monstrous erection, slips the ring it has just plucked off her finger [...]. Then seizing Roberte's fingers, he obliges her to put her own quidest in the most perfect state; in such a way that ringed, reared in all its oily sauciness, this latter is promptly mouthed by the Hunchback; to such good purpose that the Inspectress, unable to contain herself any longer, washes her spy's gullet with her wickedness ...[210]

At the heart of the trilogy lies a description that refines our subject's fantasy. Lacan noted this: 'A fantasy is, in effect, quite bothersome, since we do not know where to situate it due to the fact that it just sits there, complete in its nature as fantasy, whose only reality is as discourse.'[211] It is a highly detailed description of the ways in which Roberte is violated. But her violation is in no way questioned from the side of the Guardsman or the Hunchback, of whom we shall know nothing. How could we, given that they have no physical presence? In the scene of the violation, a question is constructed for the voyeur who wrote it: how and what does Roberte's body enjoy? This question – to which the description gives an answer through monstration – entails for Octave 'something too dreadful to endure'[212] the apprehension of which can only bring about his immediate flight. Our protagonist can only flee faced with this spectacle of the jouissance of his wife's body – a spectacle which, however, goes on attracting him, fascinating him. What exactly is it that he fears seeing, making him take flight? The chapter 'Roberte Ce Soir' responds to this question.

209 Klossowski, P., *Roberte Ce Soir* and *The Revocation of the Edict of Nantes*, *op. cit.*, p. 58.

210 *Ibid.*, pp. 57–8.

211 Lacan, J., 'Kant with Sade', *op. cit.*, pp. 657–8.

212 Klossowski, P., *Roberte Ce Soir* and *The Revocation of the Edict of Nantes*, *op. cit.*, p. 89.

In this chapter, Roberte is shown to be endowed with a phallic attribute: her *quidest*, this mark of arrogance, of 'inborn immodesty',[213] is of unprecedented proportions. It stands in a state of monstrous erection, encircled by the conjugal ring that masturbates it bolt upright. She herself notes that she has 'too generous natural endowments.'[214] The final moment even offers a parody of ejaculation ('the Inspectress, unable to contain herself any longer, washes [...]'). Roberte is also seen as she who is radically deprived of such an attribute: as Octave puts it, her *utrumsit*[215] is vast and deep, and open. In other words, Roberte appears at once to have and not to have the phallic insignia. Klossowski's narrative demonstrates what the typical statement in perversion spells out: *I know women are castrated, but still*. This *but still* is embodied by the fetish.

Let us examine the logic here: it is because Roberte is radically deprived of the phallic attribute that, for her voyeur, her *quidest* is a substitute for a phallus, an ersatz, and the terms that describe it are male terms that name its (sexual) use for a man. The scene ends in an operation of imaginary positivation: the phallus, which for the neurotic is lack, 'destined to designate meaning effects as a whole',[216] in perversion is made presence. Thus subjectified, the phallus takes on consistency by virtue of being fixed in the imaginary, becoming in a sense the (concrete) object beyond the (forever absent) object hidden by the veil. Lacan would say that it *ek-sists*, becoming, not without paradox, a $(+ \varphi)$. Hence the caricatural way in which the *quidest* is employed in Roberte. It is a phallus that is parodied, caricatured, overdone, and dramatised. Klossowski's fiction insists on the grotesquery of the sexual farce, a host of farcical operations that are mere marks trying to give body and concreteness to what stands as a structural lack, inscribing itself into the imaginary field as a minus: $(- \varphi)$. This is a fragile equilibrium, maintained as a pretense by this positivised phallus, endlessly submitted to the raising of the curtain where feminine castration reveals itself in all its

213 *Ibid.*, pp. 173.

214 *Ibid.*

215 *Utrumist* is a Latin term for the 'vaginal cavity'.

216 Lacan, J., 'The Signification of the Phallus', in *Écrits*, *op. cit.*, p. 579.

horror. The structural reason for Octave's flight arises here, which he mentions on other occasions: he 'steals away'[217] faced with what is so unbearable for him in the emergence of feminine castration. The fetish resulting from the disavowal thus upheld triumphs over (feminine) castration, said Freud.

In fine, Roberte will be sodomised by the Guardsman's enormous organ. Sodomy is the sole sexual act practiced in the trilogy. It constitutes a form of homage to the Marquis de Sade and his immoral mentor, the famous Dolmancé. In the three fictions, this is also a form of punishment inflicted on the wife. She is not unaware of it, she who speaks of chastisement, humiliation, vexation, and insult. It merely intensifies her (sexual) pleasure and swells her *quidest*. What her body enjoys in this act will be stamped with the seal of ambiguity:

> [...] Roberte does not know if it is from shame she trembles because the sentence is carried out, enormous, impetuous, scalding, between her buttocks, or whether it is from pleasure she is sweating, because this sentence does wide violence to her *vacuum*.[218,219]

Either way, the act of sodomy does not close the scene, it is rather the precondition for the ultimate description in which Octave, to the question 'what does a woman want?', 'what and how does her body enjoy?', offers unambiguously by way of reply: like a man! A woman's jouissance is a parody of virile sexual jouissance. In short, our subject's fantasy lays bare its leading edge: as bearer, *de visu*, of the phallic attribute, Roberte enjoys as a man does. However, in this scene, Roberte's essence endures as something specific, unfathomed by Octave. Our protagonist knows there is a jouissance proper to Roberte's body, this is his belief, but at the decisive instant that it is delivered in the field of the visible, it escapes him. The terms and the images employed in speaking of it derive from what inscribes male jouissance.

217 Klossowski, P., *Roberte Ce Soir* and *The Revocation of the Edict of Nantes*, *op. cit.*, p. 89.

218 *Vacuum* is a Latin term for the 'anal orifice'.

219 Klossowski, P., *Roberte Ce Soir* and *The Revocation of the Edict of Nantes*, *op. cit.*, p. 59.

This scene is unique in the trilogy of the laws. All the other descriptions will stop just short of this final moment: where the scene is seen from the outside, limited to the evidence of the visually imposed corporeal idioms. The last scene of the chapter 'Roberte Ce Soir' shows, with rare purity, the active disavowal of feminine castration that reveals Octave's position with regard to lack.

The different forms of the failure of Hospitality observed by Octave, Théodore and Klossowski can be summed up as follows:

- By identifying himself with the gazes of his guests, one after the next, at the instant of the opened door, Octave is projected into an endless spiral where the next gaze, a new viewpoint on Roberte, is always missing. The series of guests can never be a closed set. The scenes of Hospitality are forced to multiply, caught in an intensified ritual. It stands as a new version of the Danaids' bathtub!
- In becoming the gaze of a dead man (the old Guide), our voyeur is finally able to discover what common mortals do not know. But such a gaze can clearly never be cast by 'any bearer of civil status.'[220] There is no outside life for a living subject; he cannot slip behind the scenes of life and finally see it from the other side. One cannot be both on the inside and on the outside, as his nephew Antoine says.[221]
- In merging simple substance with God's gaze by means of the bodiless angel, Octave should be able to see Roberte deliver up her essence, since the absolute and eternal gaze assembles all the possible viewpoints. But such a realisation would depend on a willingness that lies beyond the control of our protagonist: 'God willing [...]'. Hypostatic union, or the Trinity, which, were they realisable, would ensure a full and entire viewing of the wife's soul, are impossible for a human nature. Tiring himself out going on as if it were possible, the husband

220 Klossowski, P., 'Le Souffleur', *Les lois de l'hospitalité*, *op. cit.*, p. 188.

221 Klossowski, P., *Roberte Ce Soir* and *The Revocation of the Edict of Nantes*, *op. cit.*, p. 11.

(he acknowledges as much himself) reduces the (divine) mystery to a mystification, and theological reasoning to a conjuring trick.

- In this central scene ('Roberte Ce Soir'), what Roberte discovers concerning her violation by the pure spirits (*Roberte Ce Soir*) can be seen or told only in terms of virile jouissance. How and what Roberte's body enjoys remain inaccessible.
- Klossowski himself warns us: his law of Hospitality has no meaning if referred to traditional terms from the code of everyday signs wherein the identity principle (i.e. ego is ego) and the principle of non-contradiction (ego is not the other) are affirmed. Only the logic of the unique sign, under whose reign our author lives (or believes himself to), along with his protagonists Octave and Théodore, allows for this impossibility to be grasped: to exchange the unexchangeable spouse. But the unique sign cannot be communicated, it is the most intense enciphering of the soul (to be understood as a silent jouissance). There is therefore a cause, a reason behind the law of hospitality, but by definition it can only remain unformulated, ungraspable in the symbolic order (and the field of concepts). Saying it or conceptualising it makes it absurd, contradictory or ridiculous.

The Unique Sign: The Name 'Roberte'

In 1965, when Gallimard published the trilogy in a single volume, Klossowski drafted a 'Foreword' and a 'Postface' in a forceful and succinct style. He writes in the first person and describes his work. These two texts are important because they reveal what is at stake in the trilogy; when it comes to understanding his writing, they are more interesting than the insipid snippets from his private life. A writer is his oeuvre, and when he says 'I', he means his oeuvre; he is speaking about his writing. What does Klossowski say about his fiction twelve years after writing *Roberte Ce Soir*, six years after *The Revocation*, and five years after *Le Souffleur*?

Our author testifies to what orders his life: 'For the last ten years I've been living, or have believed to be living, under the sign of Roberte [...].'[222] Roberte, the simple name 'Roberte', has become the 'unique sign'[223] of Klossowski's thought. His thought (his words, ideas, his flights of fancy) revolves exclusively around this name. The name 'Roberte' is a haunting word, present at every instant. It has replaced all his other activity of thought: 'I have attempted here to take refuge in my memories, recollections, the capital part of meanings and the heart, without which I could never see Roberte.'[224] Memory, recollection, and feelings feed the thoughts, allowing Roberte to be observed in various everyday situations. But writing about this is something else entirely: '[...] an obscure law prevented me from seeing [these diverse situations] so I could describe them.'[225] In order to describe, one must not see: the name 'Roberte' does not conjure the visible, but rather it blinds, producing, in thought, a methodical organisation that allows thought to hold together. This sign does not belong to the code of everyday signs. It is not one signifier amongst others. To say that it is unique is to say that it is a sign (a signifier) that is disconnected from the signifying opposition, that it is identical to itself. The name 'Roberte' almost has the status of a *letter*, in the sense Lacan gives to the letter at the end of his teaching.[226] Between the unique sign and the code of everyday signs, a struggle sets in, a radical opposition. The everyday code can only inscribe the unique sign as its fault line: the name 'Roberte' is a hole in the signifying logic. Starting off from the unique sign, Klossowski will fight, through his writing, against the conspiracy of silence that the everyday code entails: '[...] this conspiracy forms the very axis on which Roberte's body rotates [...].'[227] He adds:

222 Klossowski, P., *Les lois de l'hospitalité*, *op. cit.*, p. 7.
223 *Ibid.*, p. 9.
224 *Ibid.*, p. 7.
225 *Ibid.*
226 Lacan, J., 'Lituraterre', in *Autres écrits*, Seuil, Paris, 2001.
227 Klossowski, P., *Les lois de l'hospitalité*, *op. cit.*, p. 9.

> [...] this conspiracy is woven under Roberte's skin as much as it is in my syntax. Thus, it disputes my writing, it refuses it the right to speak. However, Roberte's skin could not so much as quiver without my syntax that is only the wrong side [*l'envers*], while the conspiracy of silence pretends to be the right side [*l'endroit*] [...].[228]

Starting off from the name 'Roberte', to write against the everyday code that annuls (because it is general and transmissible) the particularity of an experience (by definition unexchangeable), directly influences the form of the writing: it is effected on the basis of what cannot be said.

> [...] my syntax is in a situation analogous to thought without memory, operating only from the unique sign, in its vain exploration of an arbitrary name. The elimination of memory by the unique sign, this freezing of the most capital part of meanings and the heart, demands a similar autarky of syntax. [...] my syntax constitutes the fabric of Roberte's epidermis [...].[229]

These formulations are difficult, but Octave's descriptions and Théodore's attempts allow us to grasp what is at stake in them: to live under the one unique sign 'Roberte' can only lead to a kind of folly.[230] It amounts to becoming a dead man among Living, for it means cutting oneself off from all communication, from any relationship with another. To exorcise the name 'Roberte' – in other words, to write it – is to use the signs of the everyday language that permit communication. However, communicating the incommunicable, besides being a combat against silence, does not in fact annul the incommunicable, but rather thereby specifies it as such.

The interest of the 'Postface' to the trilogy lies in its specification of what the name 'Roberte' is, and how it mentally manifests itself to our writer. Klossowski comes back to the line of thought that this name constitutes: '[...] One day, while trying to relate some circumstances of my life, I was suddenly reduced to a sign.'[231] Our writer starts to describe a

228 *Ibid.*, p. 9.

229 *Ibid.*, p. 10.

230 Klossowski uses the word many times: 'folly is the loss of one's world and of oneself, in the name of a knowledge without beginning nor end'; *ibid.*, p. 346.

231 *Ibid.*, p. 333.

banal aspect of his life. Then, through the writing, a sign imposes itself. Uncovered thanks to the act of writing, the sign turns out to be the cause of the writing – a cause that is incontrovertible and active.

> The persistence of this pretext – the name – in and of itself denotes monotonous thought at the base. [...] Not writing but residing in such a continually enclosed circuit that at times all there was was an immobile circle, it seemed that thought annulled itself in the very sign that designated it.[232]

The unique sign invades thought; it abolishes life and all temporality: it is an immobile, fixed circle. Thought is rapid and follows the path of words – vagabond, it is free association. This is what the unique sign annuls: it immobilises thought. Here we have the passage from signifying logic to the screen of the fantasy where that which is nameless is enciphered in silence and now imposes itself as a haunting fullness. The jouissance localised by the set-up of the fantasy starts to show through.

This leads us to the question: 'How to live?'[233] Writing relieves this difficulty because it requires one to communicate, which itself requires movement that brings about the unique sign; writing exorcises by providing a locus. 'As soon as I would stop writing, the memory would disappear, the immobile circuit closing up.'[234] Writing breaks this circle, even if only in a partial way. What is this unique sign? Is it the 'contents of a representation'?[235] Not in the slightest: 'Memory enriches the representation of contents that are always undreamed of. But the sign pillaged and devastated my memory in order to reduce my thought to it alone.'[236] The unique sign is not taken up in the associative play of the signifying chain. It empties discourse of its speech content. How does one say it? 'This is its persistence, what I call an inaugural intensity, to the degree of which thought is designated in me.'[237] The term *inaugural intensity* deserves to be

232 *Ibid.*
233 *Ibid.*
234 *Ibid.*
235 *Ibid.*, p. 334.
236 *Ibid.*
237 *Ibid.*

highlighted. What fascinates Klossowski is not thought spoken in words and legitimised in reason, but intensity. Thought proceeds on the basis of the waxing and waning of intensities. These intensities are the dark forces of the soul – the same forces Nietzsche speaks about at length and which our writer took such pleasure in commenting on. The name 'Roberte' is inseparable from this inaugural intensity where his own being is wordlessly enciphered, with neither concept, reason nor identity – unexchangeable. 'A name – "Roberte" – was already a designation specific to inaugural intensity.'[238] The unique sign is not intensity, but rather the first designation of this intensity that must be presupposed as antecedent and therefore inaccessible as such.

Klossowski does not stop here: he then gives us a new interpretation of the name, with imagery: 'That she should meet her physiognomy through a whole sequence of gestures and situations – this is what her malice consisted of.'[239] Visions monopolise the writer. He becomes a gaze before actions and situations where Roberte's physiognomy is involved. He sees her actions and these situations, but what eludes him (because it is invisible) is what pushes him to see: the intensity particular to his being (to his soul) which a name inaugurally designates.

> But in this name *qua* sign, it did not necessarily unfold like this. There was no sequence of these gestures that I happened to describe starting from the name. The concurrence of the intensity and this name with the contact with physiognomy is however only attained from the sign in which thought is designated.[240]

Klossowski ceaselessly asserts how the designation is not the intensity, that this tying-in between sign and designation is arbitrary. The intensity is always lost:

> However, starting from the unique sign, designations of me and of the world appear perfectly arbitrary. But would such a unique sign, by any chance, designate thought

238 *Ibid.*

239 *Ibid.*

240 *Ibid.*, p. 335.

> in order to escape the arbitrary? Isn't it always ultimately arbitrary? Nothing is more arbitrary than a designation, and thus also this unique sign![241]

The fact that this contradiction between the code of the everyday signs and the unique sign can never be eradicated tears our writer apart. The more he writes under the pressure of the unique sign as an arbitrary enciphering of impulsive intensity, the more the intensity will be lacking. Klossowski sets out his subjective drama as follows:

> [...] Whatever we do, we have obeyed the code of everyday signs [...] we can no longer do without the signs that we have just used with indifference, and even to admit this we need again these same signs. Only how is it that these signs of having and being come back to us?[242]

The signifiers are in command. They attribute *being* and *having* to the subject: *here's what he is, here's what he has*. This is a vivid affirmation of the unity of the ego as owner, whilst the impulses, intensities, and forces of non-speech are called to manifest themselves, destroying all unity, all centring, all ordering regulated by the phallic signifier. Klossowski continues, answering his own question:

> Surely by an intensity that first designates itself before being that which designates. Isn't it strange that the intensity can designate itself as a thought? Would this be once again a game of the everyday signs that abuse us? When such signs only appear according to the whims of a rush of intensity? What is this indifference that prevails after their use in one circumstance or another? In order for this indifference, which was nothing other than an absence of intensity, to become itself an object of designation, wasn't a new afflux necessary? An afflux of power in the face of its own reflux! And if I speak of an absence of intensity, may I still distinguish designating intensity from pure and simple intensity.[243]

What are the effects for the subject who says 'I', who thus takes hold of himself as thought and coherence in light of the discontinuity of life which, as such, has neither meaning, order, nor goal?

241 *Ibid.*, p. 340.
242 *Ibid.*, p. 338.
243 *Ibid.*

> In the use of everyday signs, the designation of myself always supposes a stronger intensity: myself (I) constitute the sign of thought as mine, based upon which all the other designations assure the coherence of me with myself, and of myself with the world. But what happens to my coherence from the moment there is a degree of intensity when thought invents a sign by which it designates its coherence with itself, and ceases to reclaim me in the designation of myself? If it is no longer my own thought, wouldn't this sign exclude me from all possible coherence? If it still is mine, how is it conceivable that it designates itself as the absence of intensity in the highest degree?[244]

These formulations allow us to ascertain the function of the (unconscious) fantasy: it is what ensures an anchoring point precisely where the subject's vacillation becomes blurred, alienated as he is from the signifier. The fantasy is a silent fixity; the unique sign enciphers the unknown jouissance, an open window onto the real, albeit a partial and necessarily limited one. What is peculiar to our writer is that he makes the unique sign a fetish, illuminating it like the letter that traces the edge of the hole of unconscious knowledge.

> All identity rests only on the knowledge of a thinking that resides outside us – in as much as there is an inside and an outside – a thinking that consents to think of us as such from the outside. If God is inside as well as outside, in the sense of absolute coherence, our identity is pure grace,[245]

our identity stems from the absolute Other and is, by Him, either granted or not: the divine operation of grace. But 'if it is in the surrounding world where everything starts and finishes with designation, then our identity is nothing but a pure grammatical joke'[246] – the alienated signifier; the unity of the 'I' only holds firm through the grammar that says 'I', the personal pronoun, the subject of the verb (action), and its purely logical properties.

Is that all? No. In this context, the sign takes on a new value – with the shaping of the oeuvre. The unique sign becomes an equivalent. But not one equivalent amongst others: it lays itself bare as the equivalent of

244 *Ibid.*, pp. 338–9.
245 *Ibid.*, p. 337.
246 *Ibid.*

everything that may come into being: it is a stand-in for *everything*. In this capacity, it is effectively unique.

> [...] What happens in the world happens to no one, but something happens to someone which stands in for all that happens in the world. [...] 'Each of us hears only one thing, I repeated to myself ad nauseam; oh that he should speak of something else!' But the coherence of thought makes thought insatiable. Either he stays at this degree of intensity that thought designates for him, or it designates nothing for him. In the use of everyday signs, such a unique sign will always remain insinuated.[247]

This is what Klossowski refuses: this unique sign must no longer be merely insinuated. Since he thinks and writes, theorises and paints on the basis of this unique sign, then it must belong to him through an oeuvre. He must hear it, first for himself, then make it heard, communicate it, to avoid this autarkic jouissance that was driving him mad.

> Could it be that a unique sign designates all that happens – outside of me – as the only thing important to know – just as the name of Roberte covertly permitted it? [...] Subjected to such a constraint, I looked for its equivalent for a long time, and not being able to stand this to the point of going mad (by hushing up, as required by coherence of thought), it was by already becoming mad that the equivalent came to me.[248]

The unique sign would henceforth order the world and allow what is not visible in banal everyday life to be seen:

> The sign, standing in for a gesture, a situation, a word, gives rise to utterances (without any equivalent in everyday designations [...]). In this way the sign casts its shadow on the everyday reality of the world. From there it eliminates the memory that gives rise to the world. And I became obscure noticing these utterances to which the sign gave rise in all clarity, because I integrated them to everyday reality as a description, not of reality, but of the place given to these utterances by the sign.[249]

This is what describes both Octave's and Théodore's experience in the trilogy: there are two Robertes – the everyday Roberte, living and concrete,

247 *Ibid.*, p. 343.
248 *Ibid.*, p. 345.
249 *Ibid.*, p. 346.

and the Roberte linked to the unique sign of the name 'Roberte' which only belongs to the husband's imaginary scenario. Both protagonists want to verify the Roberte elaborated in the fantasy in the everyday Roberte.

> As soon as I started to describe this physiognomy even in the notation of the utterances resulting from, outside of time, this name of Roberte, and that, in these discontinuous tasks, she appeared not just as a coincidence with the name, but as a physiognomy that had been until then outside of and shadowed by this sign […],[250]

then it happens that the physiognomy has the same worth as the sign. This physiognomy will force its presence, filling up the space in both the fiction and the painting that represents it. Imposture is not far away: divulging the physiognomy that is associated with the unique sign, incommunicable[251] by definition, '[…] remains sullied by an appearance of imposture whose mere idea henceforth haunts he who divulged the sign […].'[252] From here on, Klossowski, and his characters Octave and Théodore, shall live under the same sign 'Roberte' as enhanced by the image of the physiognomy of Denise, Pierre's wife, and named 'Roberte' in the husband's fiction. As Klossowski hammers home, this physiognomy is pure silence,[253] i.e. pure enigma. An image (physiognomy) is always incomprehensible. It does not speak; it harbours a secret. Hence the necessity of exchanging this physiognomy, supported by a living, bodily agent, by prostituting the wife so that another truth may arise: quid of Roberte's essence? 'What I see I refer to the name of Roberte; I would not see in the absence of this name.'[254] What has he seen? To unpack what the name 'Roberte' allows us to see blindfolded (blinded? – and this is to be taken literally, not metaphorically: Octave/Théodore becomes a pure *gaze* object) is to find our bearings in the author's 'forest of the fantasy'[255] through his oeuvre – and its limitations.

250 *Ibid.*, p. 347.

251 'The divulgation of a sign, unverifiable in itself, is a form of delirium […]', *ibid.*, p. 348.

252 *Ibid.*

253 *Ibid.*, pp. 348–9.

254 *Ibid.*, p. 335.

255 Lacan, J., 'Kant with Sade', *op. cit.*, p. 654.

Are the laws of hospitality the locus of the unique sign? Yes and no. Yes, because they are the system in which the constraint of the unique sign may be exorcised and communicated. No, because the sign only has one locus: itself. It is an immobile circle, enciphering the shifting and impulsive intensity. It is 'the coherence of thought with itself [...].'[256] The trilogy of 'Roberte' is built on this uneliminable tension: it both is and is not the locus of the unique sign. We can only grasp what is at stake in the textual fiction of the trilogy when we refer to the tension that the contradictory formula inscribes: *Exchange the unexchangeable Roberte!*

256 Klossowski, P., *Les lois de l'hospitalité*, *op. cit.*, p. 344.

The Violence of the Gaze

The resources for broaching the art oeuvre[1] of Pierre Klossowski, who was both a theoretician of pictorial creation and a draughtsman, are limited. For him there was a radical difference between his reflections on art and his coloured drawings, and the works he proposed to his readers or viewers can be understood only by examining the context in which he placed them. This context, however, breaks with the way we are currently used to thinking and seeing: it is based on a theological orientation. To ignore this orientation, which is maintained throughout all of Klossowski's commentaries and artwork, would deprive his texts and pictures of their cutting edge, of their pertinence. As ever, our author's theological references are multiple and not necessarily homogenous. Klossowski plays with theology, making it say things it never really did.

Two remarks, dating from 1982, shall guide us:

– 'Every work of art is thus of the order of the revelation of an essence and its contemplation',
– 'Every time, there is simulacrum and dissimulation'.[2]

The question of the image is examined throughout Klossowski's work. The analyses and the images he produces, in spite of references that seem ancient or even outdated, are astonishingly contemporary. They show and tell of how an image cannot be reduced to a closed or sealed off unity. On the contrary, an image exists only because the void that brings it about, and where it is continually recharged, is not at all annulled or forgotten but is

1 An introduction to Klossowski's artwork can be found in Jacques Henric's monograph, *Pierre Klossowski*, Adam Biro, Paris, 1989. It includes a list of the artist's exhibitions, a complete catalogue of his works, and colour reproductions. Henric defines Klossowski's drawing as 'the art of the most unstable disequilibrium there is', p. 132.

2 Klossowski, P., *La Ressemblance*, *op. cit.*, p. 110.

tirelessly approached, circumscribed, and then straight away missed. Missing it in this way is not a failure or the unfortunate sign of some impotence. Missing the void is the very condition for the emergence and success of its fixed and very real trace: the image, precisely. 'For me, the image is [...] a force,[3] he would say.

Demons and *Simulacra*

Klossowski often insists that the painting solicits the body of the attentive observer. This remark requires us to return to the antique 'theology' of Hermes Trismegistus, the legendary mystagogue – to wit, to return to the collaboration of demons in the work of art.

> In the impossibility (says Trismegistus in the anonymous Neo-Platonic text *Asclepius*) of creating a soul to animate the simulacra of the gods, the souls of demons and angels were invoked and enclosed in holy images so that, thanks to these souls, the idols had the power to do good and evil.[4]

Following Trismegistus' argument on the constitution of these idols, which are *simulacra*, Klossowski holds the idea that a picture maker cannot act through his subjectivity alone. He has to strike an alliance. Here we see that the call to demons must be put in its Neo-Platonic context: they are the natural intermediaries between impassive gods and passionate men. Demons have contradictory natures. Being part men and part gods, they can serve as mediators between the two. Since no contact, no collaboration whatsoever is possible between divinity and mankind (where there is absolute heterogeneity), going via the demons is not a choice, but a necessity in order to animate the pictures as simulacra. The Neo-Platonic demons are needed, namely, to give the pictures a power, an action – a

3 *Ibid.*, p. 104.
4 *Ibid.*, p. 95.

'moral'[5] action says Klossowski – over his viewers; thanks to the demons, the pictures become active. Hence, 'these simulacra that know the future, herald it through fate, through the seer, through dreams [...] that strike men with illness and heal them'.[6]

Our author likewise brings up this reflection on the simulacra in at least three other historical references posterior to Trismegistus – references that mix polytheism with the Catholic notion of conception.

For the Romans, the *simulacrum* designated the status of a god. The simulacrum was a constructed object, made to represent a divinity. In Late Rome, these statues lined the roads throughout the city, but – most importantly – they 'gave a sexual determination to the divinities they represented. For the indeterminacy of their essence, they substituted a materialisation that was a sexualisation.'[7] Through this representation they are able to bear the stamp of sexualisation. Their *essence*, as far as their sex is concerned, remains indeterminate. In this respect their essence eludes the play of the signifier – despite its many possible representations, it remains inviolate and inviolable. The Roman simulacrum specifies the inevitable tension between the need for and the impossibility of communication, here posited as structural rather than contingent. It inscribes the contradiction between the invisibility and the inaccessibility of divine essence, and the insistent wish of its worshippers to give it a concrete, palpable, representable form for worship.

Following Varron, Saint Augustine distinguishes,[8] in his *City of God*, theatrical theology, which is part of mythology, from both natural theology, which meets the requirements of reason, and civil theology that refers to the rules of social institutions. Saint Augustine employs harsh words – 'false', 'mendacious', 'fabulatory'[9] – to criticise theatrical theology because it makes a show of the gods and goddesses. This type of theology – playful,

5 *Ibid.*

6 *Ibid.*

7 Arnaud, A., *Pierre Klossowski*, *op. cit.*, pp. 48–9.

8 A. Arnaud, who studied theology, insists on the Augustinian filiation with regard to vision in Klossowski's work. See *ibid.*, pp. 63–7.

9 *Ibid.*, p. 27.

based on make-believe and 'as if' – ridicules the divinities and their worship. By privileging image and representation, theatrical theology affirms the precedence of imposture and intellect over the power of the soul. The Christian Fathers – Tertullian, Irenaeus, Augustine – will respond to this provocation with one word: 'sacrilege'.

> What you see cannot be the divine truth, but its simulacra. What you take to be vision is but blasphemous illusion, impious images inspired not by God but by demons. 'A diabolo scilicet!' fulminates Tertullian.[10]

The aesthetic prevails over the ethical. It is this theology, however, that allows one to pass from concept to image, from the word to the given-to-be-seen. But at a cost!

The notions of Christianity have from the start been supported by the contradiction between the seeing eye (the noble organ according to the Fathers) and the Most-High in so far as he entirely escapes being seen. To admit that God can be represented and that the derived images are to be worshipped is to put an end to divine transcendence, on one hand, and to lapse into idolatry on the other, by conferring a practically divine status upon images. We know that Islam and Judaism considered this practise to be sacrilege. Their response was affirmative: *no to visual representation*. Yet Christianity was more reserved, being the religion of Incarnation. Two schools of thought surfaced in this debate: the iconophiles (and the iconodules) opted for this imaged representation. Was not man created in the image of God, did not the Incarnation[11] make the Son of God fully man? On the other hand, the iconoclasts (and the *iconomaques*) insisted on the impossibility of comparing the Creator to his creatures. Hence the prohibition issued against representation.

10 Arnaud, A., '"Nihil sine visione sive in visione omnia", Klossowski', *Revue de Sciences humaines*, 197, Lille, 1985.

11 'It is only after Christianity, indeed after the Incarnation, that images came to express the supernatural in the bodily and earthly realities that they reproduced. Hence the iconoclasts' question.' Klossowski, P., *La Resemblance, op. cit.*, p. 105.

In 787, at the Second Council of Nicaea, the question was taken up again and a 'compromise'[12] was found:

> [...] we keep unchanged all the ecclesiastical traditions handed down to us, whether in writing or verbally, one of which is the making of pictorial representations, agreeable to the history of the preaching of the Gospel, a tradition useful in many respects, but especially in this, that so the incarnation of the Word of God is shown forth as real and not merely phantastic, for these have mutual indications and without doubt also have mutual significations. [...] For by so much more frequently as they are seen in artistic representation, by so much more readily are men lifted up to the memory of their prototypes, and to a longing after them. [...] For the honour which is paid to the image passes on to that which the image represents, and he who reveres the image reveres in it the subject represented.[13]

This conciliatory definition leads to the affirmation of the inherently contradictory and ambiguous status of the image. Between the image and its divine model (*typos*), there is at once a close kinship and a radical difference. The image imposes itself as a material presence but is fundamentally incomplete: the model, being invisible, is missing.

> By more than just the means of the image, the contemplator is invited to encounter that which only offers its resemblance. The community that links the image to its model is not of the order of identity but analogy.[14]

Ambiguity reigns in the image, the 'as if', the sleight of hand. Klossowski refers to Saint Thomas on this point:

> Saint Thomas defines the image as, on one hand, something distinct from what it represents and, by virtue of this, a movement in the cognoscitive faculties and in the thing represented; and on the other, a movement in the image and in the very thing it is an image of.[15]

12 Arnaud, A., *Pierre Klossowski, op. cit.*, p. 43.

13 From 'The Decree of the Second Council of Nicaea', trans. Percival, H., *Nicene and Post-Nicene Fathers, Second Series*, Vol. 14., edited by Philip Schaff and Henry Wace, Christian Literature Publishing Co., Buffalo, New York, 1900.

14 Arnaud, A., *Pierre Klossowski, op. cit.*, p. 43.

15 Klossowski, P., *La Ressemblance, op. cit.*, p. 104.

Furthermore, the decision of Nicaea does not cancel out the Decalogue's prohibition: God cannot be seen head on, 'but only from ... behind.'[16] In a word, the image is partial, biased, and anecdotic, and only obliquely represents what one wants to see: the nature (*ousia*) or essence of God. Manipulating images (the play between the movement in the cognoscitive faculties and the movement in the thing itself) becomes an activity determined by the very status that representation actualises. This is not resolved, but rather intensified by Christianity.

The formulations from the *Asclepius* – very ancient explanations that have been forgotten today – are quite present for Klossowski. He uses words of Trismegistus to think through pictorial communication and the creation of pictures.

> Formulated some two millennia hence [...], this explanation of simulacra designed to act morally upon the viewer would never cease to come back to me each time I would stand in front of a work. [...] What relationship is there between such works and idols? How can one dare to claim that a painting or a sculpture today could stem from the same principle? This question or presupposition is aberrant in the context of contemporary production.[17]

These remarks may well be two thousand years old but for Klossowski they are still pertinent. Like the idol makers of the past, he also creates simulacra, and finds himself confronted with the terrible impossibility of creating a soul, for it remains forever outside life because of its spiritual origin. The simulacrum thus remains inert, devoid of supernatural life, reduced to a thing cut off from the divine Other. This is what our artist cannot come to terms with. He will need, 'the complicity of a demonic force' to obtain a 'moral action from the visual object produced by the artist.'[18] To do so, he will not forget his theological references: theatrical theology, the Christian Fathers, the Second Council of Nicaea, and so on.

But how is one to invoke these Neo-Platonic demons at the end of the twentieth century? Klossowski's stroke of genius is to have found the

16 Arnaud, A., *Pierre Klossowski*, *op. cit.*, p. 46.

17 Klossowski, P., *La Ressemblance*, *op. cit.*, p. 95.

18 *Ibid.*, p. 96.

contemporary forms of these old and buried demons starting off from a singular experience of pathos.

> The fact that the 'invoked' demons are only the hypostases of obsessional forces acting from a visual or pictorial artwork is apparently of very little importance to the artist, provided he knows how to obtain its effect; but precisely, the fact that he can obtain it only if he upholds the hypothesis of a demonic world analogous to these forces, to the point of treating any movement of the soul as correlative to demonic movement, constitutes the very imperative of the visual suggestion he is pursuing.[19]

Although the ancient demons have disappeared, what they used to designate – the active and constraining obsessional forces – remains untouched. The phantasm (and its logic) remains, imposing itself upon the subject. These are the subject's demons. The obsessional forces are both part of the divine Other in that they stir the soul that the subject cannot create, and part human nature because they are acting, changing, and moving – they form its base in the sealed off unit of the agent. The soul is impassive, but the *pathos* made from these forces clearly is not. Allying with these forces amounts to animating the created objects. How so?

> Thus, each time the artist is at work on a picture, regardless of its 'motif', it is to forge his own invisible model – the demonic analogue of his own emotion – thus seducing it with the 'resemblance' of its simulacrum, as well as circumscribing it by a figure whose aspect acts upon the viewer in the same capacity as his model acts upon the artist.[20]

To forge the invisible model is to make an imitation that exteriorises the obsessive constraint, so that it can exit the artist and the *topos* of his soul in order to be placed in a simulacrum that is a picture. The obsession, which is now shut away and prisoner in an outside form, is the motor behind this simulated resemblance – the artwork.

The artist has a choice: either the artwork becomes an outlet where the obsessive constraint is projected outside, or

19 *Ibid.*
20 *Ibid.*

> [...] he will have been granting, for far too long, a necessary and therefore real character to this constraint so as not to know how to acknowledge therein the solicitude of the evil genius imparted to his destiny.[21]

In one case, the obsession is an internal constraint that must be disposed of on the outside; in the other, this constraint is affirmed and now exorcised in the artwork, and therefore still present and active. It is an affirmation of magic art, to use Breton's term. The demon – and its analogical replica in the phantasm's constrictive force, according to Klossowski – is not to be cast out but to be made use of – the artist has to know how to make it an ally. In this regard, Klossowski quotes Tertullian who described the demonic strategy as follows: 'The demon was both in the thing he made seen, and in the one for whom he made the thing seen.'[22] The demon must not therefore be rejected – another dead scrap on a canvas. The demon circulates between the artist, his canvas, and the viewer.

> If therefore a like 'demonic' complicity (in as much as it is always experienced by the artist as being 'outside' his will) provokes within him the obsessional, insistent vision of something, it is because it arouses in the artist a state to which corresponds the reappearance of the obsession in the painting, but awakens in the viewer a state corresponding to this aspect.[23]

This is the magical and exorcising character of art.

> Therefore the obsession acts simultaneously but differently in the artist and his simulacrum, and in the simulacrum and its viewer. The painting as a simulacrum merely reproduces the demonic strategy. To reproduce the demonic strategy is, for the artist, to exorcise the obsession.[24]

The demonic strategy conveys a particularity of the demon: it is not linked to a body, to a unit of the agent – on the contrary, as a spirit, it circulates: it is at once hither and thither, but each time differently. It is not the same,

21 *Ibid.*
22 *Ibid.*
23 *Ibid.*, pp. 96–7.
24 *Ibid.*, p. 97.

in the sense of the identical, that is reproduced and diffracted in accordance with the reflections of a mirror; it is multiple, changing, split. It is in the capacity of difference that it is found in the artist, in the viewer and in the painting. Klossowski insists on this function of art, which is assuredly of theological origin:

> [...] the phenomenon of painting in the traditional sense is in no way the reflection of a dead star at the heart of our industrial universe – or rather, in this absence of 'world', or of a perpetually disassembled world that industry means; [...] it has precisely the prestige of a persistent reflection whose source is none other than our psyche, obscured in its respiration and rhythm; this eclipse should bring to life legions of phantasms in desperate search of their own images in which they can be placed [...].[25]

This is the status of the artwork:

> It is true that none of our collectors ever take it upon themselves to claim that the malevolent as well as the benevolent forces would ever be united or met with there – if indeed what is involved is, not a construction in accordance with laws foreign to any emotive straying, in order to obtain an object that is reassuring in its very indifference, but rather a simulacrum whose constrictive power of attraction is due to the fact that it has been elaborated under the constraint of these forces.[26]

Klossowski does not however make the hypothesis of the Freudian unconscious. Conceptually speaking, nothing could be further from him. During an interview, he replied to this question (admittedly, he was mistaken about what he believed the unconscious to be for psychoanalysis, but the interest of his reply lies elsewhere) and made a contrast between psychoanalysis and 'demonological practice'.[27] Such a practice

> does not consider possession to be an illness, but a spiritual fact. The soul is always inhabited by some power, whether good or bad. Souls are not ill when they are inhabited, but when they are no longer inhabited. The illness of the modern world

25 [Translated from] *Catalogue Pierre Klossowski*, Centre nationale des arts plastiques, Éditions la Difference, Paris, 1990, 'Anthologie des écrits de Pierre Klossowski sur l'art', p. 181.

26 *Ibid.*

27 Klossowski, P., *La Ressemblance*, *op. cit.*, p. 107.

> is that souls are no longer inhabitable, and they suffer from it! This amounts to believing that the malevolent powers can be reduced to nothing on the pretext that there is no supernatural being. That is a miscalculation. As soon as a being exists, a supernatural being exists.[28]

The demon and the obsessional psychical forces are supernatural beings. They are exterior to the subject, but without them there is no more subject.

A *Topos* for the Soul

In this context, a question remains: '[...] once the painting has been made, what sustains its action?'

> What therefore is this [...] if the only thing between the artist and his simulacrum, between the simulacrum and its viewer, is the to and fro of a 'demonic' presence which, in and of this fact, by intensifying the gaze and modifying the contemplated object, always outflanks it so as never to be confused with the object of its forging.[29]

The simulacrum is not the demon. The demon does not allow itself to be imprisoned, unless he does so fortuitously in order to animate the place where he settles – 'pathology is a topology'.[30] Here we have the reference to theatrical theology, which was so opposed by the Church Fathers:

> To rehabilitate demonology is above all, for me, to establish an authentic pathophany that is both a method and a contestation. The theatrical character of theology came to it from its belief in the human soul as a locus inhabited by exterior autonomous powers, to wit, a mental topology, pathos conceived of as a *topos*.[31]

28 *Ibid.*, pp. 107–8.
29 *Ibid.*, p. 97.
30 *Ibid.*
31 *Ibid.*, pp. 105–6.

It is needless to dream of any demonic unity – the forces are always multiple, acentric.

> However, several forces can contend for the painter's receptivity to repeat their 'strategy', but none of them will ever stand in for the entirety of all those that alternate in the artist's 'pathology'. Neither the obsessions, nor the jouissances, nor the anxieties they provoke will ever exhaust the diverse appearances they consent to take on in the paintings.[32]

It is not a matter of the viewer becoming identified with the artist's demonic forces such as they animate the painting. Something else is in question – an affirmation of the multiple:

> [...] as regards the painting, the universality of the concrete in any spectator who contemplates it, even if he is uncultured, is founded on the phantasmatic potential of each viewer; not in the sense that he finds in the painting the concretisation of the same phantasm, but rather the possibility of concretising his own. The painting provides him with the syntax to actualise any phantasmatic life: the simulacrum.[33]

The canvas awakens 'in the spectator that which he cannot speak of'.[34]

On another occasion, Klossowski will return to this analysis.

> A. ARNAUD: [...] Does the artwork maintain its opacity, will it always be incommunicable?
> KLOSSOWSKI: Isn't the universal principle of any production or creation that it offers others the means to recognise themselves while at the same time concealing its own essence? The painting is the manifestation of an idiosyncrasy. [...] The art lovers who buy it can recognise themselves therein, can find complicity there. But there is seldom any coincidence between these affinities and the artist's intentions. The painting always remains a transposition, a simulacrum. It is as a simulacrum that it satisfies the art lover who finds himself therein. The spectator and the artist do not interpret the painting in the same way because they are not projecting the same experience onto it. Pathos cannot be communicated![35]

32 'Anthologie des écrits de Pierre Klossowski sur l'art', *op. cit.*, p. 196.
33 *Ibid.*, p. 181.
34 *Ibid.*, p. 83.
35 *Ibid.*, p. 109.

We need to grasp what the artwork brings us: 'The notion of reality suddenly disappears in favour of the supernatural. Any artwork is thus of the order of a revelation of an essence and its contemplation.'[36] The artist's function is

> […] always to solicit the viewer's reactions and to choose from his own dispositions those that […] must emerge in his own space and, by invading it, prolong it; the viewer must find himself face to face with this part of himself that can only be acknowledged if exterior to him: the arm that clasps is his; he is the one who palpates such and such a body part.[37]

The simulacrum offers a locus (*topos*) that the soul, animated by the pathos of obscure, idiosyncratic forces, shall finally come to inhabit. The viewer is beside himself, his forces are exteriorised, he may come to know – and madness is avoided. The 'soul's impulsive force' is set in motion – the creature is no longer separated from his supernatural being. The proof of its emergence? A force seizes hold of the viewer, '[…] actualising something that is inactual but which […] [he] lends himself to nonetheless.'[38] The viewer's essence is actualised – his moral unity comes undone, the demon rises up from the outside and from this scene: it is the abolition of the sovereign ego, and the viewer on the other side is henceforth the frozen witness.

These remarks, which might seem surprising coming from the mouth of an artist exhibited in avant-garde galleries, are articulated in light of an opposition Klossowski often comes back to: the contrast between text and picture. There is no complementarity between them – on the contrary: they are exclusive and radically opposed. Whilst one can translate a text and, he says, one can attempt to do the same for a poem, one is bound to fail because it is ultimately untranslatable. This is the status of the picture: it cannot be translated.

36 *Ibid.*, p. 110.

37 *Ibid.*, p. 194.

38 Klossowski, P., *La Ressemblance*, *op. cit.*, p. 109.

> This holds true for the painting as for the poem: one cannot reproduce them in an idiom that is different from the one of their first conception. Translated into the idiom of the translator, it is a new poem. In what idiom would one translate a painting?[39]

There is a radical incompatibility between the picture's *making seen* and the text's *making understood*. Admittedly, the two practices in question are determined by an obsessional constraint, but its treatment differs absolutely:

> It seems that the choice of the mode of expression into one space or another is already determined by the obsessional motif. That the intention of *making seen*, rather than that of *making understood*, supposes not only that the obsession is specifically spatial, but that the space of the *making seen* renders it strictly foreign to the space of the *making understood*; or else that the corporeal sensation, for example touch, suggested by the *making seen*, brings an exclusive satisfaction to the one who projects it through his mode of expression – as soon as he has no other concern than sharing the incommunicable evidence of his motif.[40]

For Klossowski, vision is absolutely privileged. Vision takes precedence and imposes itself before an image, the secret essence of its pathos and which, by definition, cannot be said.

> Since each language has its own idiomatic expressions, and since from one idiomatic expression to another there is no common measure of experience, each mode of expression opposes its own idioms to another mode: the area of the mute gesture that speech is always seeking to exorcise, while at the same time the muteness of the gesture means to reduce speech to the silence of an irreducible motif.[41]

It is only irreducible precisely because it is not said. '*Making seen* by showing is an operation that is incompatible with *making understood* and demonstrating on the condition that nothing be shown.'[42] A logical anteriority of a 'spatial instant'[43] conditions the image and its vision and excludes, because it is sheer immediacy, the temporal sequence of conceptual reasoning. The

39 'Anthologie des écrits de Pierre Klossowski sur l'art', *op. cit.*, pp. 180–1.

40 *Ibid.*, p. 172.

41 *Ibid.*

42 *Ibid.*

43 *Ibid.*

image is 'irreversible proof', with Klossowski adding: 'I possess it at first glance by the effect produced on me.'[44] There is an image because there is this effect. In a certain way, the image is conjugated in the future perfect. From the moment an effect is produced, an image ... will have been. It is not there *a priori*; only the demons (i.e. the constrictive obsessional forces) that the image encloses and activates can retroactively constitute it – create it – as such.

The image is in no way neutral or immobile; it is fundamentally active, or better still efficient for whosoever confronts it. In this respect, one has to speak of risk. It is the life itself – of the painter and the contemplator – that is risked. Klossowskian analysis brings us to this meshing of death and image.

In the Format of the Body

The next question to attend to is that of the pictures that Klossowski actually made. What does he show, and what does he say about what he does – about this switch from writing to picturing, from the speculative to the *specular*, from the concept to the given-to-be-seen?

Klossowski's first pencil drawings date from 1953 and were reproduced in *Roberte ce soir* [the French edition]. The originals are of a 100 × 72 cm format, which is completely different from what is commonly produced for small format book illustration: 10.5 × 17 cm. From the outset our artist refused to work in a small format. In order to include his drawings in the book, published by Éditions de Minuit, they had to be considerably scaled down. Why this choice of format?

> [...] while I was making my illustrations for *Roberte Ce Soir*, I was haunted by this idea of dolls. I was telling myself that I shouldn't stay in this [10.5 × 17 cm] format because people would tell me I was drawing puppets.[45]

44 Klossowski, P., *La Ressemblance*, *op. cit.*, p. 69.

45 'Anthologie des écrits de Pierre Klossowski sur l'art', *op. cit.*, p. 192.

From his first works on, Klossowski intends to impose an almost life-size presence of the body, determined to avoid any reduction in the format that might suppress the actuality of the bare body represented. Why impose the body's presence – especially the presence of a naked woman?

> The fact that the (creator's) spatial instant is only the phantasm of the body itself, in as much as it is the seat of this resistance, that it projects and limits either as a locus that conquers external resistance or, on the contrary, as a locus imposed by the obsession itself, is the proof that founds the phenomenon of visual arts [...].[46]

The body is the locus of a combat between impulsive forces and censorship:

> Nothing in impulsive life seems to be strictly free-of-charge. As soon as an interpretation directs the process itself (the emotion's struggle to subsist despite the instinct of propagation), evaluation, and therefore price, intervene; but he who ultimately bears the cost of this, he who will pay in one way or another, is the agent constituted by the locus where the combat is fought out, where a possible or unobtainable compromise is worked out and negotiated: one's body.[47]

If the body is reduced, in the drawing, to a miniature, to a doll, this problematic falls flat. The fight over and within the agent – one's body – would become derisory – it would lose its value and its power of phantasmatic constraint.

By choosing this format at the outset, Klossowski means to establish a 'communion' with the bodily presence of the spectator:

> The figures commune immediately with the spectator's bodily presence. Large religious compositions, antique life-size mural paintings, or paintings which give the impression of being life-size, place the spectator at the level of the action of the figures. The viewer shares the same space as the characters.[48]

46 *Ibid.*, p. 179.

47 Klossowski, P., *La Monnaie Vivante*, *op. cit.*

48 'Anthologie des écrits de Pierre Klossowski sur l'art', *op. cit.*, p. 193.

Choosing a small format would have had a serious consequence:

> I think there is a bit of censorship involved in restricting the dimensions. In those times when censorship was feared, it was thought very dangerous to show things life-size [...]. I was told, 'you're doing things that are really very violent, which require us to throw ourselves onto the figures lest they throw themselves on to us.' Why did Bellmer never give rise to scandal? Simply because he worked on the scale of a goldsmith, it was almost entomology or botany.[49]

To affirm a large, nearly life-size format is to make the presence of the phantasm, actualised through the represented body, something to be reckoned with:

> RÉMY ZAUGG: *Your large figures are partners to the spectator's body.*
> KLOSSOWSKI: Yes, the viewer cannot remain indifferent: either he finds that this doesn't touch him at all and he passes on, or else it does something to him, he looks, and there's a kind of exchange between him and the figures. This is due to the human scale of the figures. A painting representing life-size figures on a bedroom floor gives the illusion that they're on an equal footing with the spectator.[50]

In Klossowski's presence, Rémy Zaugg makes the following shrewd remarks, which go unopposed:

> In your drawings, the large scale, full-length figures are carefully wrought, whereas the place of action is more suggested than represented and is limited to indications of a floor, a vertical plane, some ordinary, everyday accessories, a banister, a door, or a window. The characters stand out. The place seems to be contingent, while the characters form an entity, a block that appears to be detachable.[51]

The picture stages the (nearly) life-size body by pinning it against the wall at the height of the viewer: the characters' feet must be touching the floor.

49 *Ibid.*
50 *Ibid.*
51 *Ibid.*, p. 192.

> I started off from the idea of mural painting, with everything that that entails in terms of theatricality and the spectacular. I never forget that I'm working on a wall, thus allowing for the verticality, and not on images that could be put down like a book.[52]

Klossowski draws standing up, eye to eye with his characters, with the paper attached to the wall. Though his paper is hung like this in his studio, in galleries and museums it is always exhibited above ground level, as all paintings are.

There we have it for his first drawings which date back to 1953. For nearly twenty years Klossowski would continue making pencil drawings with life-size figures: strokes that affirm the body's invasive presence as displayed across the surface of a sheet of white paper.

From Black and White to Colour

In 1972, there is another switch. To begin with, a few drawings are enhanced with coloured pencil. Next, graphite is abandoned altogether and colour reigns, still in pencil on paper. Klossowski uses neither canvas nor coloured paint. Only paper and pencil crayons are used – and it will be like this to the end of his life. In his interviews, he often repeated his anecdote of switching to colour.

> RÉMY ZAUGG: *Why did you start adding colour?*
> […]
> KLOSSOWSKI: A dealer told me: 'but why do you rule out colour? It would be interesting.' Perhaps he was thinking it would be more commercially viable. But his remark aroused my curiosity. I actually began enhancing some of my drawings, just to see. Only I didn't stop there.[53]

52 *Ibid.*, p. 197.
53 *Ibid.*, p. 189.

Now faced with the sight of coloured drawings, how did Klossowski proceed? What did he deduce from this?

> At one point I saw I had to start over, that I had to give up pencil entirely and work as one works in painting, in other words to consider the composition from the point of view of hues, to eliminate the graphite and just keep the coloured pencil. And that's how it switched.[54]

We need to grasp what is at stake in the picture maker's work. First of all, from 1953 to 1972 he opts for large formats where the life-size figures face up to the viewer. This type of drawing, often with pornographic images, is traditionally represented in reduced form, in miniature. Our artist refuses this outright – it is the creator's refusal of the censorship of his oeuvre. From 1972 onwards, he uses only coloured pencil. The formats however remain the same.

> Of course, there is a problem: the coloured pencils are completely disproportionate to the formats I use. The work is very slow by nature. It takes me a crazy amount of patience to obtain what I think I can obtain, all the same, against all the odds.[55]

Yes, Klossowski tires himself out using coloured pencils where paint, which can spread out and easily cover large surfaces, would be the obvious choice. He roams over the surface of his characters' bodies, centimetre by centimetre. He creates slowly, little by little, going over the surface of a woman stripped bare, repeatedly reproduced: Roberte. Klossowski often brings up the complications and technical difficulties that come with this choice of using only coloured pencils – this is one of his technical obsessions.

> Naturally there are people who say: 'but why doesn't he take up brushes, why doesn't he turn to oil painting?' It wouldn't be the same. And besides, I don't do it because that would necessitate real training, and I'm not sure whether the effect would be the same.[56]

54 *Ibid.*
55 *Ibid.*
56 *Ibid.*

Opting for coloured pencils is a choice to obtain a certain effect – on the viewer. But what effect? Klossowski takes some time before answering this crucial question. He comes back to the constraints of the technique:

> [...] I believe the coloured pencil to be a justified process. To draw with coloured pencil is also to apply colour, it's not simply a drawing. A painter friend [...] was telling me that for him, my pictures are painted. Paradoxically, my pictures are made with pencil crayon, but the effect is the same as a painting, as if a brush had been used like a pencil crayon.[57]

The constraint of pencil crayon imposes the impossibility of effacing, of transforming, of truly modifying the overall layout of the picture:

> The cores of some colours are composite, they're blended. The browns, for instance. If I rub out a brown, the paper becomes reddish because the pencil's powder separates into black and red, and the black powder comes off more easily. These hitches are very disagreeable. Afterwards I find it very hard to get back a satisfying hue, density and opacity.[58]

Klossowski does not complain about these numerous constraints – he accepts them. Is he not meeting again, in the concrete exercise of pictorial work – on his feet, crayon in hand – precisely what he has been ceaselessly wanting to exorcise, to exteriorise in a specific locus: the simulacrum of the oeuvre, or the obsessive constraint of the phantasm? Does he not find, in the concreteness of his slow, measured, and countless movements, the invading constraint that he calls 'my mental visions'? The means of presentation, of *monstration*, are homogenous with its very object: to imitate and seduce the sexual demon so as to enclose it within the exterior artwork, so that it is circumscribed on the outside.

What does our artist want to obtain? To bring the wall to life, he says. '[...] and I manage this with coloured pencils. Consequently, my technique is sufficient because it allows me to get what I want in a very straightforward

57 *Ibid.*, pp. 189–90.

58 *Ibid.*, p. 190.

and relatively neat medium.'[59] By animating the wall, he manages to enclose a demon that is henceforth active. It is the demon's equivalent: the obsessional visual constraint that makes the wall move and in a certain sense come to life, contrary to the neutral and amorphous support it was to begin with. 'My drawings obey a will to figuration. It's a way of seeing and letting oneself see pathos.'[60] He adds:

> My large colour compositions are designed as mural paintings for house interiors [...]. I stick to motifs that are specifically spectacular, but in a sense contrary to the optics of today with all their processes for projecting images, holograms and special effects [...].[61]

This then is the point of his 'explanation':[62] to bring the wall to life is to animate the interior of a house.[63] It is to rediscover the tutelary powers of the ancient idols. And it is especially to inhabit the bedroom – the ultimate intimate theatre and meeting ground of living bodies. Pierre Klossowski's paintings – or 'frescos'[64] – form the architecture of a place for lost and straying powers.

59 *Ibid.*
60 *Ibid.*, p. 199.
61 *Ibid.*, p. 189.
62 *Ibid.* The title of his interview with Rémy Zaugg is 'Fragments of an Explanation'.
63 '(JUDITH MILLER): *Are your drawings frescos in pencil crayon?*
(PIERRE KLOSSOWSKI): That's what they ought to be called. So far as I know, that has never existed before. Essentially, these frescos presuppose a residence. I have some collectors who have residences where they live with my pictures. An art lover doesn't stack up valuables in bank vaults. He knows how to live with my pictures. This cohabitation is different from the reader cohabiting with a book.' 'La mutation', in *L'Âne,* Issue 28, *op. cit.,* p. iv. [The full interview is reproduced in this volume as 'Mutation'.]
64 Jouffroy, A and Klossowski, P., *Le secret pouvoir du sens*, Écriture, Paris, 1994, pp. 110–11.

Writing versus Picturing

The question that most keenly intrigues those who have interviewed our artist concerns the relationships between writing and painting. Klossowski has never – this is a decisive point – both written and drawn at the same time: 'I didn't juggle the two activities, rather I alternated them. There was the period when the pencil drawings coexisted, in fact, with the writing.'[65] During this period – 1953 to 1972 – he drew then wrote, then drew again, and so on. The introduction of colour, however, had a radical effect: it marked a definitive abandonment of writing. Klossowski would no longer write fictional narratives. From then on he would merely agree to reply, with patience and attention, to interviewer's questions.

> Then there was the discovery of colour, which corresponded to me giving up writing. By the same token, the satisfaction procured by this experience led me to sacrifice to it all the time it required.[66]

Klossowski would come back to this abandonment. It only takes on meaning when referred to the radical difference between writing and showing, between arguing and giving-to-be-seen. In a 1982 interview with Alain Arnaud, one of the finest connoisseurs of the Klossowskian oeuvre, he clarifies his choice:

> This way of expressing oneself [through coloured pencil drawings], apparently a primitive one, could not brook any simultaneity with written communication, which is always indirect with regard to the lived emotion. To wit, language, in so far as it stems from common sense, alters the particular motif with a view to general receptivity. By giving up writing, which constantly lent itself to misunderstanding, I confined myself to giving expression only through the picture.[67]

The multicoloured image clears away misunderstanding by positing itself as presence. The means chosen to carry this through absorbed all of

65 'Anthologie des écrits de Pierre Klossowski sur l'art', *op. cit.*, p. 197.
66 *Ibid.*
67 *Ibid.*

Klossowski's time, who was already elderly (sixty-seven years old in 1972). For him, the result he obtained was a success – with colour, he hit the target. What happened? What did colour introduce? He specifies this on different occasions:

> [I want] [...] to make my contemporaries feel, rather than understand, my visions [...]. In fact, I've gone from graphology to calligraphy, or rather, to hieroglyphy. I treat painting as hieroglyphy [...]. There has been an absolute break from writing. Going from speculation to the *specular*, I actually find myself under the dictates of image. Vision demands that I say everything it gives me.[68]

These sentences are well known and frequently quoted. They still have their radical edge. Visions impose themselves upon our subject; for years, he had striven to exorcise them through words, sentences and concepts. When colour emerges, set down centimetre after centimetre across the paper, something imposes itself – a genuine *tuché*.[69] Klossowski copies out his visions, he shows them. But the vision is a voracious one: it is demanding. But what does it demand? To say everything that it gives. Let us note the verb 'say', as opposed to 'show'. Saying everything is not possible. Showing, on the other hand, allows, as has been said, for co-presence. In order to say everything that the mental vision gives, one must no longer say, but show. The imperative of figuration succeeds where words fail each time. 'My drawings obey a will to figuration.'[70] On one occasion he notes: 'Reading a picture is not the same thing as reading a book. Speech and writing explain a series of facts that apparently succeed each other. My pictures take up the fait accompli without explanation.'[71] The act has taken place but one does not know (anymore) what it meant. It is shown – mute.

68 *Ibid.*

69 [TN, For an elucidation of the use of this term in a psychoanalytic context, the reader may consult Lesson V of Lacan, J., *The Seminar Book XI, The Four Fundamental Concepts of Psychoanalysis, op. cit.*, pp. 53–64.]

70 'Anthologie des écrits de Pierre Klossowski sur l'art', op. cit., p. 197.

71 'Mutation', in this volume.

> JUDITH MILLER: And yet what satisfies you in drawing is the muteness [...].
> KLOSSOWSKI: ... which gives rise to an image. To those who don't know my pictorial activity, I say that now I only think in the way the picture thinks. It's asocial, as if I'd fallen into a kind of insensibility with regard to the world around me as far as other relationships are concerned.[72]

How is this *I think in the way the picture thinks* to be understood? To be precise, it is the affirmation of mutism. Klossowski does not *say*, he no longer *writes*, he carries through his visions wordlessly. He thinks what the picture thinks; in other words, he does not think anymore: he transcribes his visual mental obsession and exhibits it without conceptual mediation.

> But it's communication all the same, whose initial egoism makes amends by inviting the viewer to participate in it. The painter is neither a hermit nor a solitary figure. For me, it's more important to *show* than to *say* what I see. Exhibiting is perhaps a defence with regard to the world we live in, to current affairs and the scarcity of understanding that is rife there. The phantasm is the obsessional and constrictive fact for all those who strive to create. Saying that I only paint to demonstrate my 'theories' is idiotic. An exhibition is not a demonstration.[73]

This exclusively pictorial practice gives us a new perspective on Klossowski's oeuvre as a whole. It allows us to grasp the place and effects of these inaugural mental images that exert an indestructible constraint and which demand, as sexual demons, a locus to exorcise them. The literary oeuvre – fictional and notional – finds its mainspring in the aftermath of this switch to drawing.

> [...] I did stop writing fifteen years ago now [October-November 1986]. I paint, and it's quite futile to look for any other relationship between my pictures and my novels besides the following: my pictures used to exist as such in my mind before I came to describe them in my novels.[74]

72 *Ibid.*
73 *Ibid.*
74 *Ibid.*

Already, in prefaces to his exhibitions in 1971 and 1972, Klossowski was underlining this point: the visions came first. For him, writing meant spelling out the pictures he had in his head. When he dedicated himself exclusively to colour, the same pictures, ever present, never entirely expelled, were shown. The obsession had in no way disappeared. Through narratives, theoretical works, and pictures Klossowski spent his life naming, conceptualising and visually presenting his insistent mental visions. Moreover, he adds that his pencil drawings were still too close to writing. Only colour constituted a break:

> It may well be that [...] [my] drawings betray a mental operation that is still too close to writing; and that by breaking away from it absolutely, they seem to be prolonging it. Because my books were only a transcription of motifs that I first lived and perceived as pictures and mute figures, all that I had yielded to in written form had to be retrieved as belonging primitively to the mutism of vision in order to communicate it in its original state.[75]

Writing and picturing become two activities cut off from each other. 'Language belongs to everyone, but not the image.'[76] The word makes for a social bond; the image creates a secret community where the singularity of a specific vision prevails. Klossowski would go so far as to say:

> My vision [...] of the bodies I draw remains subject to the 'syntax' of the space where these bodies move, just as the words they bring to the surface in the text of my books remain a function of the anatomical mutism of these figures.[77]

These visions are pure silence, and it is on the basis of this silence that words or new images are created. It would be naïve to believe that saying or showing would annul this original silence. On the contrary, saying and showing, each in their own different and specific way, bring this silence into being as a presence, as a remainder of what can be neither said nor shown. Klossowski is not so naïve as to believe that the ineffable is suppressed

75 'Anthologie des écrits de Pierre Klossowski sur l'art', *op. cit.*, p. 173.

76 Jouffroy, A and Klossowski, P., *Le secret pouvoir du sens*, *op. cit.*, p. 72.

77 'Anthologie des écrits de Pierre Klossowski sur l'art', *op. cit.*, p. 172.

by the effable, or that what cannot be represented is annulled by what is shown to be *figurable*.

> Text [...] has the flaw of including the tacit spatiality of these bodies, just as my drawings are dubious in as much as they are in charge of 'programming' the text. And despite appearances to the contrary, my drawings are drawn in a perfect ignorance of the written text, or the text to be written, just as this text speaks of their motifs as if they'd never been drawn by me, but were liable to be by whosoever would abstain from writing them.[78]

The Stereotype

A question remains in suspense: what does Klossowski picture? What does he give-to-be-seen, and above all how does he go about it? What style does he adopt? Klossowski develops a 'science of stereotypes'.[79] What does that mean? We must again begin with the simulacrum.

> The simulacrum in the imitative sense is the actualisation of something that is in and of itself incommunicable, or cannot be represented: literally, the phantasm in its obsessive constraint. [...] The simulacrum imitates what it catches in the phantasm. In this double function relative to the fact that it tends to reproduce either what cannot be said or what cannot be shown, according to social, moral or religious censoring, how does it pronounce it imitatively?[80]

Here we have the concise definition of the phantasm, as well as the question of the form it uses to show the unshowable that specifies it. In a very recent text, from 1994, Klossowski writes in answer to Alain Jouffroy – a reply that takes up afresh this tying-in between phantasm, simulacrum and *monstration*:

78 *Ibid.*
79 *Ibid.* p. 178.
80 *Ibid.* p. 174.

> By simulacrum, I do not mean a simulated picture, as has been reckoned or understood maliciously, but the picture materially simulating an interior vision, therefore one that is intimate and morally experienced (the phantasm), to wit, the constraint it exerts and thus exteriorises in accordance with the traditional rules of the image. In such a way that the emotional constraint switches round into the operation, in itself constrictive, of executing the picture.[81]

These formulations are noteworthy: 'traditional rules of the image', imitative capture. Klossowski depicts images in a realist manner, and to do so he borrows, '[...] in order to swing them round in favour of imitation, the institutional and therefore conventional stereotypes of the sayable and the showable.'[82] These stereotypes are presented on paper as a 'pantomime of spirits'.[83]

But what form does the stereotype present?

> The stereotype itself corresponds first of all to the normative schemes of our visual, tactile or auditory apprehension, a schematisation that conditions our first receptivity. Being institutionalised in accordance with social motifs that are always variable, these schemes, as stereotypes, will serve to warn of their slightest alteration by some lived fact of a perception or a phantasmagorical, monstrous or perverse receptivity.[84]

Klossowski insists, in a new way, on this specificity of the stereotype: it is

> any form schematised through use in as much as it expresses the lawfully sayable portion of a lived fact. But already the forms of tangible apprehension, in as much as they develop the habits of feeling and thinking (for example, the vision of the human body) are alerted by institutional interpretations, stereotypes therefore – the lived fact only becoming intelligible independently of its primitive, uncontrollable content.[85]

The art of the stereotype consists not of annulling or going beyond normative forms of academic representation. On the contrary, it is a matter

81 Jouffroy, A and Klossowski, P., *Le secret pouvoir du sens*, *op. cit.*, p. 58.
82 'Anthologie des écrits de Pierre Klossowski sur l'art', *op. cit.*, p. 175.
83 *Ibid.* p. 174.
84 *Ibid.* p. 175.
85 *L'Arc* journal, Issue 43, *op. cit.*, p. 19.

of choosing, absolutely, this mode of *monstration* by parodying it, exaggerating it, and over-coding it.

> The simulacrum efficiently simulates the obsessive constraint of the phantasm only by exaggerating the stereotyped schemes: going one step further with the stereotype and accentuating it amounts to acknowledging the obsession therein, of which it is a replica. And already a consummate science of stereotypes is characteristic of such varied geniuses as Ingres and Courbet, the former through his exploitation of the classic scheme, the latter by exploitation of popular imagery.[86]

The new function of the stereotype is particularly active and efficient:

> What therefore does the process of a 'science of stereotypes' consist of? Accentuating in the stereotype, to the point of excessiveness, to the point of disparity, its character of obsessive replica of the masked phantasm. In this way the stereotype itself makes a critique of its masking interpretation.[87]

To choose the stereotype is to opt to show, conventionally, what must be. Klossowski will call upon outmoded, outdated forms of stereotypes as modalities of seeing and *making-seen*. 'I've reached the point where I'm only speaking in "semblants" of forms and tonalities that I like doing with the most tasteless pompousness – as if I were leading a poor, desperate rearguard action [...].'[88] Our artist adds:

> Any invention of a simulacrum presupposes the reign of prevalent stereotypes: it's only with their decomposed elements that the making of a simulacrum manages to impose itself in turn as a 'stereotype'.[89]

This remark is important. Let us continue with Klossowski's analysis:

> Indeed, at the level of expression, as much in language as in art figuration, stereotypes are merely residues of the phantasmatic simulacra that have fallen into common use,

86 'Anthologie des écrits de Pierre Klossowski sur l'art', *op. cit.*, p. 175.
87 *L'Arc* journal, Issue 43, *op. cit.*, p. 19.
88 'Anthologie des écrits de Pierre Klossowski sur l'art', *op. cit.*, p. 180.
89 *Ibid.*, p. 175.

> left to a common interpretation: but as degraded simulacra they reflect an individual or collective reaction to some phantasm that has been emptied of its content.[90]

He adds:

> [...] as a degraded simulacrum, (the stereotype) appears as an institutional reaction provoked by the reflection of a (non-contemporary) phantasm in language as much as in art figuration. This is where the stereotype reveals its function as a masking interpretation.[91]

In other words, stereotypes are former simulacra that have passed into common use; they have become the bastardised forms of an original creation: the simulacrum, imitating the individual constraint of a phantasm. The stereotype is a cement that forms a social bond: it is a collective way of saying or seeing. Syntax – literary or pictorial – is an example of the efficient stereotype present in a society's culture. Klossowski has very harsh words for the abandonment of the science of stereotypes:

> The pure and simple destruction of the stereotype in painting, at the start of our century, heralded the rejection of the imitative and therefore exorcising role of the simulacrum, and by the same token the abandonment of the 'subject'. The picture ceased to be a simulacrum and became an *in-and-of-itself*.[92]

A consequence is deduced from this: 'Henceforth, the picture is no longer the exorcising simulacrum of some pre-existing phantasmatic obsession, since it does not imitate but draws to a close in its own "anatomy".'[93] There remains 'an arbitrary production of phantasms without any inner constraint, and therefore no longer able to morally exercise such a constraint'.[94]

For the 1970 issue of the journal *L'Arc* that was dedicated to him, Klossowski wrote a dense text, 'Protase et apodose'. He concludes it with a section entitled, '*De l'usage des stéréotypes et de la censure exercée par la*

90 *Ibid.*

91 *L'Arc* journal, 43, *op. cit.*, p. 19.

92 'Anthologie des écrits de Pierre Klossowski sur l'art', *op. cit.*, p. 175.

93 *Ibid.*, p. 176.

94 *Ibid.*

syntaxe classique' ['On the Use of Stereotypes and the Censoring Exerted by Classical Syntax']. These remarks complete the previous observations on his pictorial style.

> Undergoing the censorship of 'classical' syntax, to wit, its logical rigour exclusive of all contradictory propositions (in the image of 'anomalies'), literally amounts to reproducing the obsessional constraint of the (incommunicable) phantasm.[95]

To submit oneself to the external constraint of (literary or pictorial) syntax is to find oneself suddenly reproducing and imitating it rather than cancelling it out. The syntax becomes the equivalent chosen for reproducing the power of the constraint that the phantasm obsessionally exerts over mental life as a vision. Reproducing the obsession enables it to be placed on the outside, to be given a locus.

> Practiced wisely, the institutionalised stereotypes (of syntax) provoke the presence of what they circumscribe; their circumlocutions mask the incongruity of the phantasm and by the same token trace the contour of its opaque physiognomy. Hence the effect of disproportion between phantasmatic incongruity and its localisation in stereotyped terms that flaunt it on the pretext of conjuring it away.[96]

The stereotype enables a conjugation of that which cannot be conjugated. It contradictorily actualises the impossibility of a union: the disjunction between the (incongruous) phantasm and the code of everyday signs that excludes it. But by hiding it, annulling it, and censoring it, the stereotype delimits, in sunken relief, the unknown phantasm. The stereotype is a *veil* and in this capacity it brings out what it covers over as something missed, lost and impossible. The phantasm is painted or drawn as missing on the contours of the veil. Here we return to the critical function of this science:

> [...] the stereotype is a result of a stratifying process of the representation itself, such as it is developed on the basis of the phantasmatic constraint: the less this constraint comes to be voiced through the production of a word or an image, the more the obsessed subject [...] will be inclined to help himself to a stereotype already in

95 Klossowski, P., *La Ressemblance*, *op. cit.*, p. 11.
96 *Ibid.*

> existence, simply to signal its presence. What counts, when it comes to the future role of stereotypes, will be that which determines how the obsessive chooses one stereotype over another.[97]

To proceed any differently, by not keeping the masking and censoring forms of syntax, is a mistake because

> disarticulating the syntax in order to 'restore' the phantasm as such, breaking the forms down to reconstruct a phantasmality from it, amounts to letting go of the prey for a shadow, or to liquidating any constraint without exerting any, in the name of a futile liberty. Without the stereotypes of syntax, without any stereotype whatsoever, there is in turn no constrictive simulacrum.[98]

One could not be more incisive: the phantasm can be circumscribed only on the basis of the veil and censorship. In and of itself, it is incommunicable and ungraspable. Saying tells us that there is an unsayable; showing, that there is an unshowable. It is a question of drawing what cannot be said, writing what cannot be depicted.

The Incomprehensible Scene

It would be naïve to suppose that Klossowski offers up to view what lies hidden. Or that he brings to light that which is secret in a woman, in that teetering instant when sexual turmoil – 'animal' sensation – surges forth. The picture does not inscribe what is about to occur, and it in no way describes the act of carrying through the law of Hospitality. On the contrary, it suggests another scene, another action, another spectacle, but they are without witness, without the gaze that reveals them. That which is presented is not that which is truly to be seen: 'The spectator is put in a position of waiting: that which is [...] to be seen is still to come, but

97 *L'Arc* journal, 43, *op. cit.*, p. 19.

98 Klossowski, P., *La Ressemblance*, *op. cit.*, p. 11.

outside of the canvas: behind the closed eyes of the spectator'[99] notes Jean Roudaut in a fine text on the *Simulacra*. Klossowski – like Tonnerre – '[...] paints what one sees only with eyes shut, the other side of the curtain of eyelids.'[100] Such pictures *evoke*, and in no way *represent*.

As Octave notes, the radical violence of this staging is due to a very learned baring that does not hold to the bared, to the nudity of the body, but to 'what is in itself the least pictorial instant. The eye likes to dwell restfully upon a storyless motif, and our artist seems to unsettle this repose of the gaze by suggesting to the mind what the painting hides.'[101] This remark is decisive: the violence of the scene is not represented by the violation (e.g. of Roberte in her novels), but by a non-pictorial instant – which therefore lies off the canvas. This non-pictorial instant is what is suggested to the mind by the painted clues. The silent space of the canvas turns into time for the contemplator's *esprit*, his 'spirit'. Painting, given to the eye to feed upon, hides the violence of the scene. But the spirit says neither what it sees nor what it could see. What is effectively seen suggests only, to the mind and its demons, what is not visible. This is precisely what a picture must show: a violence spelt out or given-to-be-seen is always a simulacrum, a counterfeit of another violence which, for its part, is neither said nor visible. This is what Octave calls the 'glory of the oeuvre'.

Klossowski – like Tonnerre of course – paints characters whose actions and postures on the canvas are suspended, halted, immobilised. The suggested act is about to take place or has already taken place. The picture freezes actions and postures just a little before or just a little after this act that would reveal absolute violence. To understand this disconcerting fixity which precedes or follows an absolute violence, we can refer to Antonin Artaud and Albert Camus and their commentaries on Balthus' oeuvre. Quoting them with regard to Klossowski is possible because they

99 [Translated from] Roudaut, J., 'Les simulacres selon Pierre Klossowski', *Pierre Klossowski*, Les Cahiers pour un temps, *op. cit.*, p. 172.

100 *Ibid.*, p. 174.

101 Klossowski, *Roberte Ce Soir* and *The Revocation of the Edict of Nantes*, *op. cit.*, p. 99.

both examine precisely the effect of the *tableau vivant* on the canvas – this tableau vivant that Pierre had singled out in his brother's work in his first text on painting.

> I know not why painting [...] smells of plague, tempest, and epidemics. But it brings to light something from an electric period in history, one of those moments when the drama takes shape. Something like one of those atmospheric troughs [...] into which the advancing ship seems to be swallowed up. And there is nothing. The scenes are calm and motionless. The characters are those of a terrible brewing drama, yet they are taken unawares by the most anecdotal side of their lives.[102]
>
> That is how Artaud saw it. And Camus?
>
> Balthus [...] fixes the emotion and the scene, both at once, so precisely that one has the impression of gazing through glass at figures which a kind of spell has turned to stone, not forever but for one fifth of a second, after which their motion will be resumed. That fifth of a second is still going on as I write: that's the point, and then we realise that nature, if we look at it during that instant of stillness, is even stranger than the strange monsters that take shape in men's imagination.[103]

Klossowski himself writes:

> The representation of accessories relative to the figures in the picture creates an interval between the before and the after of the incident. The picture must suggest to the spectator what it in no way gives-to-be-seen.[104]

The spectator of our painter's pictures is thereby introduced into a scene he supposes

> not to have been destined for him. A terrible character, and one who compels him to see, playing the role of initiatory guide, is a third party between the presented work and himself. The painter is this third party who, granting himself the role of

102 [Translated from] *Catalogue Balthus*, Centre Georges Pompidou, Paris, 1983, p. 47.

103 Fox Weber, N., *Balthus*, Random House, 1999.

104 'Entretien de Pierre Klossowski avec Rémy Zaugg', *Catalogue Pierre Klossowski*, Centre nationale des arts plastiques, *op. cit.*, p. 63.

> the one who shows, shuts his eyes to convince himself he had seen: the fundamental experience is only the memory of a doubtful obsession.[105]

The viewer is compelled to see by force, led by the gaze of this terrible third party for whom this would have been destined. 'A curtain has just been drawn back for him [...]',[106] but the scene that is seen is incomprehensible, and the picture that is shown resembles a 'poster advertising some show or other'.[107] Our artist adds:

> I treat this picture (the scene known as *The Parallel Bars*) as a poster. No one, not knowing what it's about, could fail to be intrigued were I to show it in the street. People would inevitably stop and interpret it in their own way.[108]

The minutely represented details on the poster both indicate and blur the codes of readability:

> You've just seen, all of a sudden, a scene you don't understand, as often happens in life. The most striking thing is precisely the fact that you don't understand it. I play on incomprehension and not on the fact that there might have been a story.[109]

The viewer is compelled to suppose a univocal meaning or understanding of the scene. This is in fact a supposed meaning or understanding attributed to an other, for whom the scene would have been destined, and who would thus have been in the know; this eludes the viewer forever. The eye finds itself caught in an astonishing temporality that remains silent – that words can never break. He would see, on the canvas, the incident, or 'the odd news item nothing can prepare the viewer for.'[110] The illustrated incident is

> the staging of our modern discontinuity: a sudden vision of the unperceived fait accompli, between before and after. Which requires the most hysterically loyal

105 Roudaut, J., 'Les simulacres selon Pierre Klossowski', *op. cit.*, p. 172.
106 *Ibid.*
107 'Entretien de Pierre Klossowski avec Rémy Zaugg', *op. cit.*, p. 69.
108 *Ibid.*, p. 56.
109 *Ibid.*, p. 69.
110 *Ibid.*, p. 67.

reproduction of the antinomic phenomenon implicit in the odd news item: the rupture of the everyday by something apparently everyday.[111]

Modern discontinuity designates this ever present emergence of the impulsive forces that break up chronological duration, where the subject's unity (i.e. the ego) tends to be perpetuated. Discontinuity names for Klossowski the structural heterogeneity between the forces on the inside and the everyday signs that hold together the subject's fiction. This much is known: 'The code of everyday signs censors all experiential content.'[112] The emergence of these incidents on canvas, frozen in its illustration, reveals phantasmatic incongruity, and in this capacity calls upon the viewer's fundamental idiosyncrasy.

> It's in this sense that I speak of the discontinuity that our modern life is: the everyday is abruptly interrupted by something apparently everyday, *etwas scheinbar Alltägliches, das die Alltäglichkeit unterbricht*. We don't realise right away that there's an *Unterbrechung*, because something seems to be part of the *Alltäglichkeit*. But there is a break all the same, such that the incident, which is as banal as the rest, stops the course of things that had until then allowed you to bear everything. All of a sudden you can no longer stand it.[113]

The incident immediately sends us back to a *what's going on?* What strangeness, what uncanny familiarity manifests itself then! And the scene shifts. The picture becomes a rebus: at the heart of the everydayness, the obscure and the animal-like are about to be shown – between the before and the after. This is what the picture must bring about:

> Contrary to the emblematic code of mediaeval religious painting, the representation of an incident – precisely the 'odd news item' nothing prepares the viewer for – supposes a code, inscribed in the necessity of the incident, which must be discovered. Each incident, thus represented, invents its own iconic code.[114]

111 *Ibid.*, pp. 69–70.
112 'Anthologie des écrits de Pierre Klossowski sur l'art', *op. cit.*, p. 198.
113 'Entretien de Pierre Klossowski avec Rémy Zaugg', *op. cit.*, p. 71.
114 *Ibid.*, p. 56.

Gulliver and Disproportionate Optics

Klossowski's character, the painter Tonnerre, excels in showing the solecism that the hands of his female figures perform. This constant reference to the details of the body is directly connected to what Klossowski calls Gulliverian optics (from Jonathan Swift's character Gulliver). His numerous descriptions of the paintings convey this visual context, this peculiar way of seeing. This optics is the source of the insistent reference to the odd news items, whose emergence is announced by details in the painting. To explain this, our author does not hesitate to describe his first visual experience: it started with a certain psychic terrain not far from pathology:

> [...] for a long time I had been attracted to mental or art constructions that came under the category of pathology; this was in a sense that was in no way 'disinterested', one that might have drawn me to medical studies. But since I felt myself to be from the other side (a still wholly mediaeval vision, due to my catholic background, assimilating the spectacular products of the folly of religious life), I wondered by what means these constructions had been able to triumph in some cases over the tyranny of common sense. [...] This was how, long before frequenting psychiatrist or psychoanalyst friends, meaning back in my teenage years, I would prefer authors whose biographies disclosed a few anomalies: any anomaly seemed to me back then an invention of the author himself [...] to attack a hostile atmosphere.[115]

This was the period when the young man was reading Poe and Baudelaire. Next he would describe coming across Swift:

> I shan't insist on the disturbing influence necessarily exerted over any anxious child [...] by Gulliver's 'disproportional' vision; but it was with the eye of Dublin's Dean that, burying myself in Vigny's *Cinq-Mars* or Balzac's *The Chouans* or Scott's *Ivanhoe*, I latched onto fortuitous details, on the basis of which I was able to take up the matter of these books in a perfectly 'maniacal' fashion.[116]

115 *L'Arc* Journal, Issue 43, *op. cit.*, p. 9.
116 *Ibid.*

An entire image, or situation as a whole, is envisaged, observed and reconstructed on the basis of these fortuitous details, which obsessively impose themselves upon him. With what result? That of surprise, incomprehension, uncanniness, oddity, and disquiet. The fortuitous detail, through the polarisation that it implies on a part, a fragment, a bit, a portion of the envisaged reality, destroys the totality of reference – it shatters it into pieces. As the detail is disconnected from the whole of which it is an element, incomprehension takes precedence and sweeps over the young Klossowski. The detail makes him blind to the visual totality, dumbfounds him before the rationality that only the whole can deliver. This visual experience remains pertinent for him, as do its consequences:

> [...] I may say that this same 'disproportionate' vision has not only persisted but has developed in a very particular way, despite everything, right up to my most recent works. [...] I have never recovered from this vision; but it cured me of all kinds of tentative and misleading searches and wrong paths.[117]

By shifting from the whole to the part, vision finds itself immediately modified: the other parts are now broached from the point of view of the partial and the oblique. Vision changes its yardstick and the part is no longer seen on the basis of the totality. What then becomes of the totality when it is visually tracked starting from one of these fragments? What does this new point of view reveal? A genuine change of perspective is brought about, a disproportionate one that breaks with the prevalent censorship and mores. Everyday life takes a quite different turn:

> A detail detached from the context suddenly shines with an inner light that would otherwise be imperceptible; this ecstatic banality is brought to completion in the atmosphere of contemplation in which I live.[118]

117 *Ibid.*

118 Monnoyer, J.-M., *Le peintre et son démon*, Flammarion, Paris, 1985, p. 23. Klossowski was opposed to the publication of this book, which is not commercially available. On this point, see Arnaud, A., *Pierre Klossowski, op. cit.*, pp. 181–213.

Furthermore, we may note the homage Klossowski pays to his 'infirmity':[119] not only did he not recover from it, but it brought him out of the rut that stereotyped vision produces. He insists:

> [...] this 'disproportionate' vision saved me from a great deal of rallying, or position taking, or incitation to react. Perhaps today I'm not less but more 'conditioned' than twenty years ago. If no one can escape conditioning, then everything boils down to knowing what conditions us.[120]

Klossowski does not partake of a logic of symptom and complaint – he does not believe that his way out would have been to get rid of what conditions and constrains him. His goal is to know what conditions him – and to know this, he must expel the obsessions – the demons of the psyche – by finding a place for them. This is an active and curative operation of exorcism.

How does one see by virtue of Gulliverian optics? This is a vision held in a metonymical displacement, in the absorbing, dazzling and paralysing detail. In *Roberte et Gulliver*, a divertimento written in 1987, we can read Klossowski's account of this peculiar optics and what is at stake in it, namely, a method to see, say and understand. He was able to turn his 'infirmity' into a new and profoundly heuristic method of exorcism – for him. '[...] close your eyes: everything you/shall hear/you are about to see [...]'.[121] Here is the method – and it was developed for the occasion of knowing how to see 'everything a woman's siesta signifies.'[122] Roberte's, of course:

> To find in the laws of optics/a way to behave with regard to other similar creatures/and within the rules of perspective/the practice of those dissimilar/is Gulliver's invention!/In this space everything that comes closer gets bigger/everything that moves away gets smaller/as pleasures and pains go away in time/and if one comes to the foot of a monument/that from afar one might slip into one's suitcase/nonetheless among humans we shall always find/our inevitable neighbour. [...] Changing dimensions,

119 Klossowski also said 'morbid attention', 'Anthologie des écrits de Pierre Klossowski sur l'art', *op. cit.*, p. 177.

120 *L'Arc* Journal, Issue 43, *op. cit.*, p. 9.

121 [Translated from] Klossowski, P., *Roberte et Gulliver*, Fata Morgana, Montpellier, 1987, p. 11.

122 *Ibid.*, p. 14.

> dear Sirs/is Gulliver's invention!/Still, to put it into practice/one needs to make an apposite distinction/lest tragic situations arise/between truth and falsehood![123]

In this piece, Roberte is a sleeping giant that Gulliver roams over, portion by portion, moving over the beaches of her bare skin. 'We may conclude', says our character:

> if the sleeper measures full four cubits/long/thus four Gullivers – it is as much/in depth/no less in height and length/than a whole Gulliver apt by his own size/to gauge each of the parts that make up the lady/a fragment assessed by Gulliver/each time worth the woman in her entirety.[124]

This divertimento is a little farce, but it translates the staggering effect of Gulliverian optics: here the part stands in for the whole, and the totality of all the parts is judged on the basis of the infirmity of this vision that sees in miniature. As our commentator shrewdly writes:

> The laws of Gulliverian optics are not those found in physics handbooks. Phantasmatic optics, Gulliverian vision, puts everyday reality at a distance by reflecting it in a distorting mirror. Contrary to the scientific view, which puts the real at a distance so as to objectify it in the space of knowledge, the Gulliverian view puts it at a distance so as to parody it in the space of *la gaya scienza*.[125]

This reference to *la gaya scienza* and the parodying of the usual schemes of vision and everyday representation is wholly justified.

Each time Klossowski speaks of his disproportionate vision, he specifies that it has always been there as something irreducible – contracted like an incurable illness. This irreducible vision is what he calls his monomania: 'Under the guise of an "odd news item", the occurrence of a detail recorded by the monomaniacal eye. A reference to Gulliverian optics.'[126] He complements this with:

123 *Ibid.*, pp. 14–15.
124 *Ibid.*, pp. 19–20.
125 Madou, J.-P., *Démons et simulacres dans l'œuvre de Pierre Klossowski*, *op. cit.*, p. 78.
126 Klossowski, *La Ressemblance*, *op. cit.*, p. 83.

> [...] if monomania does indeed consist in tirelessly highlighting just one same thing – in showing, in the pictorial as well as written sense, just one same physiognomy – indeed, just one same scene or series of compositions – according to the infinite variations stemming from the problems inherent to the picture's structure – then this amounts to resolving these problems by virtue of the repetition, each time differentiated, of this one and same figure.[127]

Monomania is only possible starting from the detail that is imposed – and even discovered – through this new Gulliverian perspective. Monomania is the art of not being released by this ... detail. What should one do? Free oneself from this detail that gazes upon the obsessed subject? Not at all, roars Klossowski repeatedly. On the contrary, he must 'experience [...] [his] own mania.'[128] He answers his questioners on different occasions:

> It so happens that a very long time ago now I came up with an overthrow of Kant's maxim – to take as universal that which makes me, and me alone, obey an idea [...]; as I've already said, and to say it again in all sincerity, strictly speaking I'm neither a philosopher nor a novelist – but just a private individual who, compelled by monomania, long ago set about describing his experience with the sole aim of communicating it in the most precise fashion and, to give an idea at least of its persistence, has been doing no more than resume its description: the more this experience is repeated, the more it seems to him to be inexhaustible.[129]

On another occasion he would proclaim:

> Put away your tape recorder then, but remember this for the joy of my detractors: I'm neither a 'writer', nor a 'thinker', nor a 'philosopher' – nor anything else in any other mode of expression – nothing of all that comes before having been, being and remaining, a monomaniac.[130]

Klossowski will never let this idea go: 'Monomania endlessly starts itself up again. Always from the same starting point, it knows how to wait.'[131]

127 *Ibid.*, pp. 84–5.
128 *Ibid.*, p. 86.
129 Monnoyer, J.-M., *Le peintre et son démon*, *op. cit.*, p. 17.
130 Klossowski, *La Ressemblance*, *op. cit.*, p. 91.
131 *Ibid.*, p. 86.

He likewise designates himself as an 'auto-biographer', or an 'independent writer' – namely, an artist specified by a 'monomaniacal eye' where vision is concerned. Lest we forget Klossowski's affirmation: disproportionate vision is a method.[132]

Pictorial Solecism

The character Octave has a passion for the paintings of Frédéric Tonnerre in which he sees the results of Gulliverian optics applied to pictorial practice: the intensification of the detail as standing in for the whole. In his diary, he writes of his passion: 'I just live and die for the sake of beauty [...].'[133] He collects Tonnerre's paintings – or, in his words, salvages and hoards them. He is the only enthusiast of this painter, who was a friend of Courbet's. He alone knows how to *see* these realist paintings. What is there to be seen or uncovered when one pores over them at length?

The sole collector of this minor master, Octave flatters himself on 'removing the oeuvre from the gazes [...] of those who will only become miserable for not having the leisure time it takes.'[134] Indeed, Tonnerre's

132 In *La Vocation suspendue* (Gallimard, 1950), we find an excellent example of how this method allows us to see. One of the priests, La Montagne, collects sculptures. Part of his collection is a group of life-sized, polychrome statues that he bought out of curiosity, without understanding their meaning. He is unaware of their meaning because he does not see it. At one point, after a theft, La Montagne discovers a group of statuettes. Great is his surprise when he notices that these little statues are simply the replicas of his life-sized ones – and that now that he sees the statues in miniature he can immediately grasp their meaning: 'this is the Lady de la Salette [...] and here is Mélanie and Maximin'. This change of perspective and modification of proportions allowed the meaning to appear; in this new scale, La Montagne can see what before blinded him.

133 Klossowski, *Roberte Ce Soir* and *The Revocation of the Edict of Nantes*, *op. cit.*, pp. 141–2.

134 *Ibid.*, p. 126.

oeuvre, lacking in any 'taste', wilfully promoting 'bad form', demands the 'leisure time' of our protagonist – requires it to the point that he spends several hours a day casting his eyes over each canvas, savouring the 'sovereign jouissance of the oeuvre that shines out into space, where it glows in its own right.'[135] Because, for Octave, only by casting and immobilising his own gaze on the canvas can the painting take on life. Octave sees Tonnerre's paintings with a disproportionate vision, an attraction to the tiniest detail; he sees in the way that Klossowski describes himself as seeing. 'But what would a painting be if the gaze were not cast upon it? Isn't it then that it takes on life, doesn't it die as soon as one turns away, only to be reborn with the next gaze?'[136] The monomaniacal gaze allows one to see, to give life to the canvas. Without this vision, without this radical shift in perspective in which substitutions and hieroglyphs with incomprehensible rebuses emerge, in short, without this method emphasising metonymical play, the painting would remain a pointless, dead, and meaningless oeuvre. In spite of all this, the Gulliverian method, an attempt to make the painting by means of the gaze, fails. Much as Octave may have worn his eyes out and exhausted himself contemplating the painting fragment by fragment, he still remains helpless in relation to what he calls the 'glory' of the oeuvre. According to our collector, this glory of the painting is its 'real presence'. It is completely beyond him, leaving him dazed, lost, and even captive to the large apartment he hardly ever leaves anymore. A real presence in the manner of that which arises in the mystery of the Eucharist, over which he has no control – a presence that watches him while he, alone, sees the painting and describes it piece by piece. This presence, which makes up the canvas's invasive power and force, can be neither seen nor said, and yet it actively goes on being there: it is real. His monomaniacal gaze does not *totally* make the painting – within it, something always ungraspable endures: it is the *real* of presence – the *tuché* – and it drives him to start writing so as to try to bear witness to it. It must be understood that in referring to Octave's writing we are, of course, also referring to Klossowski's.

135 *Ibid.*, pp. 126–7.
136 *Ibid.*, p. 126.

The narrative's long, meticulous descriptions of Tonnerre's canvases correspond to the author's attempt to give an account of this encounter with the real. The details are imposing and blinding. This is why from this point of view the scene is incomprehensible; it can no longer be grasped in the obvious terms of rational comprehension. Hence the choice that plagues Klossowski: *either* to see with everyday stereotypes and therefore end up seeing nothing, annulling whatever might emerge or might even be there already; *or* to see with disproportionate vision, but then comprehension is lost and possible explanations and interpretations proliferate: they become fabrications and flights of fancy sparked off by these disconnected fragments. They are henceforth the 'irruption, the suddenness of an eternal instant that emerges between a before and an after [...]'.[137]

In what way do the 'unknown master's'[138] unexhibitable works make up a series? Our protagonist scrupulously establishes the annotated catalogue of his collection, quoting, as an epigraph, a sentence in Latin from Quintilian, taken from the *Institutio Oratoria*: *In gestu nonnulli putant idem vitium inesse quum aliud voce, aliud nutu vel manu demonstratur.* He translates it: 'Some think there is solecism in gesture too, whenever by a nod of the head or a movement of the hand one shows the opposite of what the voice is saying.'[139] For Octave, this is what gives order to the hoarding of his paintings, and what makes him a collector: solecism is the sole pictorial 'motif' of Tonnerre's paintings. This tirelessly shown and staged motif makes each canvas an element of his collection. The presence of these pictorial solecisms makes this master unexhibitable: the anonymous spectator sees either a *nothing* on the canvas, or an *unbearable* that makes him turn away. Solecism, in its usual definition, designates an erroneous use of syntax – in contrast to barbarism which is an error in morphology or semantics.

With such a definition, a difficulty arises: Octave wonders what relationship can be established between the painted gesture and speech. The

137 Monnoyer, J.-M., *Le peintre et son démon*, *op. cit.*, p. 23.

138 Klossowski, *Roberte Ce Soir* and *The Revocation of the Edict of Nantes*, *op. cit.*, p. 99.

139 *Ibid.*

solecism, according to Quintilian's definition, unites those things that Klossowski's entire demonstration shows to be incompatible: the image and the word, the singular and the gregarious, the immediate and the deferred. Ought one to conclude that the solecism, this error, is an articulation, a bridge between these two incompatible, heterogeneous objects: picture and writing? Octave's remarks explicitly suggest this. If there is a solecism, if something contrary is being hinted at by the figures with a precise, visible gesture, then these figures have to say something in order for this contrariness to be sensed. Being painted, however, they keep absolutely quiet. Would speech, which is presupposed in the definition of solecism, be the speech of the spectator who would speak for the mute figures, because they are painted, 'in such a way as to sense the opposite of the gesture that he sees them performing'?[140] This would necessitate an interpretative reading of what the canvas describes. The gesture, isolated by virtue of the disproportioned vision, would be calling for its decryption: here is what it indicates, what it signifies. Thus, of one of Roberte's thumbs extended downwards in one of his paintings,[141] Klossowski comments: '[...] there is all the same the woman's gesture of her down-turned thumb which signifies "knock him out", addressed to a third party [...].'[142] Interpretative decryption, which is never monovalent and definitive, stands in contradiction to the context it arises in: this painted gesture is an error in relation to the overall syntax of the painting. Without interpretation, the error cannot take on its full value, its weight.

In practically every one of Tonnerre's paintings, the same motif – which fascinates Octave – is laid bare: the unveiling of a violent act in which a woman is involved. What Tonnerre was endeavoring to express in his painting, and thus exorcise, as his collector puts it, is the 'moral repugnance and the irruption of pleasure simultaneously gripping the same soul, the same body.'[143] This tipping point – as portrayed through a woman

140 *Ibid.*, p. 12.

141 Colour reproduction in 'Anthologie des écrits de Pierre Klossowski sur l'art', *op. cit.*, p. 135. The title is *Roberte in the Role of Valentine* (1981).

142 'Entretien de Pierre Klossowski avec Rémy Zaugg', *op. cit.*, p. 56.

143 Klossowski, *Roberte Ce Soir* and *The Revocation of the Edict of Nantes*, *op. cit.*, p. 111.

in his paintings – between repugnance and pleasure intensely fascinates the painter and his enthusiast. We find here the crux of the solecism: in regard to the syntax that includes repugnance, pleasure is an error; in the syntax that is deduced from pleasure, repugnance is, in turn, an error. Two contradictory syntaxes juxtapose: the solecism, through its error, translates this contradictory encounter. Only a monomaniacal gaze can grasp this contradiction, through a detail of the solecism that always touches a fragment of the body. In fact, Tonnerre lets the eye 'feed' upon the instant of 'satisfied fright' that precedes the central scene of the violation, in which a woman discovers her own surprise during her sexual assault. Tonnerre paints what Octave is the voyeur of, when Roberte is in the arms of the guest Octave has chosen for her.

Take for example Tonnerre's painting, *Lucretia*. Octave will describe the modality of the solecism with precision – his description being valid for all the other solecisms that Klossowski's narratives and pictures are teeming with. He calls to mind the Roman heroine's dilemma:[144] if she gives in to Tarquinius, she clearly betrays her husband; if she resists, she will still be thought to have betrayed him, for, after raping her, Tarquinius will kill her to make everyone believe she was punished for being an unfaithful wife. Either choice leads to betrayal and calumny. Octave then describes this oeuvre that only he has seen. Tonnerre

144 Lucretia, wife of Lucius Tarquinius Collatinus, grandnephew of King Lucius Tarquinius Superbus, is famous for her tragic death in 508 BC, considered to be the immediate cause of the revolution that overthrew the monarchy and established the Roman Republic. During the siege of Ardea, the princes of the royal family wondered how their wives behaved in their absence. They rode to Rome at night to discover their wives thoroughly enjoying themselves at a wine party; only Lucretia was weaving with her maids. Sextus Tarquinius, son of the king, stricken by Lucretia's beauty, returned to Rome a few nights later and entered her bedroom by stealth. She awakened and he offered her two choices: she could submit to his sexual advances, or he would kill her, claiming he had caught her in an act of adultery. Lucretia yielded to Sextus, but the next day disclosed the rape to her father and husband calling on them for vengeance, and then stabbed herself in the heart before their eyes. Lucius Junius Brutus immediately called for revolt, proclaiming the decline of the Tarquins.

> [...] shows us Lucretia lying full length upon a couch, propped upon one elbow, her head, seen in profile, erect, one leg straight, the other thigh lifting in a suspicious manner, as if repelling the aggressor perhaps, but preparing the way for him [...].[145]

Klossowski's ruse is not to resolve this dilemma but to introduce a third term that reconciles the irreconcilable, the *un-thought* in the hypotheses. Lucretia says no (by refusing, her loyalty to her husband is affirmed), but is also carried away by the nascent pleasure, and, without knowing it, opens up to Tarquinius, the rapist. She says no and also shows acceptance. The solecism is found here. How does Tonnerre manifest this pictorially? Octave, while pursuing his description, guided by this point of uncontrolled irruption of pleasure in the body still overcome by repugnance, pays attention to the heroine's hand:

> Tarquin brings his face near the lady's cheeks, wrapping an arm around her waist, one hand clutching her breast while she, her other elbow raised, her hand open, tries to fend off the young man's lips as the arm upon which she is leaning reaches down toward her belly where that hand, all its fingers extended, seems less to be covering her too visible shame than to be waiting [...].[146]

This vital point glares out at our protagonist and drives him – in an intense movement of the scopic drive – to stand before the canvas and stare at it. It is a face-off. Octave is caught in a trance:

> But I return to the detail of Lucretia's panic-stricken face, to that hand which under the pretext of warding off Tarquin's greedy mouth, in the most flagrant manner presents her palm to it, to that other hand, lower down, which, far from forbidding access to the treasure, strains, reaches out its fingers [...].[147]

The solecism dramatised by Tonnerre is made pictorial 'through the position of the hands, one of which is lying and the other avowing a crime which seeps from its fingers.'[148] Here we have simultaneous moral repugnance and

145 Klossowski, *Roberte Ce Soir* and *The Revocation of the Edict of Nantes*, *op. cit.*, p. 110.
146 *Ibid.*
147 *Ibid.*, p. 111.
148 *Ibid.*

emergence of pleasure in the body. The description operates like a film in slow motion. The bodily fragments become autonomous and elude the silencing, unitary consciousness. By losing this unitary reference – that of the rational ego upheld by the grammatical fiction of the subject of the statement[149] – censorship loses its power and coerciveness. It is not that the hand that avows the crime of sexual turmoil provoked by the attacker shows what will next sweep over the entire body. Klossowski is precise: the part stands in for the whole. 'Without this slant [the hand], I affirm that nothing would be "body".'[150] The hand stands in for the whole body – this detail will remain autonomous, it will represent for the whole the irruption of turmoil that contradicts the loyal wife's conscience. In short, the hand is not an extension of the body, it is an autonomous part with its own rules. The hand becomes a 'separate intelligence'.

Octave emphasises his favourite painter's choice of solecism: This

> [...] artist often enlarges the women's hands in order to emphasise what they feel; he thereby intrigues the spectator. [...] For, in placing the back of a hand in front of an unveiled fleece, in imparting this or that expression to fingers, in modelling the palm of a hand, in stressing index and thumb, he counterpoises a spiritual agitation against the tangible mass of this or that part of the body. And there, at that point, one can measure the exact degree to which the woman is in possession of herself or finds her charms slipping out from under the control of her will, we are witness to unending expropriations of the body subjected to an outside gaze [...].[151]

Tonnerre thereby develops – and this is the paradoxical character of his painting – an art of the unveiling of concealment. Which may also be called: showing the process of masking. Gulliverian vision allows one to grasp what eludes 'normal' vision. Our commentator writes:

149 [TN, The 'subject of the statement', which Lacan develops in contradistinction to the 'subject of the enunciation', *cf.* 'Remarks on Daniel Lagache's Presentation' and 'The Subversion of the Subject and the Dialectic of Desire', in *Écrits, op. cit.*]

150 [Translated from] Lugan-Dardigna, A.-M., *Klossowski, L'homme aux simulacres*, Navarin, Paris, 1986, p. 61.

151 Klossowski, *Roberte Ce Soir* and *The Revocation of the Edict of Nantes*, *op. cit.*, pp. 111–12.

> An unexpected gesture fleetingly expresses the unspeakable part of the experience: that incommunicable moment at which consciousness [...], more or less expressed in its physiognomy, runs up against that which is irreducible in the body and sensation. For, in the end, what is 'physiognomy' [...] if not a learned equilibrium, a subtle dialectic between the reasonable constructed part [...] (where consciousness dominates) and the irrationality of personal demons expressing themselves in the pantomime [...] of bodies?[152]

For Klossowski, monomaniacal obsession takes priority over a woman's (Roberte and her models) hand. The poet Alain Jouffroy questions Klossowski on the role the hand plays, and its embodying solecism. Jouffroy counts over eighty drawings or paintings in which a hand is drawn with open palm and fingers folded. He reads there a 'blindingly obvious encrypted sign.'[153] The remark is fair, but the dialogue that follows is particularly interesting. Klossowski scarcely replies to the questions, and he lets his poet friend do all the talking and make all the associations. The latter reminds him, quoting the art historian Daniel Arasse, that in Italian there are two terms for 'detail': *il particolare*, 'an image, [...] a sign from afar in the painting, that invites the eye to move in closer, so as to see better'; and *il dettaglio*, which, on the other hand, is purely pictorial, and 'does not conjure an image [...] nor a representation, and gives nothing else to be seen besides pictorial matter.'[154] The detail in question for Klossowski is closer to the definition of *il particolare*. Klossowski reminds us of his goal: to use this detail of the hand in order to examine 'the moral state and all its nuances of temptation, seduction or repugnance.' He adds: 'independently of the signification of these situations [...] where the body of someone remains silent but whose members move, it is especially through the hands that one understands what is happening.'[155] We have singled out the following extract from the interview:

152 Lugan-Dardigna, A.-M., *Klossowski, L'homme aux simulacres*, *op. cit.*, p. 56.

153 Jouffroy, A and Klossowski, P., *Le secret pouvoir du sens*, *op. cit.*, p. 97.

154 *Ibid.*, pp. 99–100.

155 *Ibid.*, pp. 102–4. '[...] the ambiguous gestures of the hands show us what is happening "inside the figure".'

JOUFFROY: If I've rightly understood the meaning you give to the word 'mania', you never premeditate the position of the hands of each of the figures in your paintings [...].
KLOSSOWSKI: No, absolutely not.
JOUFFROY: Do those gestures occur to you naturally?
KLOSSOWSKI: Yes. But when you say they crop up nearly ninety times in my different paintings, you're the one who's telling me! Because if I so much as imagined, while composing the picture, that it was the ninetieth time I was putting the right hand or the left, or both, in that particular way, I wouldn't be able to work anymore![156]

Our artist's monomania is not a voluntary, conscious decision. It is forced upon him, and the embodied solecism in the shape of a hand is one of its effects. In this way, the solecism has a revelatory power.

For Klossowski, painter and art theorist, figuration is a truly 'fascinating game, an "incantatory" medium'.[157] It is from this original, subjective position that his theoretical texts and pictures take on meaning. From then on he will devote his life to figuring the unfigurable, to depicting the unapprehensible presences that take possession of him. It is a 'worship of images' – '[...] the image (Klossowski and his brother Balthus) dream of, whether profane or sacred, necessarily bathes in the "obscure clarity" of the sanctuary.'[158] Religious iconography is continually present. This is why Klossowski's drawn or coloured figurations have 'a theatrical, scenic, dramaturgical character – like those compositions of Füssli's where he represents scenes from Shakespeare and upon which he [...] writes the names of the actors and the roles they are playing.'[159] Indeed, our painter exclaims: *I am a dramatist*.

In 1981, Klossowski confesses what his dream then was:

RÉMY ZAUGG: Many of your drawings could be sculptural projects.
KLOSSOWSKI: If that's what you're saying, you're saying more than the truth, you're speaking of my regret. If I had the means – it would be horribly costly – I'd make my works in encrusted enamel. The statues I'd like to make – wax figures, in fact – would

156 *Ibid.*, pp. 104–5.
157 'Entretien de Pierre Klossowski avec Rémy Zaugg', *op. cit.*, p. 47.
158 *Ibid.*
159 *Ibid.*, pp. 79–83.

> be done in a realism as academic as possible, without looking for any other style or new art expression, somewhere between abstraction and concrete vision. Therefore, something utterly conventional, as conventional as can be. You're quite right; my compositions are practically sculptural projects.[160]

A few years later, with his growing notoriety, Klossowski was able to make some sculptures. Indeed possessing the characteristics he had desired and foreseen, they are late twentieth century idols in the style of Late Roman simulacra – multicoloured, even gaudy. They realise, perhaps most accurately, the theatrical theology that fascinated him as much for its symbolism as for its liturgy.[161]

Thus, our artist would not hesitate to affirm: 'ideas are important to me only at the cost of an experience, namely, a destiny. Ultimately, for me the most authentic view of what I do is seen through what I show – what I show and not what I make read.'[162] This formulation could not be more radical and definitive. He goes on to confesses: 'This is why I say: it so happens that I paint for people who only seek to read my pictures rather than look at them, on the pretext that my images put out your eyes.'[163] Blinding, dazzling images that force our eyes shut. Words emerge so that one does not see nor allow the emergence of the outside, paralysing gaze. Vision is affirmed right up to the purely subjective moment when sight becomes blurred and the gaze emerges. Our own essence is thenceforth present, piercing a hole in the illusory continuity of egoic, rational identity. Might Klossowski's painting be illusionist? Is his painting marred by anecdotalism due to his maniacal taste for detail (Gulliverian optics)? Not so. It is, on the other hand, the figured affirmation that 'only through fiction, and in no other way, does the truth manifest itself'[164] – a sentence that could have come from the hand of Jacques Lacan!

160 'Anthologie des écrits de Pierre Klossowski sur l'art', *op. cit.*, p. 191.
161 'Entretien de Pierre Klossowski avec Rémy Zaugg', *op. cit.*, p. 47.
162 *Ibid.*, p. 91.
163 *Ibid.*, p. 101.
164 *Ibid.*, p. 47.

Conclusion: Inhuman Diana

In what is perhaps his keenest text, the 1965 *Diana at her Bath*, Pierre Klossowski actualises the insistent question of the presence/absence of the gaze. This text allows us to grasp what is at stake in the act of viewing as well as in what is given-to-be-seen by the (magical) picture. He takes up the story of Diana (Artemis) and Actaeon, as recounted notably by Ovid in his *Metamorphoses*, and which remains ever-present in our memories: Diana, goddess of hunting, at her bath, is surprised naked by the young hunter Actaeon. This pivotal scene: *seeing the goddess naked*, was one of the staples of western painting and sculpture.

The contradictory attributes of the goddess are well known: 'virginity and death, night and light, chastity and seduction.'[1] She is the protector of hunters, and yet one of the finest, Actaeon, meets the fate of a hunted game animal, torn to pieces by his own hounds after she had transformed him into a stag. Diana is thus 'the dazzling and murderous maiden'.[2]

In this pivotal scene, the goddess 'presents herself to man, then slips away from him',[3] re-actualising her contrasting attributes in the very instant at which Actaeon rears his head and catches her unawares. Once again, we meet the contrast between seeing and saying, between image and text, between immediacy and concept. Actaeon did not see Diana bathing by chance, as Ovid and all antiquity supposed. On the contrary, he *wanted* to see, violating with his gaze the goddess' (forbidden) mysteries, secrets as contradictory as they are provocative. In this version/interpretation of the myth, Actaeon is no longer a hapless victim of divine fate, but he who must plead guilty at the price of his sacrifice/castration. Actaeon's (subjective)

1 Klossowski, P., *Diana at her Bath/The Women of Rome*, trans. Sophie Hawkes & Stephen Sartarelli, Marsilio Publishers, New York, 1990, p. 5.

2 *Ibid.*

3 *Ibid.*

calling is realised in the final scene, but he is no Oedipus. There is no pathos here, despite the violence done to the hero's body. The myth runs as follows, then: Diana pretends to be out of breath after the chase, she feigns fatigue, and the heat and perspiration that take hold of her. Then she undresses, quite aware of the presence of mortals around her.

> The bath that ends Artemis' hunt is the cruellest moment of our chase: we are denied our siesta, which we were hoping to taste in the goddess' arms: and if now she asserts her untouchable nature, it is to convince us all the more of the theophanic reality of her cheeks, her breasts and her buttocks [...].[4]

The forms of Diana, those that Actaeon tries to catch sight of, are merely a representation, a veil that hides the divinity from view, along with her essence which has neither shape nor consistency. Diana's nakedness is in turn but an image that bars the route to her inviolate essence. This is why Klossowski was to qualify this vision as *mad*. Did Actaeon

> really believe the maiden could be seized in her unseizable divinity? [...] Must one not indeed be mad to presume that the goddess will relax, disrobe and take her pleasure in the pool; to believe that she is bored, so exceptionally bored that she will grant you an exclusive amusement and bless you with a privilege that you will pluck like a wild berry?[5]

Actaeon's 'folly' was to have believed, or to have wanted to believe, that what the goddess represented (her body, her attributes, etc.) was the goddess herself, to have confused the divinity and her theophany, to have let go of his prey to pursue the shadow of future riches.

> It is to this object that cannot be grasped in the mirror that the specular image lends its clothes. A substance caught in the net of shadow, and which, robbed of its shadow-swelling volume, holds out once again the tired lure of the shadow as if it were substance [*proie*],[6]

4 *Ibid.*, p. 6.

5 *Ibid.*, p. 7.

6 Lacan, J., 'The Subversion of the Subject and the Dialectic of Desire', in *Écrits*, *op. cit.*, p. 693. [TN, as the translator indicates in an endnote (p. 839), *proie*, translated here

writes Jacques Lacan in an outlandish passage from 1960. What Actaeon failed to understand as being paradigmatic of the *One* is that

> the wholeness of the universe could rest on a *single* deity, nor that a feminine deity, exclusive of any male deity, might express herself in the singleness of a *closed* nature, sufficient unto herself, finding in chastity the fullness of her essence.[7]

Thus, Diana may never forge a relationship with a mortal; she is and always will be shut off, sufficient unto herself. In a word, she will be forever other, absolutely heterogeneous. She is 'Goddess beyond destiny, with whom no mortal, even at destiny's behest, could presume to join in union.'[8]

Described thus, Diana shows in the fictitiousness of the myth the impossibility of the sexual relation. The tipping point in this scene resides in the fact that this goddess from without, this Other goddess, 'becomes the perpetual excitation of the emotions subjugated on the *inside*.'[9] She becomes that which gives shape and consistency to what stirs the subject and which as yet has neither name nor form. She becomes the vision that enciphers what must be unveiled and which tortures the subject from within. She imitates on the outside the movements of the soul on the inside. Diana's nakedness is the form given to what both reveals and covers over the cause of Actaeon's desire, driving him to catch sight of what perturbs him within. Once realised, the scene of *seeing the goddess laid bare at last*, empties speech of all content in one fell swoop. Moreover, it is in this capacity that painting and sculpture have always shown this scene to be pure silence.

Conversely, what effect does this abrupt gaze produce in Diana? Klossowski describes it in the following terms: '[...] invisible Diana contemplates Actaeon imagining the goddess naked. The deeper he sinks into

---

as 'substance', generally gives 'prey' in English, but this passage alludes to Lafontaine's dog that *lâche la proie pour l'ombre*, literally, that 'lets go of its prey to pursue its shadow'. This has passed into common idiom and is used in much the same way as the English maxim 'one in the hand is worth two in the bush'].

7 Klossowski, P., *Diana at her Bath ...*, *op. cit.*, pp. 11–12.

8 *Ibid.*, p. 12.

9 *Ibid.*, p. 18.

his reverie, the more Diana assumes bodily shape.'[10] This means that the 'body, in which she will manifest herself to herself, she actually borrows from Actaeon's imagination.'[11] She wants to be seen 'as a woman, in a body which, once seen, will excite the passions of a mortal man.'[12] The contradiction lies in the following point: '[…] the wish to see her own body involves the risk of being defiled by a mortal's gaze […].'[13] If she is not to remain Other to herself, a pure disembodied enigma, Diana must go via the *One*, via Actaeon's imagination. In going via this *One*, she sheds part of her Otherness, a portion of her 'closed nature' shifts over into terms that open her up and violate her. She is no longer an absolute essence, untouched and inviolate.

To bring about the theophany, the grasping of a woman's body as elaborated in Actaeon's imagination, Klossowski supposes that Diana has made a pact with a 'demon who intercedes between the gods and humanity'[14] as he expresses it in terms borrowed from Platonic theology.

> Through his airy body, the demon *simulates* Diana in her theophany and inspires in Actaeon the desire and mad hope to possess the goddess. He becomes Actaeon's imagination and Diana's mirror.[15]

Through this demon, Diana may take on a body that appears to be that of a mortal, visible and tangible woman. Not only does the goddess achieve an appearance capable of arousing men's desire, but masked by this body she may also

> surrender herself, or experience incognito the emotions that her immutable principle precludes […]. In this way, without prejudice to her essential and invisible body, inseparable from her divine principle, impassible because impalpable, though a

10 *Ibid.*, p. 31.
11 *Ibid.*, p. 33.
12 *Ibid.*
13 *Ibid.*, p. 32.
14 *Ibid.*, p. 35.
15 *Ibid.*

> spectator [...] she witnesses her own adventures – adventures in which her chastity is put to the test.[16]

The principle of this chasteness is an emotion that, as a goddess, she is unaware of. The gods are impassive, they know neither emotion nor sensation. It is by virtue of the demon who serves as her mask and who mimes out her role that she may feign fatigue, heat, and perspiration after the hunt. She comes to experience chasteness and emotion as a result of being put to the test by mortals.

We are familiar with Actaeon's fate – here the paradigmatic fate of the voyeur and the viewer/enthusiast/spectator of what emerges as a picture – he who wanted to see and to possess the goddess. Klossowski introduces precise terms to tell of the hunter's demise: the incompatibility between the scene in which her nakedness is revealed and the words that might describe it. It is a matter of *either* seeing *or* saying, *either* vision *or* the word. This is why Klossowski's commentary on this myth is precious when it comes to exposing what is at stake in the image and what is at stake for he who goes about setting down his mind's visions in painting.

> [...] what Actaeon then sees takes shape *beyond* the birth of any words: he sees Diana bathing and he cannot say what he sees. [...] the event absorbs what remained still expressible in the apprehension. *What I saw, I cannot say what it was*. Not that what one cannot say, one might not more fully understand, nor that one cannot see what one does not understand. Actaeon, in the myth, *sees* because he *cannot say* what he sees: if he could say it, he *would no longer see*.[17]

What he wants to see is nameless. No word exists that could speak of it. What he wants to see and appropriate is not Diana's body reduced to an appearance that the demon lends her, but rather, and desperately, what lies beyond appearances, beyond this incomparable beauty. What he wants to see is the invisible aspect of the goddess: divinity itself. What the voyeur wants to see, what the painter according to Klossowski wants to appropriate, is the phallus in so far as it is absent, in so far as it is the very trace of

16 *Ibid.*, p. 38.

17 *Ibid.*, pp. 52–3.

absence. What Actaeon is striving to catch sight of stands in a relation of infinitude with regard to the field of vision that he endeavours to master by the all-powerfulness of a voracious, insatiate eye.

When Diana discovers Actaeon, she splashes him with water transforming him into a stag, and tells him – these will be her last words: '*Nunc tibi me posito visam velamine narres/Si poteris narrare, licet.*' These words '[...] provoke divulgence through language of what has just come about and at the same time show that the metamorphosis renders this indulgence impossible.'[18] Klossowski speaks of the goddess' provocation and irony:

> [...] provocation: Say it, then, describe Diana's nudity, describe my charms, that no doubt is what you're waiting for, what your fellow men would love to know! The irony: If you can tell at all![19]

Transformed into a stag, his mouth now a snout that can speak no more – his thinking muddled, a cloud descending over his concentration, his words breaking apart – a mute silence falls. Klossowski enjoyed representing this scene visually, and did so often, even making a sculptural version.

What might Actaeon have seen? At what precise moment did the metamorphosing word of the goddess issue forth? '*Nec nos videamus labra Dianae.*' Following the dictates of his demonstration, Klossowski invents this sentence, and (attributing it to Ovid) gives a commentary on it:

> With one hand she had just cast water in his face, but as she was pronouncing the sentence, already she was withdrawing the other hand from the space between her thighs, and whether as of that moment she had initiated Actaeon, or having already initiated him thus admitted him to her final rite, or whether, lastly, she thus put an end to her theophany, by this very gesture she uncovered her vermilion vulva, uncovered her secret lips: Actaeon see those hellish lips open at the very moment that the spray of water streams over his eyes, blinds him [...].[20]

18 *Ibid.*, p. 63.
19 *Ibid.*
20 *Ibid.*, p. 66.

A movement of the hand: where before she was concealing her rose-red vulva, now, by throwing the water on the hunter's face, she lays bare her secret and transforms her voyeur who will remain forever mute. In this fine description from the pen of our commentator, we read how Actaeon is reduced to the gaze object. On the one hand, he sees no more – the water blinds him – on the other hand, transformed into a stag, he can no longer speak – he is annulled as a subject, metamorphosed into a beast. Klossowski speaks of a 'gaze scrutinising the night', and 'a staggeringly wilful servitude'.[21] This pivotal scene is thus reduced to a vision, *labra Dianae*, better still, to a flash that lasts but an instant, a blinding blaze of light that suddenly abolishes the scene for he who wanted to see: *nec videamus*. The instant (in a subjective temporality outside of any exterior chronological time) at which Actaeon sees the goddess naked is ultimately the very instant at which he dies, torn to shreds by his pack of fifty hounds. The temporality at the heart of the myth sinks into the atemporal. The mental space that is ordered by the *time for understanding* converts into the eternal return of the instant: at once, inseparably and endlessly, Actaeon sees Diana at her bath, becomes a stag, and dies devoured. There is no succession between these different postures, only the reiteration of the constancy of one self-same act. The strictly limited temporal structure of this scene, its time frame boiling down to the *instant of seeing*, indicates to us its place in discourse. It is the structure of myth, but also the structure of Klossowski's oeuvre. If we follow Jacques-Alain Miller's remarks in his 1982–3 Course[22] (one of the lessons being devoted to myth), this place is that of the fantasy, i.e. the place of the real in so far as it is deduced from the dead-ends of the signifier, the same signifier that orders the coordinates of visual 'reality'. Diana and Actaeon are emblematic of the excellence of the fantasy in its fixity, its monotony, its resistance to signifying interpretation – the fantasy in so far as it is the sole window that looks onto the real of the cause. It is because it

21 *Ibid.* [TN, Klossowski writes *cervitude volontaire*, introducing *cerf*, a 'stag', into *servitude*. We have sought to render this play on words by introducing 'staggering'.]

22 Miller, J.-A., *L'orientation lacanienne II, 2, Du symptôme au fantasme, et retour* (1982–3), unpublished.

silently enciphers the jouissance of he who turns himself into a gaze, a pure gaze object, that this fantasy is equivalent to fascination. Seeing the goddess naked is a fantasy of fascination that in itself carries a fascinating character for others, since today it still stands as the vivid trace of a lost humanity, one that we can scarcely believe could ever have existed. Klossowski's oeuvre is there to remind us of this lost humanity, buried deep down, and which by his grace rises again to the surface, brilliant and intact.

This scene lays bare a subjective reversal: at the very moment the woman's bare flesh appears, at which it can be seized and appropriated, it suddenly eludes our predator/voyeur. It eludes him because it transforms him, or better still, it metamorphoses him. He becomes the prey. When the stunning image of her skin appears, he who wanted to see is transformed into a gaze. Where before he was the voyeur who wanted to see, at the end he is fascinated, immobilised, turned to stone by this skin, this nakedness that now looks back at him from without. To put it in Freudian terms, Actaeon has failed to see the absent phallus of the feminine Other. This failure is the sign that castration falls on the side of Actaeon. As far as Diana is concerned, she objects to it. Actaeon's submission to Law is affirmed: the conjunction between One (him) and the Other (her), between phallic logic and womanly jouissance, is impossible. Diana is not the other sex, but the absolute Other that bears no relation: castration. The ultimate fate of our hero, the scrap cast unto the hounds, stands as the emblematic form of castration, albeit imaginarised as being bitten, ripped apart, and torn to shreds. In this respect the myth becomes as bright as the crescent moon at night – Diana's attribute.

This is what always lies in wait for any who would contemplate and paint the elusive nakedness that harbours womanliness. This is what is in store for the painter, and his viewer. The poetry of the Baroque made no mistake about this, when it calls Actaeon, 'happiness' incarnate, in spite of the terrible fate that awaits him, and adds that Diana is 'inhuman', in as much as the secret she keeps – and which her rose-red lips give an image of (and prevent us from seeing!) in the scopic field – shall be forever real.

Pierre Klossowski's oeuvre is a literary, conceptual and pictorial means of responding to this gaze from without, put into the position of cause; an oeuvre that becomes in turn a *gaze* for its reader, its commentator, and its viewer.

JUDITH MILLER

Mutation: Interview with Pierre Klossowski

JUDITH MILLER: Is *Klossowski, l'homme aux simulacres* the work of an admirer?

PIERRE KLOSSOWSKI: Eight years ago, Anne-Marie Lugan-Dardigna published a feminist book with the editor Maspéro in which I was made to bear the cross for all the others, Sade, Bataille, Robbe-Grillet, etc. But afterwards she came round to reconsidering her initial point of view, in particular her analyses of the *Roberte* trilogy (*Les lois de l'hospitalité*), and one day she wrote me a letter of great warmth, with an eye to meeting up. We spoke, and she listened to me at great length for this book.

JM: Do you think highly of her work?

PK: Absolutely. Nevertheless, I did stop writing fifteen years ago now. I paint, and it's quite futile to look for any other relationship between my pictures and my novels besides the following: my pictures used to exist as such in my mind before I came to describe them in my novels. Indeed, it was the endlessly reiterated living presence of my conjugal model of Roberte in my pictorial compositions that freed me from fictional writing. But there again, I was straying into the androgyny proper to the character's physiognomy, to the extent that my first representations of the young Ogier were showing effects of this. Now, I had the rarest stroke of luck of finding a boy model for my pictorial work which completely changed my manner. The fantasy always exists for a painter, especially in such cases as these. It includes reminiscences, memories from college, involving the male adolescent who is the only one to occupy me now. I'm altogether ambivalent in my sensibility, there's no need to say any more about that.

The fantasy and its model

JM: What status does this model have?

PK: Having this model has made things different. It's both an obstacle and a rectification, and at the same time it makes way for a whole play of projections onto Living figure of this quite handsome young man, a man of exceptional intelligence, who has agreed to pose for me. The space of readiness that is his is serenely reflected in my recent pictures, thereby offering such an unusual reality that the paintings of my painter friends have remained quite transfixed by it. Since I've been working with this outer representation, which confirms this reality, my craft has changed, both in the structuring and intensity of the shades. People have remarked on the disproportion between the formats I favour and the coloured pencil crayons that I now use, while returning to these 'anthropometric' dimensions, given that coloured pencil, as Lamarche-Vadel has emphasised, is usually only suitable for sketches or smaller formats.

In all my transpositions, I choose subjects that my books do not narrate. Though the figures from the female, *Roberte* series, came out of this, and have a like-minded fortune, the images of boys are of a different order.

Androgynous fictions

JM: You do see a genealogy though between these female figures and the current male adolescent?

PK: Certainly, but it's not about equivocal *angels* anymore. It's well and truly about adolescents: without being a man, he's not a girl either. The ephemeral character of the charm of a child between thirteen and seventeen effaces the fable that represents his encounter.

JM: Are you the bond between Roberte and the adolescent?

PK: Yes and no.

JM: All the same, isn't it the apprehension you have of these androgynous fictions that angelises them?

PK: I would like to rule out the ridiculous discussion on the sex of angels. Ganymede was a boy. He's not transfigured but exalted as such by Zeus. In *The Baphomet*, the page Ogier behaves as a boy of his age unaware of all the idolatrous hallucinations he gives rise to in the Templars. Though one of my pictures does indeed represent the Grand Master's conversation with the androgynous Baphomet, on the other hand, in the one that shows the young page at brother Damien's bedside, I set about rendering not the fantasmatic aspect of my model, but that aspect that is really quite real.

Bernini's Angels, and Sade's

JM: Is it the equivocity of the sexual identity of your female figures, like that of the male adolescent, that makes them angels, that immortalises them?

PK: That indeed is the direction baroque sculpture took: look at Bernini's angels in Rome. Those angels are spirits, but the equivocity of the adolescent is in no way an angelic one. This ambiguity is too familiar to the Roman society of the time (think of the institution of the castrati in the Sistine) to be shocking, contrary to the taste of the French mind which is impervious to this kind of attraction.[1] Hence the drama of Sade who paradoxically breaks away from the libertinism of his time by virtue of his anomaly: to treat women as boys and boys as women. Endowed as he was with a rich

1 Note by P. Klossowski: However, the romantic generation did get to grips with this, notably in Balzac's *Sarrasine*.

feminine sensibility, did he not identify with Justine, whose misfortunes he describes as his own, just as much as with Juliette, so as to entrust her with putting his philosophy to the test? Juliette is the mental androgyne to whom he lends his brain. Unlike the Sadean pervert who in his integral monstrosity defines sensuousness, the Sadean heroine speaks reason. Sade bears a feminine richness, which I attempted to describe in *The Philosopher Villain*, which is earlier than my final version of *Sade My Neighbor*.

However, as my pictures absorbed me more and more, I removed myself entirely from his influence, whilst in the silence of the image the chords of Mozart's musical eroticism were ringing out (Kierkegaard *dixit*).

JM: Isn't not taking sexual difference into account and encouraging the lifting of censorship a way of being atheist?

PK: In Sade, yes indeed. And due to this very fact he can't see any other way out but atheism, i.e. a rationalisation of his anomaly, as I've written in some detail. Besides, how could I possibly dare to deny that Sade was an influence on me some time ago, as much through his prose as his staged situations interspersed with discourse? Being dependent on the logical language of his time, didn't Sade bring it up to date? But with what ferocious irony!

Is Jules Romains a Pornographer?

JM: Why attribute to an era what comes from the logic of language? Do you think that in fiction someone can be what is censored within him?

PK: It is the heavens, the liberation of what lies stifled within someone, and the impulses that fight each other. To put me in the same class as the supposedly pornographic painters along the lines of Félicien Rops is an absurdity. And even Félicien Rops is not a pornographer when he sets down to painting. Even Jules Romains, is he one? Who would dare claim such a thing? It's the same thing with the scenes I've staged, and the figures I've made. In sum, I used to write for the blind who could see when they read me, whilst those who knew how to read me couldn't see what I show. Now, and with the Parisian criticism especially, one cannot forget that I used to write, and people are thinking that they have to go and refer to my books to understand my pictures!

JM: What did the writer not say, which the painter makes visible?

PK: Reading a picture is not the same thing as reading a book. Speech and writing explain a series of facts that apparently succeed each other. My pictures take up the fait accompli without explanation.

The Contemplativeness of the Enthusiast

JM: You don't address the same people when you write and when you draw!

PK: Exactly. There's a contemplativeness proper to the art lover that is quite different from that of the reader.

JM: Are your drawings frescos in pencil crayon?

PK: That's what they ought to be called. So far as I know, that has never existed before. Essentially, these frescos presuppose a residence. I have some collectors who have residences where they live with my pictures. An art lover doesn't stack up valuables in bank vaults. He knows how to live with my pictures. This cohabitation is different from the reader cohabiting with a book.

JM: A fresco isn't mobile.

PK: Generally speaking, my compositions are translucent, they are made to be on a wall in a different way from how a painting is hung up like a mirror.

JM: Which can also be taken down, unlike a fresco …

PK: The fresco presupposes an architecture. A painting is an object. In material terms, it's like a piece of furniture. The fresco is not a piece of furniture. On the other hand, my first graphite drawings, like 'Roberte and the Schoolboys', were inspired by silent films on the big screen fifty years ago.

JM: Has your pictorial activity suspended your writing?

PK: For my personal satisfaction, in many respects I need to write again so as to retrieve certain periods, in a biographical sense. It's a real need. To defend myself. It's too quickly forgotten that my brother and I are from a background of painters.

An Exhibition is not a Demonstration

JM: Does your need to write correspond to finding this origin again?

PK: In the Postface to *Les lois de l'hospitalité* I explained how things come to the surface, how this need came to blossom from the pictorial point of view.

JM: And yet what satisfies you in drawing is the muteness?

PK: ... which gives rise to an image. To those who don't know my pictorial activity, I say that *I don't think any differently from how the picture thinks*. It's asocial, as if I'd fallen into a kind of insensibility with regard to the world around me as far as any other relationships are concerned. But it's communication all the same, whose initial egoism makes amends by inviting the viewer to participate in it. The painter is neither a hermit nor a solitary figure. For me, it's more important to *show* than to *say* what I see. Exhibiting is perhaps a defence with regard to the world we live in, to current affairs and the scarcity of understanding that is rife there. The fantasy is the obsessional and constrictive fact for all those who strive to create. Saying that I only paint to demonstrate my 'theories' is idiotic. An exhibition is not a demonstration. What I said about the fantasy, the simulacrum, and the constraint it expresses is true for the entire history of painting. There's a religious element that's strongly accentuated in the West by Christianity. In a general sense, art is religion's accomplice: everything that's going on nowadays goes against this.

What could be more normal?

JM: You've mentioned Balthus, allow me to spell out what's striking for an outside 'voyeur' to your exhibition. One of you is fascinated by male adolescents, the other by female adolescents. Do you talk to each other?

PK: No, never. It's not the same relationship, and our paths have evolved in completely different ways. What could be more normal than an artist constantly looking at young girls? But not so for the emotion of the one such as Socrates when he sets eyes on Charmides, inspired by *Eros paidikos* – which was customary in his time – and which Goethe said was as old as humanity itself.

JM: Would you say that only the male adolescent conveys adolescence, that there is no real female adolescent?

PK: Adolescence is a moment that becomes utterly fascinating when singled out. But boys don't blossom at the age of man, not even the epheboi, in the same way as young girls become women. On the woman's side, the relations between Diana and Callisto would be the equivalent. In one of my last series, I showed *Charmides Submitting to Socrates' Incantation*, at an age when he could disturb him before disappointing him. You can see a reproduction of it in *l'Énoncé dénoncé*.[2]

2 *L'Énoncé dénoncé* was co-edited by Marval (Paris), La Galerie Beaubourg (Paris) and Lens Fine Art (Antwerp), (1986).

JM: Do you really denounce the utterance? Is your mutation a denunciation?

PK: Yes, a little. In the very large *Revealed In the Looking-Glass* picture, which was the poster for the Beaubourg gallery exhibition and then the Toulouse exhibition, you don't know whether the man is a kind of Judex. He's not a priest, he's simply a very moral man. He wants to stop the adolescent from passing through the looking-glass, where each of them can see what is going on in their mutual apprehension.

Originally published in L'Âne, *October–December 1986*

A.R. PRICE

Translator's Postface

A translation. The word seems innocent enough. Does the translation suppose the translator? This question should give us some pause for thought.

Freud opens his metapsychological paper on the unconscious with the observation that we only come to know the unconscious after it has been 'translated into something conscious'.[1] Does the work of the unconscious imply a subject of the unconscious who wills this translation, a dream-weaver who 'does not think, calculate or judge in any way at all'?[2] Lacan would tackle this question in his late teaching, speaking of 'the ideal worker, the one Marx made the flower of capitalist economy'.[3]

Klossowski started out as a translator, in the same years that saw Lacan trying his hand at rendering Freud and Heidegger into French with varying results. Klossowski concluded, as we can read in Hervé Castanet's monumental study, that this labour is an impossible one, presupposing as it does a conversion of like into like, when no such like exists.

Like to like would give representation; and representation, as Lacan deduces from the Freudian letter, is intrinsic to the structure of the signifier. Now, it is precisely the operative field of this signifying structure that Lacan's late teaching would progressively rein in. The so-called Borromean clinic, drawing on the inter-looping rings of the Real, the Imaginary and

1 Freud, S., 'The Unconscious', in *The Unconscious*, trans. G. Frankland, Penguin Modern Classics, 2005, p. 49.

2 Freud, *S., The Interpretation of Dreams,* trans. J. Strachey, *Standard Edition, op. cit.*, Vols. 4–5, p. 507.

3 Lacan, J., 'Television', trans. D. Hollier, R. Krauss, and A. Michelson in *Television/A Challenge to the Psychoanalytic Establishment*, Norton, New York/London, 1990, p. 14.

the Symbolic, examines the modalities of connection and articulation that lie beyond the jurisdiction of representation:

With regard to the Symbolic, the vague notion of *symbolisation* makes way for a finer nuance between what is necessarily *inscribed* at the level of the signifier (through history, through writing, through sexuation, through market economy and the social bond) and what is contingently *enciphered*. The Freudian notion of the decryption of the unconscious gives ground first to an unconscious that includes its own interpretation, then to the ideal worker that encrypts jouissance into the cipher of the signifier.

With regard to the Real, this economic operation raises the question of the fantasy as the site and the condensed residue of this enciphering. Klossowski writes it with a 'ph', and in the study on which we are now commenting we read sometimes 'phantasm', sometimes 'fantasy', where it falls to the reader to determine whether in passing from one to the other we pass from like to like. A 'fabricated object', a 'fortuitous coherence', an 'obsessive constraint', an 'anchoring point' that provides 'an open window onto the real': such are the terms that allow us to tackle this enigmatic point of translation.

With regard to the Imaginary, revitalised and newly esteemed in Lacan's late teaching, symbolic demonstration is replaced by a *monstration*, a showing, designed to circumvent the tropes of the signifier. This effort of exposition, of exhibition, which employs mimicry, make-believe, and dissimulation, calls upon the reader or viewer as accomplice. What stands as a mere elusive and unconfirmed *will to translate* at the level of the hypothetical ideal worker, is here doubled by the creator's wilful forging of *simulacra* that engage the other in a silent dialogue. The reader/viewer is summoned to a locus that brings him into a mediated relationship with the phantasm. Art, the 'one mediator that can say what a phantasm "wills"', enlists the imaginary in the service of the real.

This clinic sets the context of Hervé Castanet's study, and it is a clinic that is still little known in the English-speaking world. We have not, however, opted to clutter Castanet's text with interminable signposts to this reference, and indeed up until the present Postface the reader has only been guided by a small handful of footnotes clarifying some of the more familiar

Lacanian vocabulary from the earlier phases of his teaching, most of which refer back to the 2006 translation of the *Écrits*.

Klossowski's question 'how is a singular experience to be translated into writing?' is answered in his reading of Nietzsche for whom it was a question of working backwards, going from 'conscious' semiotics to an unconscious 'semiotics of impulses', from intention back to intensity in what he calls a 'retranslation'.

Translation and retranslation give us the terms by which we may consider what is presented in Castanet's text as deciphering and enciphering, demonstration and monstration, and indeed Castanet shows us a Klossowski grappling with the cipher, the glyph ('hieroglyphy'), the figure and the illuminated letter that trace 'the edge of the hole in unconscious knowledge'.

The question remains as to whether this effort comes in the wake of the labour of the ideal worker, or whether, on the contrary, its insistence is so much more arduous because this hypothetical worker was never in fact contracted in the first place. Is it not this vacant post that necessitates the visitation by the spirited third party auxiliary (as in Octave's three-phase 'lesson' on actualising the inactual Roberte, or in the demonic complicity invoked by the icon)? Whether through the 'grammatical transcription' of the communication of idioms, or the pictorial solecism of theatrical theology, Klossowski's oeuvre constitutes an effort to translate the untranslateable, to bind the three Borromean rings together, each of which are equivalent, without ever standing in a relation of like to like.

A.R. Price, 27 July 2011

Cultural Interactions
Studies in the Relationship between the Arts

Edited by J.B. Bullen

Interdisciplinary activity is now a major feature of academic work in all fields. The traditional borders between the arts have been eroded to reveal new connections and create new links between art forms. Cultural Interactions is intended to provide a forum for this activity. It will publish monographs, edited collections and volumes of primary material on points of crossover such as those between literature and the visual arts or photography and fiction, music and theatre, sculpture and historiography. It will engage with book illustration, the manipulation of typography as an art form, or the 'double work' of poetry and painting and will offer the opportunity to broaden the field into wider and less charted areas. It will deal with modes of representation that cross the physiological boundaries of sight, hearing and touch and examine the placing of these modes within their representative cultures. It will offer an opportunity to publish on the crosscurrents of nationality and the transformations brought about by foreign art forms impinging upon others. The interface between the arts knows no boundaries of time or geography, history or theory.

Vol. 1 Laura Colombino: Ford Madox Ford: Vision, Visuality and Writing
275 pages. 2008. ISBN 978-3-03911-396-5

Vol. 2 Graham Smith: 'Light that Dances in the Mind': Photographs and Memory in the Writings of E. M. Forster and his Contemporaries
257 pages. 2007. ISBN 978-3-03911-117-6

Vol. 3 G.F. Mitrano and Eric Jarosinski (eds): The Hand of the Interpreter: Essays on Meaning after Theory
370 pages. 2009. ISBN 978-3-03911-118-3

Vol. 4 Grace Brockington (ed.): Internationalism and the Arts in Britain and Europe at the *Fin de Siècle*
368 pages. 2009. ISBN 978-3-03911-128-2

Vol. 5 Gabrielle Townsend: Proust's Imaginary Museum: Reproductions and Reproduction in *À la Recherche du temps perdu*
232 pages. 2008. ISBN 978-3-03911-124-4

Vol. 6 Lennart Nyberg: Bodies of Poems: Graphic Poetics in a Historical Perspective
187 pages. 2009. ISBN 978-3-03911-343-9

Vol. 7 Jeff Adams: Documentary Graphic Novels and Social Realism
214 pages. 2008. ISBN 978-3-03911-362-0

Vol. 8 Caroline Patey and Laura Scuriatti (eds): The Exhibit in the Text: The Museological Practices of Literature
292 pages. 2009. ISBN 978-3-03911-377-4

Vol. 9 Francesca Orestano and Francesca Frigerio (eds): Strange Sisters: Literature and Aesthetics in the Nineteenth Century
324 pages. 2009. ISBN 978-3-03911-840-3

Vol. 10 Carole Bourne-Taylor and Ariane Mildenberg (eds): Phenomenology, Modernism and Beyond
404 pages. 2010. ISBN 978-3-03911-409-2

Vol. 11 Gillian Pye (ed.): Trash Culture: Objects and Obsolescence in Cultural Perspective
264 pages. 2010. ISBN 978-3-03911-553-2

Vol. 12 Carol Adlam and Juliet Simpson (eds): Critical Exchange: Art Criticism of the Eighteenth and Nineteenth Centuries in Russia and Western Europe
420 pages. 2009. ISBN 978-3-03911-556-3

Vol. 13 Kyriaki Hadjiafxendi and Patricia Zakreski (eds): What Is a Woman to Do? A Reader on Women, Work and Art, c. 1830–1890
404 pages. 2011. ISBN 978-3-03911-116-9

Vol. 14 Emma Wagstaff: Writing Art: French Literary Responses to the Work of Alberto Giacometti
227 pages. 2011. ISBN 978-3-03911-871-7

Vol. 15 Linda Goddard: Aesthetic Rivalries: Word and Image in France, 1880–1926
323 pages. 2012. ISBN 978-3-03911-879-3

Vol. 16 Kim Knowles: A Cinematic Artist: The Films of Man Ray
342 pages. 2009. ISBN 978-3-03911-884-7

Vol. 17 Jo Carruthers and Andrew Tate (eds): Spiritual Identities: Literature and the Post-Secular Imagination
248 pages. 2010. ISBN 978-3-03911-925-7

Vol. 18 Giovanni Cianci, Caroline Patey and Sara Sullam (eds): Transits: The Nomadic Geographies of Anglo-American Modernism
350 pages. 2010. ISBN 978-3-03911-949-3

Vol. 19 Nick Havely (ed.): Dante in the Nineteenth Century: Reception, Canonicity, Popularization
343 pages. 2011. ISBN 978-3-03911-979-0

Vol. 20 Phillippa Bennett and Rosie Miles (eds): William Morris in the Twenty-First Century
323 pages. 2010. ISBN 978-3-0343-0106-0

Vol. 21 Simone Francescato: Collecting and Appreciating: Henry James and the Transformation of Aesthetics in the Age of Consumption
217 pages. 2010. ISBN 978-3-0343-0163-3

Vol. 22 Hervé Castanet: Pierre Klossowski: The Pantomime of Spirits
327 pages. 2014. ISBN 978-3-0343-0209-8

Vol. 23 Savina Stevanato: Visuality and Spatiality in Virginia Woolf's Fiction
309 pages. 2012. ISBN 978-3-0343-0241-8

Vol. 24 Paola Spinozzi and Elisa Bizzotto: *The Germ*: Origins and Progenies of Pre-Raphaelite Interart Aesthetics
310 pages. 2012. ISBN 978-3-0343-0298-2

Vol. 25 John Harvey: The Poetics of Sight
Forthcoming. ISBN 978-3-0343-0723-9

Vol. 26 Rina Arya (ed.): Contemplations of the Spiritual in Art
264 pages. 2013. ISBN 978-3-0343-0750-5

Vol. 27 Shannon Hunter Hurtado: Genteel Mavericks: Professional Women Sculptors in Victorian Britain
348 pages. 2012. ISBN 978-3-0343-0756-7

Vol. 28 Adrianne Rubin: Roger Fry's 'Difficult and Uncertain Science': The Interpretation of Aesthetic Perception
287 pages. 2013. ISBN 978-3-0343-0791-8

Vol. 29 Harry Heuser: Immaterial Culture: Literature, Drama and the American Radio Play, 1929–1954
374 pages. 2013. ISBN 978-3-0343-0977-6

Vol. 30 Judith A. Kidd: Behind the Image: Understanding the Old Testament in Medieval Art
279 pages. 2014. ISBN 978-3-0343-0993-6

Vol. 31 Outi Remes, Laura MacCulloch and Marika Leino (eds): Performativity in the Gallery: Staging Interactive Encounters
261 pages. 2014. ISBN 978-3-0343-0966-0